WITNESSING
WATERLOO

24 Hours, 48 Lives,
A World Forever Changed

DAVID CRANE

WILLIAM
COLLINS

D0230047

William Collins
An imprint of HarperCollins*Publishers*
1 London Bridge Street
London SE1 9GF
WilliamCollinsBooks.com

This William Collins paperback edition published 2016

First published in Great Britain as *Went the Day Well? Witnessing Waterloo*
by William Collins in 2015

1

Copyright © David Crane 2015

David Crane asserts the moral right to
be identified as the author of this work

A catalogue record for this book is
available from the British Library

ISBN 978-0-00-735838-0

All rights reserved. No part of this publication may be
reproduced, stored in a retrieval system, or transmitted,
in any form or by any means, electronic, mechanical,
photocopying, recording or otherwise, without the
prior permission of the publishers.

This book is sold subject to the condition that it shall not, by
way of trade or otherwise, be lent, re-sold, hired out or otherwise
circulated without the publisher's prior consent in any form of
binding or cover other than that in which it is published and
without a similar condition including this condition being
imposed on the subsequent purchaser.

Printed and bound in Great Britain by
Clays Ltd, St Ives plc

MIX
Paper from
responsible sources
FSC
www.fsc.org   FSC™ C007454

FSC is a non-profit international organisation established to promote
the responsible management of the world's forests. Products carrying the
FSC label are independently certified to assure consumers that they come
from forests that are managed to meet the social, economic and
ecological needs of present or future generations,
and other controlled sources.

Find out more about HarperCollins and the environment at
www.harpercollins.co.uk/green

Contents

PART II

Went the day well?
We died and never knew.
But, well or ill,
Freedom, we died for you.

John Maxwell Edmonds

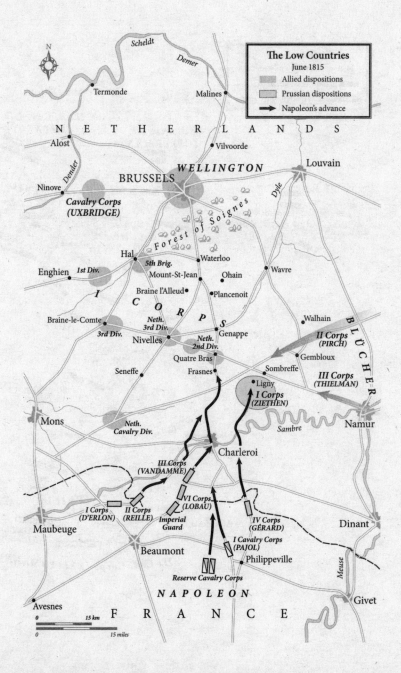

N

Scheldt

Demer

Termonde   Malines

N E T H E R L A N D S

Alost   • Vilvoorde

Louvain

Denter

Ninove

BRUSSELS   **WELLINGTON**

Cavalry Corps
(UXBRIDGE)

Dyle

Forest of Soignes

Hal   *5th Brig.*   • Waterloo

Enghien   *1st Div.*   Mount-St-Jean   • Ohain   • Wavre

I   Braine l'Alleud   • Plancenoit

C O R P S   Braine-le-Comte   *Neth.*   • Walhain
3rd Div.

   3rd Div.   Nivelles   *Neth.*   Genappe   **B L Ü C H E R**
   2nd Div.   **II Corps**
   (PIRCH)

Seneffe   Quatre Bras   Sombreffe   Gembloux

   Frasnes   • Ligny   **III Corps**
   (THIELMAN)

Mons   *Neth.*   *I Corps*   Namur
   Cavalry Div.   *(ZIETHEN)*

   Sambre

Charleroi

III Corps
(VANDAMME)

VI Corps
(LOBAU)

I Corps   **II Corps**   *Imperial*   **IV Corps**   Dinant
(D'ERLON)   *(REILLE)*   *Guard*   *(GÉRARD)*

Maubeuge

Beaumont   *I Cavalry Corps*
   (PAJOL)

   • Philippeville

Avesnes   *Reserve Cavalry Corps*   *Meuse*

N A P O L E O N   Givet

0   *15 km*   **F R A N C E**

0   *15 miles*

The Low Countries
June 1815

   Allied dispositions

   Prussian dispositions

   → Napoleon's advance

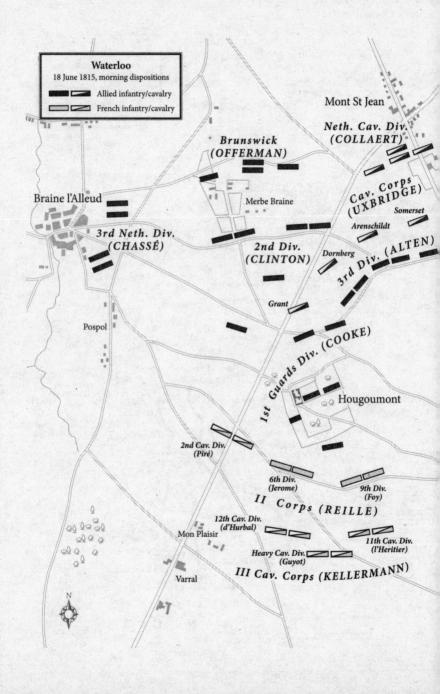

Waterloo
18 June 1815, morning dispositions

Allied infantry/cavalry
French infantry/cavalry

Mont St Jean

Neth. Cav. Div.
(COLLAERT)

Brunswick
(OFFERMAN)

Merbe Braine

Cav. Corps
(UXBRIDGE)

Braine l'Alleud

Somerset

Arenschildt

3rd Neth. Div.
(CHASSÉ)

2nd Div.
(CLINTON)

Dornberg

3rd Div. (ALTEN)

Pospol

Grant

1st Guards Div. (COOKE)

Hougoumont

2nd Cav. Div.
(Piré)

6th Div.
(Jerome)

9th Div.
(Foy)

II Corps (REILLE)

12th Cav. Div.
(d'Hurbal)

Mon Plaisir

11th Cav. Div.
(l'Heritier)

Heavy Cav. Div.
(Guyot)

III Cav. Corps (KELLERMANN)

Varral

N

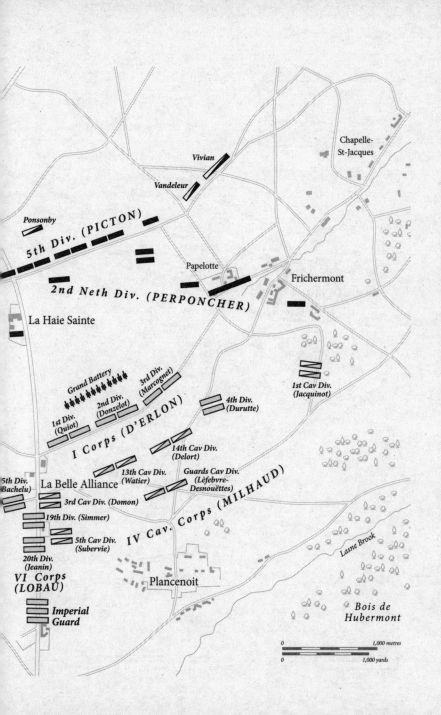

Chapelle-St-Jacques

Vivian

Vandeleur

Ponsonby

5th Div. (PICTON)

Papelotte

2nd Neth Div. (PERPONCHER)

Frichermont

La Haie Sainte

1st Cav Div.
(Jacquinot)

Grand Battery

3rd Div.
(Marcognet)

2nd Div.
(Donzelot)

4th Div.
(Durutte)

1st Div.
(Quiot)

I Corps (D'ERLON)

14th Cav Div.
(Delort)

13th Cav Div.
(Watier)

Guards Cav Div.
(Lefebvre-
Desnouëttes)

5th Div.
(Bachelu)

La Belle Alliance

3rd Cav Div. (Domon)

IV Cav. Corps (MILHAUD)

19th Div. (Simmer)

5th Cav Div.
(Subervie)

IV Cav. Corps (MILHAUD)

20th Div.
(Jeanin)

VI Corps
(LOBAU)

Plancenoit

Lasne Brook

Bois de
Hubermont

Imperial
Guard

0   1,000 metres

0   1,000 yards

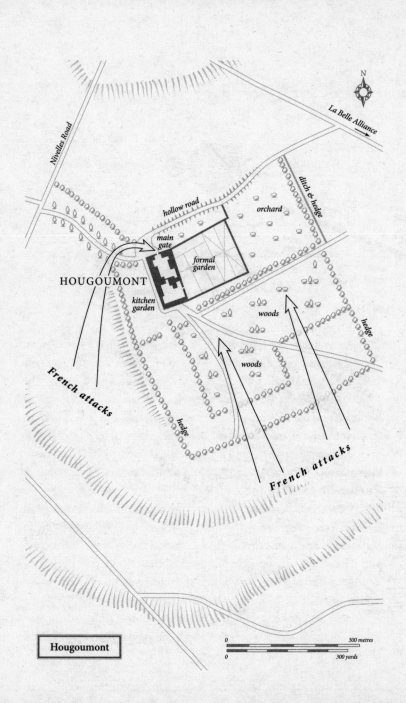

N

La Belle Alliance

Nivelles Road

hollow road

orchard

ditch & hedge

main gate

formal garden

HOUGOUMONT

kitchen garden

woods

hedge

French attacks

woods

hedge

French attacks

Hougoumont

| 0 | 300 metres |
| 0 | 300 yards |

Prologue

'There exists a highly respectable school of liberal thought which
does not deplore Waterloo. We are not of their number. To us
Waterloo is the date of the confounding of liberty.'

Victor Hugo, *Les Misérables*

On any Sunday or holiday around the end of the Napoleonic Wars,
the naval pensioners of Greenwich Hospital, dressed in their
tricorn hats and blue uniforms, could be found under a tree near the
Observatory in the Park, their telescopes set up, their old yarns of
Trafalgar and the Nile primed for retelling, waiting for trade. From the
summit of the hill on which they stood the view stretched northwards
over the marshes towards Barking church and Epping Forest, and westwards across a forest of masts and docks to the London of Wren, St
Paul's and Westminster Abbey.

It was a sight to make a foreigner quail at the trading might of a
modern Tyre – there might be more than two thousand ships lying in
the Thames at any one time – but for the Sunday holiday-makers who
had made their way up Observatory Hill there was a more macabre
demonstration of Britain's naval power. For the last four hundred years
crimes at sea had been punished with all the symbolic pomp the
Admiralty could manage at Wapping's Execution Dock, and for the
price of a penny, the pensioners' customers could hire a telescope and

take their fill of the latest victims of naval justice, their bodies tarred and chained, and hanging in iron cages from a gibbet at the river's edge as a warning against piracy.

On one such holiday in the early summer, while the hawthorn was still out and the great elms and chestnuts of Greenwich Park were looking their best, the humorist and poet Thomas Hood had paid his penny to see the sights and was sitting beneath the trees near the Observatory, watching the early-comers queue to take their turn. In almost every instance the first thing they asked to see were the 'men in chains' across the river on the Isle of Dogs, but there was one exception – a young woman he had watched climbing the hill on the arm of her husband, a swarthy-looking able-bodied seaman 'with a new hat on his Saracen-looking head, a handkerchief full of apples in his left hand, with a bottle neck sticking out of his jacket for a nosegay' – and it was this pair who caught Hood's attention.

When it came to their turn, the sailor asked one of the 'telescope-keepers' to point out the men in chains for his 'good lady', but she told him that 'she wanted to see something else first'.

'Well!' he wanted to know. 'What is it you'd like better, you fool you?'

'Why. I wants to see our house in the court, with the flowerpots, and if I don't see that I won't see nothing. What's the men in chains to *that*? Give us an apple.' There was nothing he could say that was going to change her mind, and while he consoled himself with his bottle she took an apple out of the bundle and told the pensioner to turn the telescope towards Limehouse church.

'Here, Jack! Here it is, pots and all!' she suddenly screamed. 'And that's our bedpost. I left the window up o'purpose as I might see it.'

Jack himself took an observation. 'D'you see it, Jack?'

'Yes.'

'D'ye see the pots?'

'Yes.'

'And the bedpost?'

'Ay, and here Sal, here, here's the cat looking out of the window.'

'Come away, let's look again.' And then she looked, and squalled, 'Lord! What a sweet place it is!' And then she assented to seeing the men in chains, giving Jack the first look.

Anyone familiar with Bruegel's painting of the Fall of Icarus, with the labourers in the foreground pressing on with the ploughing, unconscious or utterly indifferent to the drama unfolding behind them, will hardly need the reminder but Thomas Hood's Sal is still a useful warning about the way we see history. For all those nineteenth-century Britons who grew up with the memory of Waterloo, 18 June 1815 could only mean one thing, and yet for the men and women who lived through that day, carrying on their ordinary Sunday lives, going to Greenwich Park or church, oblivious to the fact that on the other side of the Channel the greatest single act of Sabbath breaking in British history was unfolding, it was a different story.

He didn't think he would ever recover from this, a tragic Thomas Fremantle wrote in his diary after being bowled out for a duck in a school match at Eton, and it is this profoundly human mix of the extraordinary and the everyday, that gives the day of Waterloo its peculiar, haunting character. For two long weeks in the June of 1815 the country had been forced to live in that anxious limbo between events and report, and even as Wellington's rain-sodden army was retreating towards Brussels for the final, decisive battle, men and women across the country were still going to the theatre and science lectures, still working in the fields and the factories, still reading and writing their sermons, still applauding the Duke of York's winners at Ascot and buying their lottery tickets, blithely unconscious that there was such a place as Waterloo, or that the children who would be born that Sunday would be born into a different Britain from the Britain that for the last twenty years had struggled with Revolutionary and Napoleonic France.

I should like to have been able to say that this book was the story of Britain's pots and cats and chained men on this, the most important day in its nineteenth-century history, but that might lead to the wrong expectations. This is not a social history of the kind that tells what people wore or the time at which they ate, but a book about the intersection of the private and public spheres, about the ways in which individuals are touched by remote events, and how much – or how little – of what we usually think of as mainstream history actually impinged on the lives of ordinary men and women who witnessed Waterloo.

'And what should they know of England who only England know?' Rudyard Kipling asked in the last heady days of Empire, and the same question might just as well be posed of the Britain that defeated Bonaparte. The Regency age carries with it such brilliant aristocratic and literary associations that it is very hard to look past them, but this was as much the age of the Highland Clearances and brutal misery as of Byron, Prinny, and Almacks, an age of such violent cultural, intellectual and economic extremes and contrasts that it is difficult to believe that the events described here took place in the same century let alone the same country.

This is a book about that country, the Britain that fought Waterloo and the very different Britain that emerged triumphant from it, and if it says more about the casualties of victory than it does about its rewards then that is because the latter hardly need spelling out. For another hundred years the country would bask in the rich afterglow of victory, and yet while successive generations could grow up with the comforting assurance of God's special dispensation for his chosen people, there was another Britain – the Britain of the prison and the poorhouse glimpsed here through the smoke of battle and the burgeoning mythology of Waterloo – that would never see the fruits of a war that had framed, blighted or ended their obscure lives.

This is the unique fascination of Waterloo, the chance it gives to see the country at that crucial moment in its history, fixed in all its trivial and mundane detail in the diaries, newspapers and letters of the time as firmly as Pompeii in the ash of Vesuvius. In the aftermath of the battle, Britain might enjoy prestige and power of a kind it had never known before; but if one could go back a day or even hours, if one could just go back to the Saturday evening of 17 June, to the Britain that 'Mr Stevenson, engineer' had buried in a time capsule at the opening of the new lighthouse at the Point of Caswell that morning – to a Britain that did not know it was going to win – did not know that the 'Age of Waterloo' was starting – a Britain that was no more united than the Edwardian Britain that would rush to war a hundred years later, what kind of country would we see?

I have begun the story of that night at the London home of Charles and Mary Lamb, where the fragile crust that separated Regency civilisation from brutal reality was at its thinnest, because their story is, in miniature, the story of the age itself. What lay behind the stuccoed elegance of Nash's facades or the dazzling swank of Lawrence's portraits on show at the Royal Academy this Saturday? What irresistible pressures for change were building up behind the matchless beauty and numinous historical resonance of England's landscape? What would you have seen, if you could have looked through that telescope at Greenwich? Which lives, which stories unfolding that night, carried with them in some embryonic form the suggestion of the future?

And, finally, what was the Britain like that was in part created out of the mythology of Waterloo? For the men who fought it and the families who grieved it was a fight for freedom but for a great swathe of radical Britain it was the death knell of all their hopes. Which was it? Was Hugo, speaking as much as a liberal as a Frenchman, right? Or could the soldiers who fell along the Mont-Saint-Jean ridge at Waterloo die with the same confidence in their cause as their successors in Flanders a century later? The object of this book is to tell the story of that day and open out these questions. It shifts hour by hour, between Britain and Belgium, prison and palace, poet and pauper, though a warning note should be added to the timeframe of the events described. There are specific times here that we know from journals or memoirs or written orders, but how accurate they are is impossible to say. In Britain there would be no standardised time until the coming of the railways in the middle of the century – there might be anything up to twenty minutes difference between local mean time and Greenwich Mean Time – and when it comes to Belgium nobody can agree even so far as the time the battle began. Some contemporary accounts give it as early as nine in the morning, some recent historians as late as one in the afternoon. British officers' watches would probably still be on London time, which explains why British accounts of the battle tend to place events earlier than French sources, but even within the allied ranks there was no synchronisation of watches that might narrow the gap. I have placed it – out of probability as well as narrative convenience – late in the morning as most of Britain was going to church and Sal and her tar were fondly looking at their cat.

PART I

The Tiger is Out

'The pilot who is carrying us into Liverpool, told us of
Bonaparte's return to Paris ... Even in this age of tremendous
revolutions, we have had none so appalling as this ... When
Napoleon was rejected from France, every man in Christendom,
of honest principle and feelings, felt as if a weight of danger had
been lifted from his prospects – as if he had a surer hope of
going down to his grave in peace and leaving an inheritance to
his children. But now the whole complexion of the world is
changed again ... God only can foresee the consequences.'

George Ticknor, 11 May 1815

In the early hours of 7 March 1815, the representatives of the five Great
Powers meeting at Vienna to deliberate the future of post-Napole-
onic Europe wearily adjourned the latest round of discussions. They
had not solved the tricky problem of what to do with the king or the
Kingdom of Saxony, but as they went to bed that night, they could, by
and large, feel fairly satisfied with what they had done.

There were still outstanding issues and open sores – in Germany, in
Italy, in Switzerland, with the Catholic Church, with disgruntled minor
sovereigns and bitterly disappointed liberals and patriots – but if
nobody had everything they wanted, nobody either had gone to war.
Over the past six months there had been any number of potential flash-

points that might easily have led to bloodshed, but with an inimitable mixture of diplomacy, frivolity and old-fashioned horse-trading that marked the Congress of Vienna, Bourbon France had again been integrated into the brotherhood of civilised nations, Prussian and Russian territorial ambitions accommodated, British concerns over the Low Countries met and the principle of legitimacy – tempered with a brutal streak of realpolitik – firmly reasserted without recourse to arms. 'May security, confidence and hope revive everywhere,' read a draft declaration drawn up by the British, 'and with them peaceful labour, progress in industry, and prosperity, both public and private! May sombre anxiety for the future not awaken or bring back the evils whose return the sovereigns would wish to prevent and whose last trace they would like to efface! May religious feeling, respect for established authority, obedience to the law and horror of everything that might disturb public order once again become the indissoluble ties of civil and political society! May fraternal relations, mutually useful and beneficent, be re-established between all lands! ... And may homage at last be rendered to that eternal principle that there can be for nations as for individuals no real happiness but in the prosperity of all!'

It was an idealistic, if improbable dream – disinterest had been remarkable by its absence from the Congress – and even as the tired plenipotentiaries made their way to their beds or their mistresses on the morning of the 7th, couriers were on their way to Vienna to tell them the dream was over. At six that same morning the Austrian Foreign Secretary Count Metternich was woken by his valet with a despatch from Genoa marked 'Urgent', and within hours the whole of Vienna knew the worst: Napoleon Bonaparte, exiled by the allied powers to the island of Elba just eleven months earlier, had 'disappeared'.

Neither the Austrian consul in Genoa nor the British representative in Florence had any idea where he was gone, but the money at Vienna was on Italy. In the rearrangement of Europe, Napoleon's old marshal

4

Joachim Murat had somehow clung on to the throne of Naples, but as British frigates desperately scoured the Mediterranean for some sign of the Great Disturber, Bonaparte himself, along with the small force of his old Imperial Guardsmen and Polish lancers that had been permitted him in his island exile, was landing on the French coast to reclaim his crown.

The 'Tiger', as the great portrait painter Sir Thomas Lawrence, with a Blake-like mix of awe and fear had called him, was again loose and when two days after Vienna the news reached Britain the country was swept up in a storm of excitement, speculation and fear. 'What times we are living in,' the ageing, half-cracked Mrs Piozzi – Dr Johnson's Hester Thrale – wrote from Bath, a city, like some Regency Gomorrah, desperately searching Revelations to learn of its impending fate. 'The events come forward as Scripture says they will do, like Pangs of Parturition; every Pain sharper than the last … I was a sad Blockhead to leave Faber's Books upon the Prophecies behind me … they are so sought after now … While Buonaparte remained on Elba nobody thought of them: it must be very gratifying to the Author – That *He* should be immediately looked up to when all the Folks are wondering, and thinking What will come next? What will come next?'

It was a question that was being asked across the country, and for all the reliable intelligence that anyone had one that was as likely to be answered in Revelations as it was anywhere else. The first reports of Napoleon's escape had not reached London until 9 March, and by then the news was more than ten days out of date and the desperate 'adventurer' who had landed near Antibes with barely a thousand men was already halfway to Paris and, 'God knows how, and in the twinkling of an eye', as *The Champion's* editor, John Scott, reported from France, 'up again and in all his meteor-like intensity shaking from his "horrid hair" portentous flashings over the astounded world'.

Antibes, Grasse, Castellane, Grenoble, Lyons – a man would need 'the wings of a demon' to keep pace with his progress, the *Edinburgh*

Courier told its alarmed readers. No sooner had one shock been absorbed than there was another to face. On 7 March, Lord Fitzroy Somerset had written from Paris that there was nothing to fear for himself or his pregnant wife, but by the time the letter reached his brother in England the 'monster' that Marshal Ney had vowed to bring back in a cage was again emperor in his old capital and Louis XVIII once more on his way into exile.

'What a dreadful prospect is thus suddenly opened to mankind! What dismay must not these tidings strike into the hearts of hundreds of thousands of human beings in every station of life,' the great reforming lawyer, Sir Samuel Romilly, had written in his diary, and yet even as London held its breath and hoped, Europe was already mobilising for war. 'Napoleon Bonaparte, by again appearing in France with projects of confusion and disorder,' the Congress of Sovereigns famously declared, 'has deprived himself of the protection of the law, and in consequence has placed himself without the pale of civil and social relations; and, as an enemy and disturber of the tranquillity of the world, has rendered himself liable to public vengeance.'

After less than a year of quiet, Europe was again in arms, and as the sovereigns at Vienna returned Napoleon's protestations of peace unanswered, and the Duke of Wellington left the Austrian capital for Brussels to take command of the allied army in the Low Countries, a bewildered Britain took stock of the new reality. For more than twenty wearying years it had been at war with either Revolutionary or Napoleonic France, and for half the population those few delusory months sandwiched between Napoleon's abdication and escape were virtually the only peace they had ever known.

For as long as many could remember the aspirations and hopes of a whole nation had effectively been put on hold. In terms of battlefield deaths the British Army would lose more lives on a single day in 1916 than it had in these twenty years combined, but by any other measure than a butcher's bill it had been a 'total war', consuming the energies and talents of the whole country, changing the land and shrinking distances, stifling reform and reaching into every facet of life in a military and economic struggle that had left Britain with the undisputed command of the world's trade, a national debt of £861 million, one in five of the population on the poor rates, and a whole thwarted generation longing for political change. 'In 1814 a war which had lasted so long that war seemed our natural state was felt to be over,' wrote the Edinburgh lawyer, Henry Cockburn, recalling the sense of a new beginning that Napoleon's exile just eleven short months earlier had seemed to promise; 'from this moment the appearance of everything was changed. Fear of invasion, contempt of economy, the glory of our arms, the propriety of suppressing every murmur at any home abuse, the utter absorption of every feeling in the duty of warlike union – these, and other principles, which for twenty years had sunk the whole morality of patriotism in the single object of acknowledging no defect or grievance in our own system, in order that we might be more powerful abroad, became all inapplicable to existing things.'

Nobody who had not lived through that first heady summer of 1814, insisted the painter Benjamin Haydon, could have any inkling of what it was like to feel a whole country's exhilarating sense of liberation. For the first time since the phoney peace of 1802, ordinary men and women had been able to travel abroad again, and as naval and Peninsular officers married, and their wives got pregnant and the country's women caught up with fashions, and British artists saw Old Masters they had known only from prints, Britain looked forward to a world un-shadowed by war. 'All the town was out to see them,'[1] the great Victorian engineer, James Nasmyth – just a lad at the time – recalled of the magical night when the whole city of Edinburgh, generous in victory to a beaten foe, had turned out to watch the passage of French prisoners from the castle down to their transports at Leith; 'they passed in military procession through the principal streets, singing as they marched along their revolutionary airs, "Ça Ira" and "The Marseillaise." The wild enthusiasm of these haggard-looking men, lit up by torchlight and accompanied by the cheers of the dense crowd who lined the streets and filled the windows, made an impression on my mind that I can never forget.'

In the year since then peace had delivered on few of the hopes of Cockburn and his fellow liberals – the brilliant Summer of Sovereigns of 1814, when London had been *en fête* for the Emperor of Russia and crowds pulled Blücher's carriage through its streets, was already a fading memory – but to a great swathe of the country peace at any price was better than more death, taxation and hardship. 'We are at the moment smarting under an almost intolerable load of taxation, incurred in fighting other peoples' battles and in dictating to other nations whether they shall have for their ruler King Stork or King Log,' the *Liverpool Mercury* had protested bitterly when the first news of Bonaparte's escape reached England. 'Such idle squabbles have deeply injured our moral character, almost exhausted our national resources; and reduced a great portion of our population to a state of ignominy or dependency ... To enter into a new war, under such circumstances, must entail upon our country a complication of evils, which cannot be thought of by the philanthropist or the patriot, without the most melancholy forebodings.'

It was perhaps predictable enough that Liverpool merchants, who had scarcely finished toasting the end of hostilities with America, were against another war, but what astonished George Ticknor, an engaging and well-connected young New Englander in Britain for the first time, was the breadth and depth of opposition. He had been taken up in Liverpool by the littérateur and philanthropist William Roscoe, and armed with introductions had made his leisurely way down to London via the Hatton parsonage where the man known as the 'Whig Johnson' – the redoubtable classical scholar and pedagogue Dr Samuel Parr – left him in no doubt that it was not just mercantile Liverpool that was against the war. 'I am for Napoleon versus the pilferers of his pensions and the kidnappers of his person,' Parr declared, 'for the army and people of France versus any and every foreign power, which should presume to oppose their sacred right to choose their own sovereign – for brave men versus assassins – for wise men versus blundering monsters – for insurgents in one country versus the confederate enemies of freedom and independence in all countries – for the countless many versus the worthless few – and finally, for a reasonable peace versus unnecessary, unjust and inhuman war.'

For all the rhetorical flourishes, here was the genuine voice of old Whiggery, and ranged alongside Parr was a rainbow coalition that reached from the usual radical suspects at one end to all those children of the Romantic age clinging on to a hero-worship that no crime, betrayal or excess of Bonaparte's could ever quite eradicate. From London's clubs to the Royal Academy, from the pages of *The Examiner* and the columns of *The Times* to private letters, the debate raged on – it was a war against Liberty, it was a war against Tyranny, it was a Tory war, it was a Necessary war, it was a war for Autocracy against Humanity, it was a war for Christianity against Barbarism – and neither side had any monopoly on the violence of its opinions. For every William Godwin preaching the 'extirpation' of the allied soldiers, there was a Wordsworth damning 'That soul of Evil … from Hell let loose'; for every vinegary old radical like William Blake's wife demanding the head of poor, mad King George or Byron looking forward to seeing Castlereagh's adorning a French pike, there were loyal theatre audiences ready to cheer anything remotely royalist to the rafters.

In spite of all the white noise of angry protest in Parliament and in the liberal and radical press, there was a groundswell of patriotic support for the war for which a deeply unpopular government and a despised Prince Regent had only the French to thank. Through the spring of 1815 there had been violent and widespread rioting over the imposition of Corn Laws, but there was no race quite like the French – 'vain, insolent, shallow … tender without heart, pale, fierce, and elegant in their looks, depraved, lecherous, and blasphemous in their natures!'– and no enemy like Boney to make John Bull forget the price of bread or the weight of his taxes and roll up his sleeves for another fight.

There had never been any doubt, either, in the minds of Lord Liverpool's Tory government that they would have to fight, and as Britain moved smoothly on to a war footing, and soldiers lobbied for employment and made their wills, and cheering crowds waved goodbye to transports carrying troops to Belgium, and the borders of France were closed and intelligence dried up, the country steeled itself against the coming storm. Since the first battles of the 1790s, parents and wives had lived in permanent dread of the news the *Gazettes* might bring them, and now again they found themselves trapped in that old, familiar limbo of apprehension and suspense, fighting over the last newspaper or pushing their way through the agitated scrums around booksellers to read the latest placard pasted in the windows.

There would not have been a town in Britain that was not sending its soldiers to Belgium during those weeks of May and early June, hardly a household that was not holding its breath, because never since the Armada had the hopes and fears of the whole country hung on the outcome of one event in the way that they did on the eve of Waterloo. At the height of French invasion scares eleven years earlier the whole country had been caught up in the demands of total war, but these early summer days in 1815 were different again from anything that the country had known, different in immediacy, different in the fissures revealed in society, and different, above all, in that sense of suspended time – William Wilberforce's 'fearful interval' – during which a schizophrenic nation, one face pointed towards Belgium and the other hell-bent on its ordinary pleasures, waited for the first news that hostilities had commenced.

* * *

It was on one such day in the middle of June, a Saturday that had seemed like any other that month, at some time after ten in the evening that a middle-aged man might have been seen walking down Chancery Lane in the direction of the Thames. At the bottom of the lane he crossed over to the south side of Fleet Street, and pushing his way through a small wicket gate in an archway beneath a big painted sign for the 'Waxworks' paused at the doorway of an old, brick-built terrace house on the right-hand side of Inner Temple Lane.

After the brightness and noise of Fleet Street, there would have been something almost palpable in the silence of the Temple, as if the City itself held its breath, listening to the muffled sounds of lives that went unheard or unnoticed on the other side of Temple Gate. Fifty yards to the west the Coalhole Tavern would be steeling itself against the raucous arrival of the actor Edmund Kean's 'Wolf Club', but for the moment the Inns of Court was a world apart, the still centre of a London that never slept, hidden away between the teeming flow of river life to the south and the 'bustle and wickedness' of Covent Garden to the north; between the political and social heartland of Westminster to the west and the City to the east.

It would have been odd if anyone had noticed Henry Crabb Robinson – with his long plain face, boxer's nose and receding hairline there was nothing remarkable about him – but if Robinson was Everyman he also knew *everyone* and in that lay his solitary claim to fame. As a young man he had shared in the political excitement of the 1790s until time and necessity had sobered him, and at the age of forty-five he was a jobbing barrister on the Norfolk circuit of no particular ambition, a Boswell manqué with nothing of his genius or his vices; a decent, good-natured, worthy, middle-aged bachelor on the long, slow downhill road from youthful, Godwinian radicalism to respectable, philanthropic, Victorian liberalism.

The old red-brick terrace that dated back to the days of the Commonwealth was rich in the kind of literary associations Robinson loved – Dr Johnson had lived at No 1 when he had first come down to London, Boswell in a typical act of homage at No 2 – and for the last six years Inner Temple Lane had been the home of Charles Lamb and his sister Mary. As a young boy Charles had fetched the family's water from the pump in the gloomy garden at the back of the house, and if the water only came with brandy these days, Hare Court was still as near to a place of childhood safety as anywhere in their haunted, restless lives that the Lambs would ever know.

Lamb loved the London that lay just the other side of the Temple Gate – its streets and playhouses, its churches and markets, its lighted shops and pretty milliners, its drunken bucks, tradesmen, whores and beggars, its coffee houses, bookstalls and print shops, its scuffles and pickpockets, even 'the very dirt and mud' – but he needed Hare Court and the shelter of the Temple precinct. In his younger days he had liked to fancy himself a Londoner in the robust eighteenth-century mould of a Johnson or Boswell, but Lamb was a spectator at the feast rather than a participant, a connoisseur and collector of the city's sights and sounds, happiest and most secure when he could pull up the drawbridge and, surrounded by his friends and his mildewed books and his old furniture and the comforting ghosts of childhood, listen for the distant voice of the watchman or the muffled cry of 'Fire'.

With its three dusty elms and dusty sparrows and graveyard gloom, situated just yards away from his beloved Fleet Street, Hare Court was not just Lamb's metropolitan ideal but his ideal of the countryside too. From their old lodgings in King's Bench Walk there had been a distant view across the Thames to the Surrey Hills, and save for the Temple Gardens or a walk along London's New River, that was as close as the most doggedly un-romantic of all the Romantics liked 'dead Nature' to come. 'I don't much care if I never see a mountain in my life,' he had written to Wordsworth fifteen years earlier, fending off an invitation to join him and his sister Dorothy for a holiday in the Lakes. 'Your sun and moon and skies and hills and lakes affect me no more … than as a gilded room with tapestry and tapers, where I might live with hand-some visible objects. I consider the clouds above me but as a roof, beau-tifully painted but unable to satisfy the mind ... My attachments are all local, purely local ... The rooms where I was born, the furniture which has been before my eyes all my life, a bookcase which has followed me about (like a faithful dog, only exceeding him in knowledge), wherever I have moved, old chairs, old tables, streets, squares, where I have sunned myself, my old school – these are my mistresses.'

For the last forty-five years this had been the whole circumference of Lamb's world – the Temple, Christ's Hospital, Bishopsgate, the clerks' office in the East India Company – and the only world he had ever wanted. From time to time he and his sister Mary would be forced to move a few hundred yards in one direction or another, but it was only here among the clerks and Benchers of the Temple, in the prelapsarian world of their childhoods, that he was at home and as safe as he could ever be from the horror that for the last twenty years had shadowed the quiet, external tenor of their lives.

The horror had begun one Thursday afternoon in September in 1796, as a young seamstress was preparing dinner for her family in their cramped Holborn rooms just to the north of the Temple. For some reason that the coroner's court could only guess at, the girl had suddenly seized a knife that was lying on the table, and baulked of killing her child apprentice, had turned on her bedridden mother and savagely stabbed her through the heart before the child's screams could bring their landlord. 'It seems the young lady had once before, in her earlier years, deranged, from the harassing fatigues of too much business,' the *Morning Chronicle* reported; 'as her carriage towards her mother was ever affectionate in the extreme, it is believed that in the increased attentiveness, which her parents' infirmities called for by day and night, is to be attributed the present insanity of this ill-fated young woman.'

The fragile and harassed young woman was Mary, the bout of madness lasted only days – the coroner's court found her insane but released her to her brother's care – and for almost two decades that had been his life. Every few years rumours of their old tragedy would surface and the Lambs would be forced to shift their lodgings, but for nineteen heroic years Charles Lamb had fought to keep the world and his own incipient madness at bay, collaborating with Mary on her children's stories and *Tales*, carrying her straitjacket for her on her sad, voluntary exiles to the Hoxton asylum whenever another attack threatened, and rising each day for thirty-three years to the drudgery of the East India Company accounts department to ensure that there would be a refuge to which she could return.

Over the years the loss and the perpetual anxiety for both Mary and his own mental state had taken its toll on Charles – it was there in the face, in the lines of suffering, the sadness in the smile, the misanthropic edge to his humour, the alcohol, the dark, unnerving depths that lay just beyond the bubbling shallows of his talk – but perhaps the strangest thing of all about Mary's illness is that she never felt any guilt for what she had done. In the first days after the attack she had come to believe that a benevolent providence had ordained her mother's death, and at some subconscious level madness remained almost as much a release as an affliction for her, an escape from the dull chrysalis of a spinsterish middle-age into a brilliant, fantasy past through which she glided with the abandoned licence of some dazzling court beauty of the age of Queen Anne and Congreve.

No one was more gentle or self-effacingly 'feminine' than Mary in her sane periods – the only woman of complete sense he had ever known, William Hazlitt claimed – and no one more brilliant or abandoned in her madness. It would have been less disquieting had their friends been able to see her insanity as something utterly unconnected with her 'real' personality, but nobody who heard her ravings – brilliant disjointed flashes of wit, sparkling jewels wrenched from their settings – could doubt that she was never so free as when she was in her straitjacket and never so restrained as when well.

Even for the most seasoned Lamb-watcher, in fact, it was hard to be sure who was looking after whom in Hare Court, or who had sacrificed most to create one, indivisible being out of the wreckage of their damaged lives, but no household in London ever attracted more loyal friends. For those who did not know the history of mental illness there was always something inexplicably odd about Charles, but for his discreet and inner circle of devotees, his defensive carapace of jokes and puns and antique flights of humour, eccentricities, reckless bursts of levity and bouts of helpless drunkenness – the 'between the acts' of his 'distressful drama' as he engagingly called them – only added a note of vulnerability that bound them even more protectively to him.

There were more glamorous, more distinguished, more powerful literary salons and coteries to be found in London – the room above Murray's bookshop in Albemarle Street where, under the malignant Thomas Gifford, the Tory *Quarterly* was hatched; the great Whig Holland House set where Sydney Smith sang for his supper – but nowhere could you meet with such a mixed crowd of people as at Lamb's. If Charles Lamb had any politics they were certainly on the liberal side of the debate, but that had never stopped his friends spanning the full gamut of political opinion, from Utopian revolutionaries-turned-Tories such as Southey, Coleridge or Wordsworth at one end of the spectrum, to the likes of Hazlitt, Godwin, Leigh Hunt and the radical journalist and satirist William Hone at the other.

The Lambs' was also the place where the age of Johnson met the age of Dickens and Browning in its embryonic state, and for Crabb Robinson this was its great charm. Robinson knew that the two great 'beasts' in the Lamb menagerie would not be there tonight, but he was seeing Wordsworth for breakfast in the morning, and in some ways it was easier when he was not there, less high-minded and, somehow – Robinson hated to let anything cloud his admiration of the man he recognised as the greatest poet since Milton – less constrained by the presence and dues of genius.

Coleridge was away too, in Wiltshire, writing – or at least talking, as only Coleridge could talk – and Hunt would be busy at the *Examiner*'s office deep into the night; but so long as there could be one evening without Hazlitt and talk of Bonaparte, Robinson did not mind who else was there. He was painfully conscious that he got the worst of an argument with Hazlitt over the whist tables the last time they had met, and for a barrister it was doubly galling to be bested by a man 'who was not just wrong but offensive in almost all he said'. 'When pressed he does not deny what is bad in the character of Buonaparte,' he had confided to his diary that night, part in anger, part in sadness at their parting of ways, 'and yet he triumphs and rejoices in the late events. Hazlitt and myself once felt alike on politics, and now our hopes and fears are directly opposed. Hazlitt is angry with the friends of liberty for weakening their strength by going with the common foe against Buonaparte ... Hazlitt says: "Let the enemy of old tyrannical governments triumph, I am glad, and I do not much care how the new government turns out ... His *hatred*, and my fears, predominate and absorb all weaker impressions."'

There seemed to be no one, in fact, that Hazlitt had not offended these last weeks – Charles Burney over the review of his sister Fanny's latest novel, Wordsworth with his attack in last week's *Examiner*, Hunt who had been forced to disown the article – but not even Hazlitt could spoil the pleasure Robinson always felt as he made his way up the steep flights of stairs to the Lambs' chambers. He was probably too late now to take a hand of whist but after the recent hash he had made of his cards that was probably no bad thing, and it was only deep into the evening, when they were done with cards and the tables put away, and the drink had begun to do its work, that the place came fully alive in all its strange, unruly charm.

The Lambs' Temple garret was a warren of small, shabby rooms under the roof and two sitting rooms on the third floor below. Charles Lamb had set aside the smaller of the rooms for a library so grimy that

Robinson could never bring himself to go in, but the 'state room' would be looking as it always did for one of their soirées, with their old, petted servant Becky loading the sideboards with food and porter, while Mary glided in her quiet, measured way among the party and Charles – his hair, as black at forty as at twenty, the one grey and one brown eye already bright with fun and battle – sat like some diminutive, half-tipsy Quaker under the low, smoke-stained ceiling among his Hogarth prints, with his forbidden brandy and forbidden tobacco, and talked and stammered and joked and punned and drank to keep at bay the demons that no talk could hold off for ever.

Even by Charles Lamb's standards, Robinson thought, they were an odd lot that evening: old Burney talking whist as if he had never watched Captain Cook being murdered or abandoned his wife for his sister; the poet Charles Lloyd, holding on to his sanity by the slenderest of threads; the ageing '90s radical George Dyer, in the same rusty, threadbare suit of black, the same dirty yellowed wisp of muslin around his throat, the same trousers that stopped short of his ankles and the same battered shoes that he had been wearing when Lamb had first seen him in the library at Christ's Hospital thirty years before. But as Robinson made his way among the old familiar faces there was one man he found himself watching with an interest that had more curiosity in it than he would have cared to admit.

The stranger had been buttonholed by Lamb, who was bent on securing his interest for another old Christ's Hospital friend, an epileptic clerk in the Temple with a wife and four children who had fallen on hard times, but for once it was not Lamb who held Robinson's interest. He knew who Basil Montagu was of course – everyone at the Bar did – and he knew the story of his mother's killing, but to see him here in the flesh, the refined and almost effeminate image of his father, old Lord Sandwich, was like watching one of Lamb's Hogarths come to life and Medmenham Monk turn Methodist preacher to denounce the vices of his youth.

Circumstances had combined, in fact, to make Basil Montagu – the illegitimate son of a notorious aristocratic rake and an opera singer murdered by a rival lover – more interesting than a reforming barrister with a specialist practice in bankruptcy had any business being. Montagu had been only nine when his mother's clergyman-murderer was hanged at Tyburn in front of the biggest crowd since the clergy-man-forger Dr Dodd, and his life since had been in miniature the movement of the age itself, an ascent – or descent, depending on your politics – from aristocratic bastard through Jacobin revolutionary and Coleridgean Romantic to Benthamite reformer, teetotalling vegetarian-ism and a gradualist faith in the slow triumph of liberal parliamentary reform.

As much as Byron or Prinny, or any of the more flamboyant arbiters of the age, Montagu embodied the spirit of a Regency England caught between a past it was trying to escape and a future that stubbornly refused to be born. There remained something of the ancien régime about him that Robinson did not quite like, but as Basil Montagu stood there among the smoke and fumes of Lamb's chambers, talking confi-dently of the inevitable triumph of reform, exchanging tales of life on the Norfolk circuit and offering his copy of 'Bentham on Evidence', Robinson was looking at the past and listening to the future.

It would be a long night at the Lambs', and as midnight approached and old Captain Burney – the apostolic link with the world of Johnson, Boswell, Reynolds and 'The Club' – talked cards, and Mary smoothed ruffled feathers, and Charles took poor, gullible George Dyer aside to explain in confidence that he had it on the best authority that Lord Castlereagh was the mysterious author of *Waverley*, London slid into its nocturnal mode. 'Dear God!' wrote Wordsworth, 'the very houses seem asleep; And all that mighty heart is lying still,' but he was wrong. London never slept. Across the water in Belgium, Wellington's army lay shivering in the freezing, drenching rain to the south of Brussels; and in London people were still dying and being born, footpads were still working the streets, thieves still casing properties, gamblers still at the tables, 'fashionables' still at Lady Salisbury's, wives who were now widows, mothers and fathers who were now without sons, still streaming home from the theatres, mercifully unconscious of the drama unfolding on the other side of the Channel.

Everywhere, the great and small acts of life were being played out. At the Theatre Royal in Covent Garden, where thirty-five years earlier, Basil Montagu's mother, Martha Ray, had been shot through the head by James Hackman as she climbed into her carriage, they had been watching *The Fortune of War*. At the Royal Amphitheatre, on the other side of the river, there had been 'a Real Horse Race and a Real Fox Chase' among the twenty-one scenes of Astley's new equestrian pantomime. On the west side of Hare Court, Kean's Wolf Club were just beginning the serious business of the night. A little farther past the Coalhole in the Strand, as old George Dyer hurried away to be the first with Lamb's news of Castlereagh, the printers would be putting to bed the next day's *Examiner*. In Bedford Square to the north of their office, Henry Hallam's wife – the mother of Tennyson's Hallam of 'In Memoriam' – had gone into labour. To the west, the hated Duke of Cumberland, just arrived in England to persuade Parliament to increase his allowance on his marriage to his German mistress, was walking home from Carlton House. To the east, London's notorious Recorder, Sir John Silvester, the defending lawyer at Hackman's trial thirty-five years earlier, was leaving a banquet at the Mansion House. A street away, behind the blank forbidding walls of Newgate gaol, a young woman Silvester had sentenced to death nine weeks earlier lay in the condemned cell waiting on the 'fount of royal mercy' that was the Prince Regent to learn her fate. At 13 Piccadilly, the newly married and pregnant Lady Byron was lying awake and awaiting the return of her husband, while across in Whitehall, his former mistress, dressed as a page, scribbled away furiously at the longest suicide note in history.

And beyond London, spreading out in concentric rings across the blackness of the country and the farms and villages and towns of Britain, thirteen million souls lived out their own separate lives in this strange phoney pause in the nation's life. At Hoxton, where Mary Lamb had spent so many months, officers and soldiers in the military asylum, forgotten victims of twenty years of war, lay, two to a cot, in their own stale urine. Somewhere out in the darkness, among the two million on parish relief this night, another mad old soldier, the Tortoise Man, would be asleep under his upturned barrow. On the south coast at Arundel, where the mighty Howard clan were gathered at the Duke of Norfolk's castle, workers would be toiling through the night putting the last touches to the stands for the celebrations of the 600th anniversary of Magna Carta. At Wigan, a young boy, mauled that afternoon by a tiger at a menagerie, lay in agony with his face torn off. In Glasgow a gang readied themselves for the next day's robbery of a textile shop and on the Isle of Harris, in the brief darkness of a Scottish midsummer night, a bloodied bundle lay unseen beside a pathway.

And beyond Britain's shores, out in the Downs, the thirty-one sail of the largest East India fleet ever assembled lay unseen in the mucky night. Off the coast of France, Sir Henry Hotham's blockading squadron waited and watched. At the entrance to Botany Bay the *Northampton Transport*, with its 111 female convicts on board, was ending its six months voyage. In Brussels, Charles Burney's sister, Fanny D'Arblay, lay fully clothed on her bed and waiting to flee. And as the rain poured down and the lightning flashed, a Scottish servant girl called Emma was carrying a folded note upstairs to the back room of a secluded town-house in Antwerp. The day of Waterloo had begun.

Midnight

Belgium

One of the strangest aspects of life in Belgium in these weeks and days before Waterloo is that people knew no more of what was going on than they did in Britain. It did not take a military strategist to realise that the first engagements of any campaign would occur in Flanders, but exactly when and where Bonaparte would strike was anyone's guess.

From the day that the Congress of Vienna declared him an outlaw Bonaparte had only two options in front of him, and one of those was in reality no option at all. With the allied armies advancing on the French frontiers from the east and the north-east he could in theory play the Fabian and simply wait in the hope of the allies falling out, but the only realistic, if slim, chance he had ever had of survival lay in taking on the enemy armies before they could unite, beating them in battle, and forcing the coalition to the negotiating table. If he simply sat and did nothing the sheer weight of allied numbers would inevitably overwhelm him. Military, political and geographical logic as well as time all pointed to a pre-emptive strike in the Low Countries before a Prussian army and a motley Anglo-Dutch force under the command of Wellington could invade France. In terms of national morale it made sense to fight any campaign on foreign soil, and with the loyalty of the Belgian population, only recently separated from France and joined with Holland in the United Kingdom of the Netherlands, very much in question, an allied defeat in Flanders – and a defeat, especially, for the British paymasters whose gold was financing the coalition armies – opened up all sorts of potential political dreams.

Nobody could be quite sure of the real extent of Bonaparte's support in Belgium but it was not something Wellington ever felt it safe to ignore. There was clearly a deep resentment among its Catholic population at being forcibly lumped together with Protestant Holland under an Orange king, but if the experience of English travellers was anything to go by, that was nothing compared with the hatred that twenty years of French aggression and the destruction of their industry and trade through Bonaparte's Continental system had caused. He had ruined their lace-makers, he had bankrupted their merchants, he had despoiled their art, he had taken their young men for his armies – '*Il a mange tout*,' one traveller was told; 'he cannot live without war, nor can the French; it is their trade; they live by it; they make their fortune by it; they place all their hopes in it; they are wolves that prey upon other nations, they live by blood and plunder.'

Bonaparte's hopes were not entirely fantasy, however, because a year of peace had brought no more contentment to Europe than it had to Britain. The end of war had been greeted across an exhausted continent with pretty well universal relief, but the return of old rulers, old rivals and old ways had performed their predictable alchemy on popular feeling, and one quick, decisive victory might conceivably be all that was required.

If Bonaparte could have heard Wellington on the subject of the 'infamous army' he had under his command he would have had even more reason to be confident of his prospects. Wellington had finally left Vienna for his Brussels headquarters at the end of March, but even after more than two months of pressuring the government in London for reinforcements, his Anglo-Dutch army was still the most vulnerable of Bonaparte's potential enemies, a rag-bag of Peninsula veterans, untried British battalions, Hanoverians, Nassauers, Brunswickers and Dutch and Belgian units spread out across a wide expanse of the Belgian countryside to the west of Brussels.

Wellington's army was never as bad as myth or Wellington would have it, though, and there was never any intention that he should fight the campaign alone. To the south-east of his positions were Marshal Gebhard von Blücher's Prussians, and if they might not have been the army they had been under Frederick the Great, the defeat at Jena in 1806 had sparked a wave of military reforms that had turned them into a formidable and determined enemy of Bonaparte and all things French.

Between the two allied armies, Wellington's with his headquarters in Brussels and Blücher's with his at Namur, was a force of around two hundred thousand men, but between the far right of the Anglo-Dutch and the far left of the Prussians lay something like one hundred and fifty miles of country, and in that gap lay Bonaparte's best hope. It would never be possible for him to defeat their combined forces with the 120,000-odd men who made up his Army of the North, but if he could get between them, and pick each of them off separately, with the numerical superiority on his side, he would confidently back himself to come out on top.

With the benefit of hindsight, in fact, there was only one direction that Bonaparte would take in 1815, one area where the campaign would unfold, but Wellington had neither the benefit of hindsight nor in this instance even of foresight. The quality of his intelligence work in the Peninsula had made an important contribution to his success, but at this crucial juncture in European history, it for once failed him, leaving him utterly in the dark as to Bonaparte's movements or intentions.

Bonaparte had left Paris in the early hours of 12 June, and as he headed north to join his army, an unsuspecting Brussels went on very much as it had since the first news of his escape from Elba had reached it three months before. There were rumours on the 14th that something was afoot but there were always rumours in Brussels, and as the hours ticked away towards the greatest battle of the nineteenth century, men and women were still pouring into a city that in those three hectic months had been transformed from a continental bolt-hole for indigent British émigrés into a cross between a military cantonment and Vanity Fair.

Among the unemployed soldiers and soldiers' wives, commercial travellers, casual tourists, earnest Cambridge students, clergymen, invalids and antiquarians who made their way to Brussels in these early June days was a newly married woman of twenty-two called Magdalene De Lancey. On the face of it the new Lady De Lancey was everything Brussels society could have wished for, and yet if she was certainly grand enough on her mother's side to have taken her place in the city's expatriate aristocratic society, Magdalene Hall was as much her father's daughter as her mother's: the reserved, slightly awkward and stubbornly brave child of a family as famous in Scottish scientific and intellectual circles for its eccentricity as it was for its brilliance.

Magdalene's mother, Helen, was the gentle and long-suffering daughter of the Earl of Selkirk, and her father Sir James Hall of Dunglass – the fourth baronet – one of the more unusual products of Edinburgh and Scotland's golden age. Sir James had inherited his title and estate on the Berwickshire coast at the age of only fifteen, and after university at both Cambridge and Edinburgh had set off on the Grand Tour in the last days of the ancien régime, exploring rocks and meeting fellow scientists, hatching crackpot architectural theories, studying farming methods and talking mathematics, mathematics and mathematics with a young Corsican army cadet studying at Brienne called Napoleon Bonaparte.

It says something both for and about Sir James Hall that he had no memory of Bonaparte (the Emperor Napoleon, on the other hand, after more than thirty not entirely empty years, could clearly recall the first 'Englishman' he had ever met) but if this forgetfulness seems a tad casual Napoleon was not the only French tyrant that he had known. On the fall of the Bastille in 1789, Sir James had again crossed the Channel to be in Paris, and there he and his consumptive, republican brother-in-law, Lord Daer, had thrown themselves into revolutionary politics, attending the Assembly and Jacobin Club during the days and dining with Robespierre, Sieyès or Tom Paine at night during those last, fateful weeks of the doomed Bourbon monarchy and the '*cochon*' Louis's flight to Varenne.

Republican, atheist, Jacobin: these were not the kind of credentials to make a man popular in the paranoid Tory Scotland of the 1790s, and even in good Whig circles the suspicions that Sir James was not quite all there would never entirely go away. There had always been a question in the family as to whether he would turn out a man of genius or an idiot, and with the jury still out on it when he died, something of the same suspicions would always hang over his children. 'He was the second son of Sir James Hall,' the brilliant memoirist Elizabeth Grant – the 'Highland Lady' – wrote of Magdalene's older brother, Basil, 'a man not actually crazy, but not far from it; so given up to scientific pursuits as to be incapable of attending to his private affairs … [Lady Helen] was a sister to the Lord Selkirk who went to colonise America. How could the children of such a pair escape. Their eldest son was a fool merely; Basil, flighty … the third, Jamie, used to cry unless Jane or I danced with him – nobody else would. Three or four beautiful girls died of consumption … two were idiots out at nurse somewhere in the country, and one had neither hands nor feet, only stumps. I used to wonder how Lady Helen kept her senses; calm she always looked, very kind, she always was, wrapped up her affections were in Basil and the two daughters who lived and married – Magdalene … Lady De Lancey … and Emily, the wife of an English clergyman.'

The 'fool' of an eldest boy was, in fact, a painter and scientist of some distinction, Basil a lionised traveller and writer, and Sir James himself the president of the Scottish Royal Society, and yet it was anything but a cushioned world in which Magdalene Hall had grown up. As a young man her father had rowed the great geologist James Hutton around the shore by the Halls' Dunglass estate, and if the young Magdalene, watching another sister sink into the grave, had ever wondered what kind of God could allow such suffering, her childhood walks along the cliffs at Siccar Point could have offered no easy consolations. 'On us who saw these phenomena for the first time, the impression made will not be easily forgotten,' the mathematician John Playfair wrote of the moment when he and Hall – two Doubting Thomases of the new science – saw for themselves in the folds and stacks of Siccar Point the indisputable physical evidence of the infinitely old, pitilessly indifferent universe that Hutton's geology and Herschel's telescopes were conjuring into existence: 'What clearer evidence could we have had of the different formations of these rocks, and the long interval which separated their formation, had we actually seen them emerging from the bosom of the deep? We felt ourselves necessarily carried back to the time when the schistus on which we stood was yet at the bottom of the sea, and when the sandstone before us was only beginning to be deposited ... An epoch still more remote presented itself, when even the most ancient of these rocks, instead of standing upright in vertical beds, lay in horizontal planes at the bottom of the sea, and was not yet disturbed by that unmeasurable force which has burst asunder the solid pavement of the globe. Revolutions still more remote appeared in the distance of this extraordinary perspective. The mind seemed to grow giddy by looking so far into the abyss of time.'

For a young child of the Scottish Enlightenment schooled in the rigours of such a universe – the daughter of an atheist and the sister of two 'idiot' girls – it had been an improbably romantic path that had brought Magdalene Hall to Belgium. She had only met her husband for the first time a few months before, but six years earlier, her brother Basil, then a lieutenant with HMS *Endymion* taking part in the evacuation of Sir John Moore's exhausted army from Corunna, had rescued and befriended a young, very tired, very dirty and unshaven army officer. 'We divided the party among us,' he later recalled, 'and I was so much taken with one of these officers, that I urged him to accept such accommodation as my cabin and wardrobe afforded. He had come to us without one stitch of clothes beyond what he wore, and these, to say the truth, were not in the best condition, at the elbows and other angular points of his frame. Let that pass – he was as fine a fellow as ever stepped; and I had much pride and pleasure in taking care of him during the passage.'

The threadbare army officer Basil Hall befriended was William Howe De Lancey, the twenty-seven-year-old, New York-born, English-educated scion of an American Huguenot family who had paid with their wealth and estates for their loyalty to the British crown during the American War of Independence. At the time of Corunna De Lancey was already a promising lieutenant colonel on the staff, and in the six years since he had consolidated his reputation as one of the most gifted of Wellington's young officers, ending the war with the Talavera, Nive, Salamanca, St Sebastian and Vittoria clasps to his Peninsula Gold Cross and a KCB to underline the trust Wellington had in his abilities.

In the inevitable way of war, sailor and soldier never met again, but the rising star of the army never forgot the naval lieutenant who had shared with him his cabin, linen and razor. On the abdication of Bonaparte in 1814, De Lancey had been appointed to a position on the staff in Scotland, and by the late spring of 1815 – Jane Austen's Admiral Croft would have approved – had met, courted and wed the second of Sir James Hall's three daughters, Basil's sister Magdalene.

Sir William and Lady De Lancey were at the Dunglass estate near Siccar Point on their 'treaclemoon' – as Byron, just escaped from his own honeymoon nightmare farther south on the bleak Durham coast would have it – when the news of Bonaparte's escape and De Lancey's recall reached them. On assuming command in Brussels, Wellington had wanted as many of his old Peninsula officers as he could muster, and high on his list to replace the wretched quartermaster-general the army had foisted on him was William De Lancey. 'To tell you the truth, I am not well pleased with the manner in which the Horse Guards have conducted themselves towards me,' Wellington had complained to Lord Bathurst, the Secretary for War; 'It will be admitted that the army is not a very good one, and, being composed as it is, I might have expected that the Generals and Staff formed by me in the last war would have been allowed to come to me again; but instead of that, I am overloaded with people I have never seen before; and it appears to be purposely intended to keep those out of my way whom I wished to assist me.'

The duke would not always get his way with appointments – and the newly married De Lancey was not at all sure he was ready to resume his career at his old rank – but Wellington was ready to fight for him and by 16 April, Major General Torrens was writing to reassure him that his new QMG was 'on his way out ... I told him the very handsome and complimentary manner in which you asked for his services, and assured him that nothing could be so gratifying, in my view of the case, to his military and professional feelings, as the desire you expressed to me of having him again with you.'

The new Lady De Lancey had followed Sir William south to London and then, on 8 June, across to Brussels where for one brief week they were billeted on the fourth floor of Count de Lannoy's house overlooking the Parc. De Lancey had been confident even then that it would be another month before there could be any fighting, but the newlyweds were taking no chances with the time they had together, cocooning themselves in a world of their own, walking out only when the rest of Brussels was dining, dining when the rest of Brussels was walking, utterly oblivious to the fears and rumours that filled the air or to the cavalry reviews, assignations and race meetings that made up the lives and the diaries of the rest of Brussels' British population.

It was not a regime to make a new bride much liked by fashionable Brussels – especially not the bride of a man as popular as Sir William De Lancey – but that was the last thing to worry Magdalene. In the months to come she would add a faintly pious gloss of gratitude for the memory of these few days together, but there was an unabashedly worldly joy in the way she seized her brief happiness, an implicit sense in everything she said and did that a whole lifetime had to be crushed into these few hours and an entire world into their Brussels rooms. 'I never passed such a delightful time, for there was always enough of very pleasant society,' she recalled, 'I used to sit and think with aston-ishment of my being transported into such a scene of happiness, so perfect, so unalloyed! – feeling that I was entirely enjoying life – not a moment wasted. How active and how well I was! I scarcely knew what to do with all my health and spirits. Now and then a pang would cross my mind at the prospect of the approaching campaign, but I chased away the thought, resolving not to lose the present bliss by dwelling on the chances of future pain.'

There had been a 'small alarm' on the afternoon of the 14th that had come to nothing, and even deep into the afternoon of Thursday 15th – 'the happiest' day of her life it had been until then – the only thing to disturb them was a three-line whip that would take him away from her for the early part of the evening. The De Lanceys had been invited to a ball that night at the Duchess of Richmond's that they could safely miss, and as they dallied away the afternoon in their rooms overlooking the Parc, putting off the moment when he would have to dress for dinner with General Alava, there seemed no reason to think that that evening or that ball would be any different from any other that filled the aristo-cratic Brussels life that they had so determinedly avoided. 'We little dreamt that Thursday was the last we were to pass together, and the storm would burst soon,' she remembered, 'Sir William had to dine at the Spanish Ambassador's, the first invitation he had accepted from the time I went; he was unwilling to go, and delayed and still delayed, till at last when near six, I fastened all his medals and crosses on his coat, helped him to put it on, and he went. I watched at the window till he was out of sight, and then I continued musing on my happy fate; I thought over all that had passed, and how grateful I felt! I had no wish but that this might continue; I saw my husband loved and respected by everyone, my life gliding on, like a gay dream, in his care.'

She was mistaken. While Wellington's quartermaster-general idled away the afternoon with his young bride, and the commander of his 4th Division sat in the Richmonds' garden assuring their daughters that nothing was in the offing, Bonaparte had crossed the border and Charleroi was in French hands. The duke had, in his own words, been 'Humbugged'. Moving with all his old clandestine speed and decision – the borders had been sealed since 7 June, with coaches immobilised, fishing vessels held in port, letters intercepted – Bonaparte had spent just three days on the road from Paris and by the 14th was with his Army of the North concentrated around Beaumont. On the 15th, the anniversary of Marengo, he had issued his memorable orders of the day and by 11 a.m. was in Charleroi reviewing his advancing troops. Ahead of him, to his right, were the Prussians under Blücher. To the left, scattered across a wide area of the Belgian countryside, Wellington's army. And between them, guarded only by a small allied force at Quatre Bras, the road to Brussels.

In his anxiety to escape envelopment Wellington had guessed wrong. No British general likes being separated from the Channel and in his conviction that any attack would come from his western flank he had opened up a gap between the two allied armies. Now all he could do was plug that gap. At five in the afternoon orders were issued for his scattered army to prepare to march, and by seven, as Brussels rang to the first sounds of bugles, Magdalene De Lancey knew that her dream was over. 'When I had remained at the window nearly an hour,' she recalled, living again those last moments of happiness before the husband of two months metamorphosed into the soldier and another small, private life was swallowed up in the drama of war, 'I saw an aide-de-camp ride under the gateway of our house. He sent to enquire where Sir William was dining. I wrote down the name; and soon after I saw him gallop off in that direction. I did not like this appearance, but I tried not to be afraid. A few minutes after, I saw Sir William on the same horse gallop past to the Duke's, which was a few doors beyond ours. He dismounted and ran into the house, leaving his horse in the middle of the street. I must confess my courage failed me now, and the succeeding two hours formed a contrast to the happy forenoon.'

At around nine, 'Sir William came in; seeing my wretched face, he bade me not be foolish, for it would soon be all over now; they expected a great battle on the morrow ... He said it would be a decisive battle, and a conclusion of the whole business ... He said he should be writing all night, perhaps: he desired me to prepare some strong green tea in case he came in, as the violent exertion requisite to setting the whole army in motion quite stupefied him sometimes. He used sometimes to tell me that whenever operations began, if he thought for five minutes on any other subject, he was neglecting his duty. I therefore scrupulously avoided asking him any questions, or indeed speaking at all. I moved up and down like one stupefied myself.'

For all Brussels it had been a long, sleepless night, punctuated by the endless reveilles echoing through the streets, by the sounds of aides coming and going, messengers galloping into the darkness, and of an army mustering for war. De Lancey had put in place plans for Magdalene to leave for the safety of Antwerp, but as dawn broke and they stood for the last time at their window together and the last plumed Highland bonnet disappeared through the Namur Gate, and the sound of the bagpipes and fifes finally melted away, Magdalene De Lancey did not need to have gone to school at Siccar Point to fear the worst.

It would have been strange, in fact, if she had not wondered, as the carriage carrying her and her maid Emma rolled northwards towards Antwerp, whether the intense happiness of those few days in Brussels had only been given her to be snatched away again. Her husband had made her promise though that she would listen to nothing until she had heard directly from him, and for the next two days she was as good as her word, immuring herself in the rooms at the back of the Laboureur Inn, windows tight shut against the world, and telling herself that the sound of cannon was the distant roll of the sea on her family's Dunglass estate.

She had stayed up deep into the night on Friday, waiting to learn whether she was a widow or a wife, but no message had come. Through the Saturday, too, as the streets of Antwerp echoed to the ominous rumble of carts and rumours of war, she continued her vigil, her doors locked, her maid forbidden to go out into the town or repeat anything she had heard. She had told herself over and again that De Lancey would be safe – she had kept her word not to listen to any rumours, she had kept her side of the bargain – and exactly on the stroke of midnight, as the Sunday of 18 June dawned and the rain lashed against her window, she had her reward. It was only a few hurried lines that her husband had sent, written at Genappe on the Charleroi road south of Brussels. There had been a battle, fought on the 16th, he told her, and 'he was safe, and in great spirits'; 'they had given the French a tremendous beating'. Whether, though, Quatre Bras was to be the final battle, William De Lancey did not say. In Belgium the day of Waterloo had begun.

1 a.m.

Cut

It was raining in London too as a man in his early thirties, unshaved and wild looking, stumbled out through the wicket gate at the top of Inner Temple Lane, and turned down Fleet Street into the Strand.

William Hazlitt was drunk and had every intention of staying drunk for as long as he could. For the best part of a year he had had to live with the humiliation of his hero Bonaparte, and he was not the man to sacrifice his moment of angry triumph now that the people's time had come and the 'Child Roland of the Revolution' – 'the Colossus of the age', the 'prostrate might and majesty of man', as he saluted Bonaparte – had 'risen from the dead' to scatter the Bourbon 'spiders and toads' from beneath his giant shadow.

There was an astonishing violence about Hazlitt's anger – the violence of the boxing ring that he so much loved, the violence of a man jabbing and jabbing his opponent to a bloody pulp – that was part a matter of principle and part personality. There was no political writer in Regency England who was so honest in his hatred of tyranny, but in Hazlitt everything that was best and worst were inextricably mixed, the strong stems of English libertarianism hopelessly entangled with the weeds of anti-popery, the fine intelligence mired in an abject and

33

humiliating sensuality, the blazing hatred of injustice rooted in an innately suspicious, misanthropic character that was as slow to forgive a kindness as it was a slight.

Even at the best of times Hazlitt's was a face you could watch for a month and not see smile – the lined, wary face of a man who expected to be dunned or robbed at every moment, the face of Caius Cassius who 'quite saw through the deeds of men' – and he had not had the best of evenings. It had been a long time since he and Charles Lamb had seen the world through the same eyes, and yet even now if there was one place where Hazlitt might hope to be welcome, where his anger might be dissolved in the alcoholic haze of his host's good nature – one place, in his mind, where the only sensible woman in all London was to be found – it was at the Lambs' chambers in Hare Court.

He could hardly have been surprised that old James Burney had turned his back on him after the mauling he had given his sister Fanny's novel in the *Edinburgh*, but what business a prosing turncoat like Robinson had cutting him was another matter. Hazlitt did not need lecturing on Wordsworth by anyone, and was there anything he had said in *The Examiner* that was not true? Would the 'patriot' Milton have written 'paltry sonnets' upon the 'royal fortitude' of the old mad king? Would Milton have suppressed his early anti-war poems to spare the sensibilities of a blood-besotted nation? Would Milton – to whom Wordsworth, 'the God of his own idolatry', so liked to compare himself – have traded in every principle of his youth to become a Tory Government's Distributor of Stamps for Westmoreland?

Hazlitt hated the Tories and their placemen and their pensioners, hated the hired pens of the government-controlled press, hated the mental servitude into which the nation had sold itself, and above all he hated the renegade liberal with a violence that had all the bitterness of the disappointed acolyte behind it. It was absurd to expect anything more of some shuffling, tuft-hunter of a lawyer like Robinson, but it sickened him that the men who had taught the 'dumb, inarticulate ...

lifeless' child that he had once been to think and feel, the men who had once hailed the new dawn of freedom in France, were these same 'Jacobin renegados' – Wordsworth, Coleridge, Southey – who now filled the niches of Robinson's pantheon.

He told himself he had 'done' with them, but he was fooling himself – he could no more have done without them than he could have done without oxygen – and the memory of what they had meant to him and the world their poetry had opened up only made their apostasy the more intolerable. Hazlitt had been scarcely more than a boy when he had first met Coleridge, but he could never forget the day he had got up in the dark to walk the ten miles to Shrewsbury to hear him preach 'Upon Peace and War', the sound of his voice rising from a plain Unitarian pulpit 'like a stream of rich distilled perfume'. It was, he remembered, as if poetry and philosophy had met, 'Truth and Genius had embraced' and a young man had heard the 'music of the spheres'. After seventeen years he could still recall the text, the 'Siren's song' of the voice, the 'strange wildness in his look' as if it had been yesterday: 'He talked of those who had "inscribed the cross of Christ on banners dripping with human gore". He showed 'the fatal effects of war, drew a striking contrast between the simple shepherd boy, driving his team afield, or sitting under the hawthorn, piping to his flock, "as though he never should be old", and the same poor country lad, crimped, kidnapped, brought into town, made drunk in an ale house, turned into a wretched drummer boy, with his hair sticking on end with powder and pomatum, a long cue at his back, and tricked out in the lonesome finery of the profession of blood.'

There was not a thought or feeling he had ever had, Charles Lamb would say, that he did not owe to Coleridge, and for the son of an obscure dissenting minister of Irish origins, cribb'd and cabin'd in a remote Shropshire village, that day had come with all the force and absoluteness of an evangelical conversion. Hazlitt had grown up in the fine, rational Republican Unitarian tradition that boasted Milton and

Priestley as its torch-bearers, but here for the first time in a Shrewsbury pulpit were truths and a language that his dry, difficult and honourable father, 'poring from morn to night' over his Bible and Commentaries in the internal exile of Wem, could never teach him. 'I had no notion then that I should ever be able to express my admiration to others in motley imagery or quaint allusion, 'till the light of his genius shone into my soul, like the sun's rays glittering in the puddles of the road … that my understanding did not remain dumb and brutish, or at length found a language to express itself, I owe to Coleridge.'

Hazlitt had honoured that debt in private and in public with the great hammer blows of his prose and if honouring it now meant going into the ring with the men who sold out to the old Tory idols of God and King and Law, then he was ready. For more than two hundred years his England had defined itself as a nation by its opposition to Popish tyranny, and there could be no truce now with an English government and its hireling army bent on restoring a malignant Bourbon tyrant to 'pollute the air' and squat, toad-like, on 'the corpse of human liberty'. There was only one issue for Hazlitt: did the people belong, like cattle, to a family, or were they free? Beside that all else was irrelevant.

The Tory press branded him a Jacobin. It was a title he was proud of. To be a true Englishman now, to stand in the great tradition that stretched back through the political martyrs of the 1790s and down the long line of Whig history to Milton, the Commonwealth and the Reformation, was to be a Jacobin, and 'to be a true Jacobin,' – Hazlitt's battle cry had never rung clearer or more urgently – 'a man must be a good hater'. 'The true Jacobin hates the enemies of liberty, as they hate liberty, with all his strength and with all his might, and with all his heart and with all his soul … He never forgets or forgives an injury done to the people, for tyrants never forget or forgive one done to themselves … He makes neither peace nor truce with them. His hatred of wrong only ceases with the wrong. The sense of it, and of the bare-faced assumption of the right to inflict it, deprives him of his rest. It stagnates in his blood. It loads his heart with aspics' tongues, deadly to small pens. It settles in his brain – it puts him beside himself. Who will not feel all this for a girl, a toy, a turn of the dice, a word, a blow, for anything relating to himself; and will not the friend of liberty feel as much for mankind?'

It was a lonely eminence to stand on, but he was used to that. 'Hating,' he acknowledged with a haughty, Miltonic defiance, was 'the most thankless of all tasks'. He had not heard Mary Lamb's parting remark to Robinson – Robinson was lucky, she had murmured to him, that he had so many friends that he could afford to cut them – but it would have come as no surprise to Hazlitt. Solitude was the price of truth and he was ready to pay it. No defender of 'the people' expected so little of that 'toad-eating creature man'; no champion of liberty felt so little affinity with his political allies; no husband ever had less sympathy from the wife who walked home silent at his side. Lamb, at Hazlitt's wedding, had had trouble stopping himself giggling, but there had not been much cause for giggling since. His heart, 'shut up in the prison house' of 'rude clay', had never found 'a heart to speak to' and in his lonely, angry pride he knew it never would. His soul, too, might remain 'in its original bondage' but that understanding – the power of words – that Coleridge had unlocked in the dumb angry child of dissent was still his and he would still use it. Ten years before, when news came of Bonaparte's victory at Austerlitz, he had walked out into a Shropshire night and watched the evening star set over a poor man's cottage with a sense that here was a new Bethlehem and a new era being born. Now, somewhere in Belgium, that star was about to rise again.

As they reached the top of Queen's Street, Hazlitt and his wife turned off from St James's Park, and right again into York Street. They were home. It was a house he rented from the dry, mechanical, utilitarian Bentham, but the garden had once been Milton's and the home of English liberty. And so long as Hazlitt lived there it would be still.

2 a.m.

Dance of Death

In these early hours of Sunday morning a woman in her late twenties called Charlotte Waldie sat alone in her room in Antwerp's Laboureur Inn. Her brother and sister had long since gone to bed, but even after two sleepless nights Charlotte had no intention of missing out on anything. As the rain lashed against the window panes and the thunder rolled in the distance she sat listening to the 'dismal sound' of a coffin lid being nailed down in a room below and waited for the inn to fall quiet.

Charlotte Waldie had been born of a Scottish father and an English mother on the family estate by the Tweed River, near the ancient abbey town of Kelso. In her later accounts of these days in Belgium she would always sign herself 'An Englishwoman', but underneath that rather cool description was a child of the turbulent Scottish Borders, a glowing patriot of the school of Walter Scott with an inexhaustible appetite for experience, a gift for prose of a breathless, heady kind, a travel writer's eye for detail and an unashamed habit of seeing the whole world as copy for her pen.

On Sunday 18 June, Charlotte Waldie had been in Belgium for just six days. She had sailed from Ramsgate with her brother and sister on an overcrowded packet on the afternoon of the 10th, and thirty-six stifling and miserable hours later, had been rowed ashore from their becalmed boat in the dead of night, unceremoniously carried through the waves and dumped somewhere on the sands of the Belgian coast near Ostend.

The family had been forced to leave servants, barouche and baggage behind when they abandoned the packet for their rowing boat, but Charlotte Waldie was not a gothic novelist for nothing, and anything tamer would probably have been a disappointment. The Waldies had no more idea than anyone else in Britain or Belgium of what might be happening on the other side of the French border, and after the English tourist's customary genuflections in the direction of High Art and Rubens – and an audience in Ghent with the woefully unromantic 'Louis le Désiré' – had arrived in Brussels just in time to hear that Bonaparte had crossed the border and to follow half of the expatriate population in their panicked stampede from a city suddenly under threat.

Only hours earlier, Brussels had seemed a place of 'hope, confidence and busy expectation', but as the first, confused reports from the front came in and the sound of cannon – twenty miles away? ten? five? no one could be sure – rolled across the now deserted Parc, Brussels turned on itself in a frantic struggle to get the last horse, carriage or cart out of the city before the French arrived. 'Old men in their night-caps, women with dishevelled hair,' Charlotte had watched the chaotic scenes in the courtyard below from her room in the Hôtel de Flandre, 'masters and servants, ladies and stable boys, lords and beggars; Dutchmen, Belgians, and Britons, bewildered garçons and scared filles de chambre; all crowded together, jostling, crying, scolding, squabbling, lamenting, exclaiming, whipping, swearing and vociferating'.

It had been a day of mayhem and fear, of crowded roads, of rumour and counter-rumour, of victory and defeat – the Prussians had held the French, the French had destroyed the Prussians, Wellington was wounded and the British defeated, the French were in retreat, Brussels was in French hands – and now, twenty-four hours later, as the sound of hammering ceased and the Laboureur Inn fell silent, Charlotte Waldie slipped out of her room and down the stairs to see for herself the other side of war. 'It was a solemn and affecting scene,' she recalled as she entered the same small chamber where Magdalene De Lancey had rested for an hour and which now contained 'the last narrow mansion of a brave and unfortunate prince'. Tapers were burning at the head and foot of the coffin, and the room was now empty except for 'two Brunswick officers who were watching over it, and whose pale, mournful countenances, sable uniforms, and nodding black plumes, well accorded with the gloomy chamber. It was but yesterday that this prince, in the flower of life and fortune, went out into the field of military ardour, and gloriously fell in battle, leading on his soldiers to the charge. He was the first of the noble warriors who fell on the memorable field of Quatre Bras. But he has lived long enough who has lived to acquire glory.'

The coffin was that of Frederick William, Duke of Brunswick, the cousin of the Prince Regent, the brother of Queen Caroline, a favourite uncle of the Princess Charlotte, and one of the first casualties of Hazlitt's battle between liberty and legitimacy. For the last six years the duke had held the rank of lieutenant general in the British Army, but it was as a hero of the German struggle against Bonaparte that he had made his name, raising, equipping and commanding his famous force of 'Black Brunswickers' in a quixotic and doomed bid to reclaim the duchy lost after the death of his father at Jena in 1806.

With his flat, coarse potato of a face, his great side-whiskers and a nose that would have graced a Hanseatic merchant, it would be difficult to imagine a less romantic-looking figure than the duke. And yet in spite of everything that his sister Caroline could do to taint it, romance still clung to the Brunswick name. 'The Brunswickers are all in black,' the engagingly uxorious Sir Augustus Frazer, in command of

Wellington's horse artillery, had written home to his wife, after admiring the duke's hussars at the great review in May, 'the Duke having, in 1809, when the Duchess died, paid this tribute of respect to his wife. There is something romantic in this. They are to change their uniform when they shall have avenged themselves on the French for an insult offered to the remains of the Duke's father. Is this chivalry, or barbarity?'

It was a wonderfully nineteenth-century thought that the two things might be opposites – another prince dressed in black had very little trouble squaring them – and Wellington for one would have settled for something more barbarous than the army of young boys that Brunswick had brought with him. In the weeks since arriving in the Belgian capital, Wellington had complained endlessly of the 'infamous army' he had been given to do the job, but by the time it had at last become clear that the French advance towards Quatre Bras and Brussels was not a feint, he was in no position to pick and choose whether it was his old Peninsula veterans or the raw and untested Brunswickers who would get him out of the fix he had got himself into.

That had been late on Thursday 15th, and that night anyway the duke had other things to do. He must have known as well as anyone that Bonaparte's brilliant advance had not shown him at his best, but he had promised the Duchess of Richmond she could have her ball ('Duchess, you may give your ball with the greatest safety, without fear of interruption,' he had superbly told her) and he was damned if anything the French did now was going to show him up for a fool.

He had his other reasons for going to the Richmond ball that night, or would find them with hindsight – morale, psychology, a show of British sang-froid, a 'marker' for wavering Belgians – but the answer was probably no more complicated than pride. Throughout his career he had had to live with the carping of opposition politicians who hated the Wellesleys, and yet it was a very long time – probably the Siege of Seringapatam in the spring of 1799 and his first major battle – since he had had to justify or explain himself to his own officers and he had no intention of doing anything to undermine the extraordinary hold he had over them now.

'Nobody can guess Lord Wellington's intentions,' Uxbridge's sister Lady Caroline Capel had written just a week earlier, '& I dare say Nobody will know he is going till he is actually gone.' If the women of Brussels did not know what he was doing then certainly no one else was going to. For an old Peninsula-hand like Sir Augustus Frazer there was nothing new in this, but for those who had never been around the duke before, there was something almost shocking in the dominance he exerted over officers who in any other situation and under anyone else were figures of substance in their own right. 'Our movements are kept in the greatest secrecy. We know nothing that is going on,' the Reverend George Stonestreet, the most unmilitary of Guards' chaplains, wrote from 1st Division Headquarters to his brother-in-law, a broker in the City always keen for his own reasons to know what was happening in Belgium. 'General Officers, even those commanding divisions are *kept* in ignorance by the great Duke ... I am astonished to find *the fear* which exists, of *at all offending* the Duke; and the implicit submission and humility with which Men of talent courage and character shrink before his abrupt, hurried and testy manner.'

If anyone knew what was on his mind it was likely to be his latest dalliance, the pale and anorexically thin Byron cast-off, Lady Frances Wedderburn Webster, but it would have taken a brave man to have asked the duke what he was doing at the ball. Lord Fitzroy Somerset, Wellington's secretary, had not understood why the army had not marched immediately that Thursday afternoon, but when it came to the point he was no bolder than the rest, tamely conceding that 'as it was the place where every British officer of rank was likely to be found, perhaps for that reason the Duke dressed & went there'.

He was right in that at least, almost everyone but the De Lanceys was there. And if it might have been argued – and it was in angry Whig and opposition circles – that Wellington's officers might have been better off with their regiment, nothing so vividly encapsulates the strange air of unreality that marked these last days before Waterloo. It was here at a rented house in the rue de Blanchisserie in the early hours of the 16th, as Wellington sat on a sofa and talked with Lady Dalrymple Hamilton, and the Duke of Brunswick gave a sudden, violent shudder of premonition, and Gordon Highlanders demonstrated their reels to the duchess's guests, that the cumulative oddity of what would soon be dubbed 'the 100 Days' took on the surreal, climactic air of a macabre Regency Dance of Death. 'There was the sound of revelry by night,' Byron famously would write,

> And Belgium's capital had gather'd then
> Her Beauty and her Chivalry, and bright
> The lamps shone o'er fair women and brave men;
> A thousand hearts beat happily; and when
> Music arose with its voluptuous swell,
> Soft eyes look'd love to eyes which spoke again,
> And all went merry as a Marriage bell;
> But hush! Hark! a deep sound strikes like a rising knell.
>
> Within a window's niche in that high hall
> Sate Brunswick's fated chieftain; he did hear
> That sound the first amidst the festival,
> And caught its tone with Death's prophetic ear;
> And when they smiled because he deem'd it near,
> His heart more truly knew that peal too well
> Which stretch'd his father on a bloody bier,
> And roused the vengeance blood alone could quell.

Even as the ball broke up into a hundred hurried farewells, the bizarre air of unreality still hung over Brussels. From the window of her hotel on the Parc the newly arrived Charlotte Waldie had watched a soldier turn back again and again to embrace his wife and child for a last time, and yet as the dawn exodus of Wellington's army began, and market carts and vendors bringing their cabbages, cauliflowers, peas and early potatoes in from the surrounding countryside added their own note of burlesque to the sombre occasion, it was almost impossible to take in the fact that this really was war. 'Soon afterwards the 42nd and 92nd Highland regiments marched through the Palace Royale and the Parc,' wrote Charlotte Waldie, 'with their bagpipes playing before them, whilst the bright beams of the rising sun shone full on their tartan bonnets. We admired their fine athletic forms, their firm erect military demeanour and undaunted mien. We felt proud that they were our countrymen: in their gallant bearing … Alas! We little thought that even before the fall of night these brave men, whom we now gazed at with so much interest and admiration, would be laid low.'

As the sound of the last fife melted away from a suddenly silent Brussels, the first units of the army entered into the gloom of the dense Soignes Forest that stretched out to the south on either side of the Charleroi road. It might have occurred to some of the more experienced troops that this would be no road to retreat along if things went badly, but in the warm still of the morning, with no sound of canon ahead to concentrate the mind, and Guards officers, coats open, snuff boxes in hand, trotting towards the battle along the cobbled chaussée in their smart cabriolets as if they were making for Epsom or Ascot, it was hard to believe that there was a French army less than twenty miles away.

It was partly a failure of imagination, it was partly sang-froid, part show and part utterly genuine, but at the bottom of it all was a supreme confidence in the man who led them. Over the last few months Wellington might have seemed more interested in his love affairs than in Bonaparte, but the moment the fighting started he was always a different man; the 'Beau', as his staff called him, gone, and the general worth a division against any enemy back in command. 'Where indeed, and what is not his forte?' Augustus Frazer asked his wife. 'Cold and indifferent, nay apparently careless in the beginning of battles, when his moment of difficulty comes intelligence flashes from the eyes of this wonderful man; and he rises superior to all that can be imagined.'

That 'moment' had come. But if he knew exactly where he wanted to fight his battle – he had used a thumb to mark out a long low ridge, crossing the Charleroi road just south of the Soignes Forest, on the Duke of Richmond's map only hours before – the time had long gone when he could fight the enemy on the ground he chose. The last report he had was that the French were already in Frasnes near Quatre Bras, and with the Prussians about to be engaged at Ligny to the east of the crossroads and the bulk of his army still marching from the west, the only force that stood between Bonaparte and Brussels was the reserve strung out behind him along the main north–south Charleroi road.

Wellington was certainly luckier than he deserved. A combination of inertia and confused orders and priorities had wasted an overwhelming French advantage and meant that Quatre Bras was still in allied hands when he reached the crossroads at ten. The army opposing a token allied force of 7,000 troops was three times as strong in men and still more in guns, but Wellington knew that if they could hold the critical line of the chaussée linking Quatre Bras and Ligny three miles to the east until fresh units arrived, the odds must slowly but inexorably swing his way.

There was nothing pretty about the battle that followed, nothing scientific – shot, grape, shell and musket, hand-to-hand fighting in the woods and long rye; wave after wave of cavalry breaking against British squares – but gradually a battle that should have been lost before it had begun started to move Wellington's way. Over the next hours the issue still remained in doubt, but as each unit arrived and was thrown in the odds had already begun to shift. As night fell, with the woods to the south-west of the crossroads and the farm buildings straddling the

Charleroi road again in allied hands, the field was Wellington's. At savage cost Quatre Bras had been saved and the road to Brussels held.

Over the battlefield a giant and perfect pyramid of smoke, visible for miles, hung like a funeral pall. Around the crossroads, where the foul-mouthed Sir Thomas Picton, Wellington's great 'fighting general' from the Peninsula, had rallied the 28th with the battle cry of 'Remember Egypt', and where Wellington had leaped a hedge of bayonets into the safety of a Highland square, lay the dead and wounded of both sides. French casualties were over four thousand, allied closer to five. In the course of the action, the 92nd – the Gordon Highlanders – whose sergeants, only hours earlier, had been reeling for the Duchess of Richmond's guests, had lost five commanding officers. The 42nd, the Black Watch, had suffered some 300 killed and wounded; the 69th from Lincolnshire more than forty per cent; the 30th very nearly as many, the Guards' heavy losses clearing out Bossu Wood, the Dutch and 'death's-head' Brunswickers the same. 'In no battle did the British infantryman display more valour or more cool courage than at Quatre Bras,' wrote Edward Cotton of the 7th Hussars. 'Cavalry we had none that could stand the shock of the French; the Brunswick and Belgian cavalry, it is true, made an attempt, but were scattered like chaff before the wind by the veteran Cuirassiers … The British cavalry had had a long march, some nearly forty miles, and consequently did not arrive until the battle was over. The gallant Picton, seeing the cavalry driven back, led on our infantry in squares into the centre of the enemy's masses of cavalry, facing charging squadrons with squares, and in line against heavy columns of infantry.'

Even though that old combination of Picton and the British infantryman had bailed Wellington out, it was no victory. To their left, long after the guns fell silent at Quatre Bras, the sound of cannon continued in the direction of Ligny. The allies had secured the road to Brussels but the French in their turn had prevented them joining up with the Prussians. It was, at the best, a draw. Deployed across a forward slope, and facing the main body of Bonaparte's Army of the North, Blücher's Prussians had been badly beaten, and as they retreated north and east towards Wavre, Wellington had no choice but to retire as well.

It was a dejected army that buried its dead, and on Saturday 17th, under cover of cavalry and of an apocalyptic storm, began their withdrawal towards Brussels. The rains had turned the paths and fields into canals and quagmires, but at 2 a.m. on this Sunday morning, as the thunder crashed and the rain lashed down, and the Duke of Brunswick lay in his coffin, they finally halted along a ridge just south of the Soignes Forest. The 92nd, or what was left of them – one colonel, one major, four captains, twelve lieutenants, four ensigns, twelve sergeants and about 250 rank had failed to answer the roll call – had stopped near a farm building called La Haye Sainte, taking up their position on either side of the Brussels road. The name would have meant nothing to them, but then except perhaps for Wellington and De Lancey it would have meant little to anyone. On the day before, Sir Augustus Frazer, in command of the army's horse artillery, had been told that Wellington was heading towards a place called Waterloo. He could not even find it on his map. What, he asked, was its real name? He was about to find out. The 'trumpet of fame', as Edward Cotton called it, would never sound as it should for the dead of Quatre Bras, but Wellington would have his battle where he had wanted it.

3 a.m.

A Dying World

The short midsummer night was over on the tiny Isle of Scalpaigh.
From the highest point on the island, Skye and the dark line of the
Ross-shire hills would have been visible in the distance, but if anyone
was stirring down by the shoreline they had not yet seen, lying beside
a cairn on the rough track that led from the MacLennans' stone house
to the family well, a torn and bloodied bundle that contained the
remains of a newborn child.

It was the Sabbath with all that meant in the Scottish islands, and if
the star that the young William Hazlitt saw over a Shropshire cottage
had ever shone above the heather thatch of the thin scattering of croft
houses that lined the narrow sound separating Scalpaigh from Harris,
it had long since set. Thirty-odd years before, the retired captain of an
East Indiaman from Berneray had bought Harris from his MacLeod
cousin and settled crofters here, glimpsing in the sheltered, rocky inlets
of its eastern coastline with its infinite supply of kelp and teeming
abundance of fish – cod from November to June, ling from June
through to September, dog fish during the calm summer months, skate
and eel, oysters, herring and salmon in every bay and loch – a Hebridean
cornucopia that need never fail.

Captain Alexander MacLeod of Berneray was a landlord and inno-
vator in the great tradition of doomed philanthropists and improvers
who over the next 150 years would bedevil the Highlands and Islands
of Scotland. He had originally made his fortune as captain of the
Mansfield and in his late fifties established himself at Rodel at the
southern tip of Harris, where he built a large, handsome house and set
about improving a wonderful natural harbour with everything needed
for a year-round fishing industry. 'Within the bay of Rowdill, on the
north side, there is an opening, through a channel of only 30 yards wide
to one of the best sheltered little bays in the Highlands,' reported the
elderly John Knox, another philanthropic improving Scot, after visiting
Rodel in 1786, 'from which, on the opposite side, there is an opening of
the same dimensions to the sea. This has water for vessels to enter or
depart at any time of the tide, and Captain MacLeod had deepened the
south passage to fifteen feet at common spring tides. The circumference
of the little harbour or bason is nearly an English mile, and here the
ships lie always afloat, and as safe as in Greenock dock. Here the
Captain has made an excellent graving bank, and formed two keys ...
where ships may load or discharge afloat, at all times of the tide.'

This is the voice of a pragmatist and surveyor talking – Knox was
reporting on the west coast for the British Society for Extending the
Fisheries, part of that earnest eighteenth-century effort to claim the
Scottish Highlands for civilisation – but for all his commercial instincts,
MacLeod was a romantic and Rodel a place to dream. On the hill above
the harbour a sixteenth-century MacLeod had rebuilt the church of St
Clement's, and in some crucial sense Alexander was as much a throw-
back as a sign of things to come, a relic of an idealised world of 'Charity,
Piety, integrity of life' and social responsibility that if it had ever existed
had been dealt its death blow at Culloden.

And yet if there can be few more beautiful places in Britain than
Rodel on a June morning, with a view stretching away southwards
down the long line of islands towards Barra, and eastwards to Skye and

the distant mainland, Harris was as much a place of blighted hopes as it was of dreams. Forty years earlier the Young Pretender, Charles Edward Stuart, had sought refuge on Scalpaigh during his flight into exile after Culloden, and in the decades since the failure of the '45, Harris had struggled to come to terms with the shifting, harder, commercialised relationship of owner and tenant and the vanguard of the sheep that would signal the end of the old Highland order.

There were the mainland canals to navvy on and there was still the army – there were women on the island this Sunday morning who did not yet know they were widows of Quatre Bras – but even in the good years it was a harsh life for the crofter. 'All the bread is generally consumed by the end of June,' the Reverend John MacLeod had recorded in 1792, 'and such as then cannot afford to purchase imported meal, subsist chiefly on the milk of their cows and sheep, with what fish they may chance to catch, till their wants are relieved by the first fruits of their potato crop early in harvest.'

It is a tragic irony that of all the measures Captain Alexander MacLeod introduced to improve these lives – the house, the school, the better tracks, the fishing stations, the boat yard, the Orkney yawls, the restored church of St Clement's – his abiding legacy to them was one of bitter hardship and failure. In the early days of his ownership there had been some spectacular success with commercial fishing, but when he died in 1790 it was not the 'silver darlings' of the herring trade or a balanced island economy that interested his absentee son and grandson but the easy fortunes to be had out of the inexhaustible supply of kelp in the myriad bays and inlets of Harris's rocky eastern coastline.

It would prove a dangerous dependency for the islanders but for an absentee landlord only concerned with the short-term the profits were immense – landlords would go to court to dispute possession of an outcrop of useless rocks – and the young Alexander MacLeod had been lucky in his timing. In the years before the outbreak of war with France the seaweed had principally been used in the islands to fertilise the soil, but with the disruption of trade and the end of crucial and cheaper imports from Napoleonic Europe the mineral-rich kelp ash used in the glass and soap industries suddenly soared in value.

Along the exposed western side of the island, where the Atlantic winter storms threw up vast dumps of kelp down its long line of white, shell-sand beaches, the harvesting was a simple if occasional business, but on the eastern 'bays' it was another matter. In the past these inhospitable inlets had only been used for summer grazing, but the fortunes to be made in kelp shifted the whole focus of the economy from west to east, from the sporadic collection of sea-ware for manuring the crofters' fields to its systematic farming for the precious ash.

It was a brutally harsh and primitive life for the crofters who had been resettled along the northern shore of East Loch Tarbert, but as long as the war had continued they had at least been able to survive. The huge bulk of the profits inevitably disappeared off the island to line the pockets of MacLeod's absentee heirs, and yet if the work was grim and unhealthy – backbreaking hours spent thigh-deep in the cold sea felling the kelp or tending the pits that burned along this shoreline with their sullen, acrid, blinding smoke – kelp offered the only way, short of emigration, or Quatre Bras, out of the inflationary Malthusian spiral of mounting rents, higher food prices and rising population of which the crofters were the helpless, inarticulate victims.

It was to one of these small isolated settlements on the shore of East Loch Tarbert, perched precariously between the sea and the stark lunar interior of North Harris, that some ten years earlier a young girl from the other side of the island called Eury MacLeod had come to work. There had almost certainly been the odd hovel on this site before old Alexander MacLeod's days, but like Urgha and Carriegrich to the west of it, Caolas Scalpaigh survived as a reminder of those heady days of the captain's fisheries projects, when it seemed that the silver darlings could never fail and that Harris was set to harvest its own improbable bonanza of war.

There were twenty crofting lots at Caolas Scalpaigh when war had ended in 1814, with their rental fixed to the stretch of shore rather than to the size of the holding, and it is likely that the Malcolm MacLeod, for whom Eury had come to work, was her relative. The MacLeods held crofts No 2 and 3 at this time, and if that might have made them marginally better off than the rest of Caolas Scalpaigh, an exorbitant rent of £9 a year – by far the highest in the whole settlement – still left them tottering on the edge of a disaster that only the kelp could keep at bay.

For more than ten years Caolas Scalpaigh had been Eury MacLeod's whole world, the view through the smoke of the kelp pits over the narrow sound to the Isle of Scalpaigh the limits of her horizon, when sometime in the early summer of 1815 she discovered that she was pregnant. She had a vague sense that she had not conceived before the previous Martinmas, 11 November, but beyond that and the name of the father – Roderick Macaskill, a twenty-five-year-old crofter's son from Caolas Scalpaigh who had since left the island to find work as a labourer on the construction of the Caledonian canal – she could not even have told anyone how old she was.

She was never able to say when she first realised her condition, and she had certainly told no one when on the 14 May 1815 – Whitsun – she had left the house of Malcolm and Marion MacLeod and crossed the narrow sound to live with her sister and her brother-in-law on the Isle of Scalpaigh. It is just possible that she hoped that somehow she could have the child undetected on the near-empty island, but there seems something so dumbly and hopelessly passive about Eury MacLeod's whole story that it is hard to imagine that calculation ever entered into it.

There was only one house of any size on Scalpaigh, the MacLennans' house – where in the days when Donald Cameron had been tacksman, the Young Pretender had hidden for four days during his flight into exile – and it was near here, on either Friday 16th or the Friday before, that Eury MacLeod had crawled out of her brother-in-law's house in the middle of the night and given birth to a stillborn baby boy. By the time the scattered remains were found on the 19th it was impossible to know how long they had been lying there, and long before Eury would be well enough to give any coherent account, exhaustion and fever had reduced her recollections to a blur from which only the barest facts ever emerged.

'At the time the Declarant came to ... her sister's house,' read the official statement taken down in English from Eury's confession by the Rodel schoolmaster for the Sub-Sheriff, and read back to her in her native Gaelic, 'her sister's children [she said] were ill of a fever and that her sister attended them, that about twenty days after her going to her sister's house the Declarant was herself attacked by the fever, which confined her to her bed.' For four or five days Eury had been too ill to move, but 'on a Friday evening' – which Friday she could not say – she had 'found herself very much pained', and putting on her 'cloaths' and letting herself out of her sister's house, had followed the track to near the MacLennans' store house 'where she was delivered of a male child'.

The boy was stillborn, 'not having come into its full time', and 'finding the child dead ... and being unable to bring it home', Eury had wrapped her petticoat about the body tying the string about the middle. 'She had laid the child by the side of a stone on the road to the MacLennans' well, and had then gone back to her sister's, intending, she told the schoolmaster, to come back for the child's body the next morning 'but she was too ill to do so'.

In these early hours of 18 June, as she lay beneath the heather thatch of her sister's house, still too weak to recover her dead child, she will have known little of this. Nor would she know the charge hanging over her: 'That albeit, by the laws of this and every other well governed Realm,' read the preamble, 'Murder, and more especially the Murder of a child by its own mother, is a Crime of an heinous nature, and severely punishable ... the said Aurora MacLeod did in a field near to the stone house occupied by Murdoch MacLennan, Tacksman of Scalpay ... and at or near to a cairn of stones in said field, bring forth a living and full term male child, and she did there immediately after the birth, wickedly and feloniously bereave of life and Murder the said child, by the Strangulation, or bruising the head and body thereof, or by other means ... unknown, and she did thereafter expose the body of the said child ... where it was afterwards found, much mangled and mutilated by dogs or other animals.'

Already her distinct Gaelic identity, and even her name, were dissolving in the maw of British justice. The small child who had come down to Caolas Scalpaigh to carry peat and draw water for Malcolm MacLeod was now the declarant 'Aurora' MacLeod. She would never see either Caolas Scalpaigh or her Lewis birthplace of Balincoll again. In front of her lay the short boat ride to Rodel, the schoolmaster and Sheriff-Substitute, Stornoway, the Tolbooth gaol at Inverness and the September assizes. Even the concealment of a pregnancy was a crime in itself, and when her trial finally came round – a young, sick girl, saddled with a name that would have meant nothing to her, in a court whose language she did not speak and where her only Tolbooth companion was another Lewis girl who had strangled her baby and thrown it in a loch – all that remained was the sentencing. And even that she did not get. There is no record, in fact, of what happened to Eury – Aurora – MacLeod. For some reason Aurora's sentencing was reserved to the High Court of Judiciary at Edinburgh. There seems no obvious explanation for this postponement, and somewhere between Inverness and Edinburgh – a final, gratuitously appropriate touch – she would simply disappear, leaving only an entry in the Discharge Book of the Inverness Tolbooth and a cancelled minute in the records of the Edinburgh High Court of Judiciary to mark the obscure end of her short, invisible life.

All that, though, was still ahead of her. Behind her she would be leaving a dying world, caught up in its own inexorable, resistless tragedy of the Clearances, the death of the kelp trade, and emigrations. And beside the track up to the MacLennans' well, this Sunday morning – tragedy and symbol rolled into one – lay the stillborn body of her child.[1]

4 a.m.

I Wish It Was Fit

There was no more sign of Hazlitt's bright star of liberty, or any other star, rising over the sodden slopes of Flanders this Sunday morning than there was on the Isle of Scalpaigh. To the old Peninsula men who remembered the nights before Salamanca and Vittoria, the thunder and lightning were omens of victory, but for the exhausted young boys of the 14th of Foot, Buckinghamshire farm lads in the main and still mostly in their teens, hungry, soaked to the skin, caked in mud, and un-bloodied in war, there was only the cold, numbing rain and fear.

'What a sight to we old campaigners, but more particularly to the young soldiers,' wrote home one Peninsula veteran, William Wheeler, camped with the 51st of Foot in a cornfield just beyond the 14th at the far right of the allied line that stretched out along the defensive ridge nine miles to the south of Brussels; 'being close to the enemy we could not use our blankets, the ground was too wet to lie down, we sat on our knapsacks until daylight without fires, there was no shelter against the weather: the water ran in streams from the cuffs of our Jackets, in short we were as wet as if we had been plunged over head in a river. We had one consolation, we knew the enemy were in the same plight.'

Along the whole length of the line, officers and men were making the best of whatever shelter they could find, hunkering down under hedges or beneath cannon with only their pipes, brandy, gin and sheer exhaustion to anaesthetise the misery. 'It was as bad a night as I ever witnessed,' recalled another campaigner, a cavalryman from the 7th Hussars, who had already fought one bruising action against French lancers that day while covering the infantry withdrawal from Quatre Bras. 'The uproar of the elements seemed to have been the harbinger of the bloody contest. We cloaked, throwing a part over the saddle, holding by the stirrup leather, to steady us if sleepy; to lie down with streams under us was not desirable, and to lie among the horses not altogether safe.'

It ought to have been impossible to sleep in such conditions, but a public school was perhaps as good a training in discomfort as a Scottish glen, and sixteen-year-old Ensign George Keppel of the 3rd Battalion of the 14th of Foot could not have stayed awake to save his life. From the day he had disembarked at Ostend, Keppel seemed to have done nothing but march and counter-march across Belgium, and it was late in the afternoon of the 17th, after one last weary haul from Nivelles, that his colonel had pointed out to him 'a spot in the distance' that he had never heard of, called Waterloo.

Had the young George Keppel been in any condition to take the long view of things, however, or just a fraction more self-important, he might have seen the hand of destiny at work in the bizarre chain of events that had brought him to an obscure Belgian village. His great-uncle Frederick had been a Bishop of Exeter and Dean of Windsor during the early years of George III's reign, but with the exception of that genial, pluralist blot on the family honour, the Keppels had traditionally been courtier-warriors since they had arrived with 'Dutch' William in 1688, generals and admirals who had played their part in almost every British conflict from Oudenarde and Ramillies to Dettingen, Fontenoy, Culloden, Havana and Quiberon Bay.

While his father, the fourth earl, was something of a disappointment – a Whig courtier and racing man destined to spend most of his life waiting for the return of the good days – the young George, with all the easy, good-natured charm of the first earl, the spirit of his great-uncle who had circumnavigated the globe with Admiral Anson, and the liberal, populist instincts of all the staunchly Whig Keppels, was a throwback to a freer and more robust age. In the spring of 1815 he was still a schoolboy at Dr Page's Westminster; but school had never been much more than a minor distraction for him, an alternative London address equally handy for the theatres or duck shoots, a convenient base from which he could as easily slip off to see the Princess Charlotte as join in with the mob stoning his father's Portland Street house during the anti-Corn Law riots.

If the eighteenth century, in all its dubious and scandalous licence, survived into the early nineteenth century anywhere, it was in the English public schools, and pedigree and character had equipped Keppel to enjoy its freedoms to the full. In the memoirs of other Westminsters of only a slightly later generation, the talk is all of 'shadows' and 'substances' and the other ludicrous arcana of public school life, but in Keppel's we get the authentic taste of an aristocratic Regency London, a world of prize-fighting, carriage-racing, bull-baiting, mail-coach driving, badger-drowning and the great clown Grimaldi – a world, in short, closer to that of his grandfather's days than to the God-fearing institutions that would soon be taking shape in the dreams of George's Winchester near-contemporary, Thomas Arnold.

There was not an ounce of malice, or what Arnold would darkly think of as 'vice', in the young Keppel, only boundless animal spirits and a happy, democratic talent for mixing as easily with gallows-bound ruffians down by the river as the heir presumptive to the throne. If he thought about his future at all it was in the vaguest terms of a career in the law and maybe a safe family seat in Parliament, but at the age of fifteen the Bar or the House of Commons – or anything in fact beyond the immediate confines of his schoolboy's London world – all seemed to belong to a period with which he need not unduly concern himself.

Even the escape of Bonaparte from Elba had made almost no impression on a lad more interested in the exotic Madame Oldenburg's hats than in politics, but in the mock-heroic drama Keppel liked to make of his life, their planets had already begun to converge. From his first days at Westminster he had used Abbot Livingstone's wall in Great College Street to get in and out of Mother Grant's boarding house, and on a night in the middle of March 1815, just as 'another truant on a larger scale' was about to enter Paris, George had slipped quietly back through Dean's Yard after a night at the theatre to find waiting for him the rope ladder that the school Crispin – 'Cobbler Foot by name, an old man-of-war's man' – had run up for precisely these eventualities.

It was a well-rehearsed routine – the scaling ladder hanging down on the street side, a convenient lean-to that the school authorities ('not wise in their generation', as Keppel sadly recorded) had kindly provided on the drop side, a straw dummy tucked up in his bed – and there seemed no reason to think anything was wrong. He had made his way over the wall without any difficulty and got safely back to his room; and it was only when he opened his door to find his bedding flung back and the straw doppelgänger strewn across the floor that he knew he was in trouble.

In the past he could invariably rely on his old childhood playmate, the Prince Regent's capricious daughter and heir presumptive, Princess Charlotte, to come up with a lie on his behalf, but this time there was no way out. The next morning he had been 'sorely puzzled' at the silence which greeted him when he went into school, but 'the mystery' was solved the next day when a letter from his father informed him that his 'school days had come to an end', along with another 'from Dr Page … recommending him to choose [a profession] in which physical rather than mental exertion would be a requisite'.

If nothing in his school career became him quite like the leaving, his father was never likely to see it that way, and retribution was fast. His older brother, Lord Bury, was already in the army and bound for Belgium, and the first that George knew that he was going to be joining him was when the next day Bury greeted him with the cheery news that from now on George would have to call him *Sir*.

A week earlier or a week later and George would almost certainly have been safe, but his timing could not have been worse, and he got home to find that his father had procured him a commission into the 14th of Foot. The first two battalions of the 14th were already on service in India and Italy, but in 1813 a third battalion had been raised and when the news from Elba reached London, the existing order to disband was hastily revoked and the battalion – the youngest and least experienced in the whole British army – was ordered for Ostend and the Low Countries.

Keppel was still well short of his sixteenth birthday, but as another brother disarmingly put it, there were 'plenty of us' Keppel children, and one younger son more or less was not going to make a lot of difference. In 1809 the three-week-old Henry – a future Admiral of the Fleet – was already in his father's footpan for burial in the garden when a faint whimper brought the nurse, and sentiment was in equally short order when the young Ensign Keppel of the 14th of Foot, tricked out in his new uniform and as proud of its single-fringed epaulette as any Coleridgean dupe of a shepherd boy, presented himself to his unimpressed mother at a ball hosted by the Marquess of Lansdowne. 'Holding the King's Commission, I looked upon myself as a man, and was what young ladies would call "out",' he remembered: 'My first gaiety was a great *reunion* at Lansdowne House. A less gay evening I have seldom spent. I still wanted two months of sixteen, and my fair complexion made me look still younger. In my excessive bashfulness I thought that every one whose eye I met was speculating upon what business a mere schoolboy could have in such an assembly. To complete the confusion, I encountered my mother, who, still young and hand-some, did not care to see a second grown-up son in society. "What, George!" she exclaimed; "Who would have thought of seeing you here? There, run away, you'll find plenty of cakes and tea in the next room."'

For all his pride in his commission, the 'Peasants' of the 14th of Foot were not a fashionable lot and in any normal situation they would not have been allowed abroad, let alone on active service. The one saving grace for Keppel was that half of them were scarcely more than boys themselves, but even in a unit where fourteen of the officers and 300 of the rank and file were under the age of twenty, Keppel was the 'baby' of the battalion, 'dry nursed' by his seniors and saluted by his men with the kind of half-stifled smile that had had him hiding in embarrass-ment when he first joined them for embarkation at Ramsgate.

In spite of all the subsequent marching, however, it had not been a bad introduction to his new profession – there were always chance encounters with Westminsters, or an old 'fag-master' who had given him a 'terrible licking for hiding in the coal-hole', to make him feel at home – and above all they were going to get to fight. In the usual run of things the 14th would have been kept to garrison duties, but they had been saved from that by Lord Hill and on the evening of Saturday 17 June, Keppel and the rest of the battalion found themselves instead on the ridge of Mont-Saint-Jean queuing for their gin ration as part of the 4th Division's 4th Brigade of Infantry.

The gin was pretty well the last thing Keppel could remember. His luggage had disappeared along with a baggage train two days earlier, but after the long march he was too tired to care about that, or anything else, and the next thing he knew was that it was two o'clock in the morning and he was lying flat out 'in a mountain stream' with his soldier-servant Bill Moles shaking him awake.

That had been two hours ago. Just behind where he lay was a cottage. As he went in he found three men sitting round a fire they had made out of broken-up chairs and tables, drying their clothes. Without speaking they made room for him. It was only when they put their uniforms back on that Keppel realised that one of them was Colonel Sir John Colborne – 'afterwards General Lord Seaton GCB' – and an old colleague of his brother's in Spain. He was offered breakfast, but, 'hungry as I was', it was too 'infinitesimally small' to accept. It was a reminder, though, if a Keppel had ever needed one, of why he was there.

He was there because he belonged. Caste might trump rank, but it also brought with it its obligations and it was on the battlefield that they were met. For all his youth, as the second son of the 4th Earl of Albemarle, George was the beau ideal of what the Wellington army officer ought to be. Brought up from birth in an atmosphere of privilege, deference and noblesse oblige, with all the sanctions of habit, authority, wealth and the law arrayed behind him, he was the perfect instrument of command in a species of warfare that required only physical courage of its junior officers and blind obedience of its soldiers.

For the French officer who had carried the flaming sword of liberty, equality and fraternity to every part of Europe there was something morally repugnant about this. He would have been hard put to say what offended him most about Keppel, the aristocratic pedigree that outraged the meritocrat in him, or the utter ignorance of military matters that riled the professional man of arms. To the radical press at home, too, it was deeply offensive that an army was willing to sacrifice the lives 'of hundreds of gallant countrymen' to an outdated class system. And yet if he knew nothing else, Keppel knew the small print of the contract his class had made with society. 'Mihi hodie, Tibi cras' – 'Me today, You tomorrow' – a sign over the entrance to a military cemetery in the Far East warned Britain's redcoats and after Quatre Bras no officer in Wellington's army needed reminding of that. Five days earlier, Keppel had spent his sixteenth birthday at the Grammont race meeting with some fellow Westminsters. He had watched young Lord Hay, the darling of Brussels, dressed in his jockey's silks, sitting in the scales, weighing out before a race. He 'had hardly ever seen so handsome a lad', he remembered, and now Hay was dead. It was a sobering thought.

George Keppel was brave – he would have behaved bravely whether it was naturally in him or not – but he was also young and he hated the wait. And now, as dawn was about to break, he could not get out of his head a story his father had told him. The earl had been speaking to the Bristolian bare-knuckle fighter, Henry 'Game Chicken' Pearce, just before his great battle with Daniel Mendoza for the Championship of England:

'Well, Pearce,' Albemarle had asked, 'How do you feel?'

'Well, my Lord,' answered Pearce, 'I wish it was *fit*.'

As George Keppel emerged from the cottage, still cold and hungry, his uniform drenched through, he stared out into the blackness towards the French lines and found Pearce's words echoing and re-echoing in his brain. He too wished the fight was *fit*.

5 a.m.

A Trellis of Roses

It had probably been as well for Hazlitt's temper, as he and his wife walked home from the Lambs', that he could not see into the offices in Maiden Lane on the north side of the Strand where that Sunday's *Examiner* was being put to bed. On a good Sunday the newsboys would have collected their bundles an hour ago, but at times of crisis such as these, when foreign intelligence from Paris and the Low Countries was crowding home news off its sixteen, tight-crammed pages, the printers would be working deep into the early hours in a rush to get the paper on to the streets.

It had been a busy week both in and out of Parliament – the Budget; the annual loan; Wilberforce's Slave Registration Bill; the Rosebery divorce; Lord Elgin's petition for the purchase of his Greek marbles; the last Sunday of the Royal Academy exhibition; violence in Ireland, the usual slew of bankruptcies, an art robbery, the birth of a son to the Countess of Albemarle – but it was a small paragraph tucked away at the bottom of the third page that would have attracted Hazlitt's ire. 'The writer who is at present supplying our Theatrical Department,' it read, 'closed some masterly observations on Comus last week, with an attack on the tergiversation of some living poets, from which as far as Mr

Wordsworth is concerned, we are anxious to express our dissent. If Mr WORDSWORTH praises any body, whom upon the whole neither the writer in question nor ourselves might think worthy of the panegyric, we are quite convinced, by the whole tenor of Mr WORDSWORTH'S life and productions, that he does it in a perfectly right spirit.'

If the disclaimer might have annoyed the 'writer in question', it would not have surprised him, because no two men who had so much in common could have been so far apart in temperament as William Hazlitt and James Henry Leigh Hunt. *The Examiner* and its editor were every bit as sceptical of Tory politics and placemen as Hazlitt himself, but Leigh Hunt was a Cavalier to Hazlitt's Roundhead, a Suckling and not a Hampden, a poet of gentle, airy graces and high spirits, of fine and unworldly impulses, whose virtues and vices had yet to atrophy into the calculated helplessness that Dickens made such lethal use of in his portrait of Henry Skimpole.

Even at his angriest Hunt was a mocker not a 'hater'. Where Hazlitt was all angry principle, Hunt was all exquisite feeling, a febrile, nervy creature, strung like some Aeolian harp to vibrate to the joys and sorrows of the world. In another century Hazlitt would have been found in the stocks with the Leveller John Lilburne or on the pyre with William Tyndale, but the hypochondriacal Hunt was not the stuff of which martyrs are usually made. It is one of the rummer ironies of the age that this Sunday, while the driven, misanthropic Hazlitt was free to add another brace of enemies to his score, the 'mawkish, unmanly namby-pamby' editor of *The Examiner* was still paying with his shattered health for the oddest, most whimsical stand ever made against Tory tyranny and mediocrity.

Hunt had not been strong enough to bring in his own copy to the offices this Sunday – two years in prison had left him an agoraphobic wreck too frightened to leave the safety of his own rooms – but *The Examiner* still, as ever, bore the imprint of his personality. The paper unquestionably owed its business stability and probity to the character of his brother John, but when any reader thought of *The Examiner* – the townsfolk of the young Thomas Carlyle's Ecclefechan, for instance, who would queue excitedly for the mail-coach that brought the weekly edition to them – if anyone recalled its campaigns against army flogging, or the sale of army commissions to boys like Keppel, or the abuses of the theatre, then it was Leigh '*Examiner*' Hunt and the distinctive, accusatory symbol of the pointing index finger with which he signed his articles that he thought of.

The Examiner had been in existence for seven years by 1815 – 18 June was Edition Number 390 – and in that time the Hunts had turned it into London's and the country's leading Sunday newspaper. By the end of the Napoleonic Wars, the *Observer*, the first of the 'Sundays', had declined into little more than a government propaganda rag, and for anyone looking beyond William Cobbett or such partisan heavyweights as the Whig *Edinburgh Review* or John Murray's Tory *Quarterly*, the 'impartial opinion' on politics, theatre, literature or the arts promised by Leigh and John Hunt's *Examiner* provided a new, fair and commanding voice in British public life.

In the political climate of the day, however, such success had its dangers. In their original prospectus the Hunts had proudly trumpeted their independence of all 'party', but Lord Liverpool's was not a government to brook anything that even remotely smacked of opposition, and in 1812 a series of legal skirmishes over *Examiner* articles had finally come to a head with a libel trial provoked by Leigh Hunt's attack on that 'Adonis in loveliness' and 'Conqueror of Hearts', the bloated and painted fifty-year-old Prince Regent. 'What person, unacquainted with the true state of the case, would imagine,' Hunt had demanded in response to an absurd panegyric on Prinny trotted out in the government press, 'in reading these astounding eulogies, that this *Glory of the People* was the subject of millions of shrugs and reproaches! That this *protector of the Arts* had named a wretched Foreigner his Historical Painter … That this *Maecenas of the Age* patronised not a single deserving writer! … In short, that this *delightful, blissful, wise, pleasurable, honourable, virtu-ous, true and immortal PRINCE*, was a violator of his word, a libertine over head and ears in debt and disgrace, a despiser of domestic ties, the companion of gamblers and demireps, a man who has just closed half a century without one single claim on the gratitude of his country or the respect of posterity.'

For an 'artless' and retiring soul who knew nothing of politics, as his counsel, the Whig politician Henry Brougham, insisted at his trial, Leigh Hunt had chosen his target well, and the government in their turn did all they could to turn him into a martyr. The verdict had been a foregone conclusion even before the two brothers came to trial, and in the February of 1813 they were sentenced to two years imprisonment, John Hunt to the House of Correction at Cold Bath Fields in Clerkenwell, and Leigh to the Surrey gaol in Horsemonger Lane, Southwark, where nine years before Colonel Despard and his fellow conspirators had been hanged and beheaded for high treason.

Horsemonger Lane was not Leigh Hunt's first experience of prison. His earliest memories were of the family's room in the King's Bench where his father had been incarcerated for debt, and imprisonment brought out that odd mixture of resilience and whimsy that was the hall-mark of his character. He had been housed on arrival in a garret with a view – if he stood on a chair – of the prison yard and its chained inmates, but it was not long before a doctor had him moved to an empty room in the infirmary and there, in the midst of all the human hopelessness and despair that a London gaol was heir to, he turned his back on reality and created his own Arcadian retreat. 'I turned [it] into a noble room,' he wrote in his *Autobiography*, 'I papered the walls with a trellis of roses; I had the ceiling coloured with clouds and sky; the barred windows I screened with Venetian blinds; and when my bookcases were set up with their busts, and flowers and a pianoforte made their appearance, perhaps there was not a handsomer room on that side of the water … Charles Lamb declared there was no other such room, except in a fairy tale.'

His wife and child had been allowed to move in with him – another child would be born in the prison – and Hunt had not stopped at the Venetian blinds. There was a small yard outside his room that he shut in with green palings, and there in his own small and hidden kingdom, he planted his flowers and saplings and apple tree and entertained Lord Byron and Tom Moore as if some poor wretched country girl, guilty of infanticide, was not waiting execution only yards away.

Byron and the Irish poet, Tom Moore, were not the only visitors, and for the two years that Leigh Hunt and his long-suffering family were in Horsemonger Lane, the Surrey gaol enjoyed a celebrity comparable with anything that Lamb or Holland House had to offer. The government had set out to teach the Hunts a lesson that all radical London would heed when they sent the brothers to prison, and instead they had turned a minor poet and journalist into a hero of the left, and the old infirmary washroom into a literary salon where you were as likely to meet Jeremy Bentham or James Mill as Lord Byron, the scowling William Hazlitt as the self-effacing Mary Lamb, the novelist Maria Edgworth and the painters David Wilkie and Benjamin Haydon as a politician like Henry Brougham, or the future editor of *The Times*, Thomas Barnes.

Although it seems somehow typical of the born survivor he was that, while John languished in a cell sixteen feet by nine without books, pens, paper or company, Leigh Hunt entertained and wrote sonnets and read Italian poetry, it was not all roses and trellises at Horsemonger Lane. In the years ahead Hunt's stock would plummet with many of those who had supported him through these years, but for the younger generation of Romantics such as Keats and Shelley, his painted idyll, set in the heart of the massive walls of a prison synonymous with government tyranny, was not a piece of escapist whimsy but a symbolic gesture of political defiance, an assertion of the freedom of the imagination, the independence of the word, the integrity of the arts, of everything in fact that *The Examiner* stood for and for which Lord Chief Justice

Ellenborough – the champion of the pillory, the judge who sentenced Despard to death, and the perennial scourge of the liberals – had condemned the Hunts to gaol.

A liberal metropolitan elite were not the only ones who saw it in this way, and long before the Hunts left gaol, *The Examiner*'s 2,000 subscribers had trebled and quadrupled in number, with the printers unable to keep up with demand. The government had believed that with the brothers locked up the paper would fail, but the Hunts had somehow managed to keep it going and in February 1815 – just a month before Bonaparte's escape from Elba – they had emerged from their separate prisons unreformed, uncowed and unrepentant in their determination to find the Prince Regent as ludicrous as ever.

If gaol had been the making of Leigh Hunt and *The Examiner*, elevating him to a place in the literary and moral life of the country that nothing he would do could hope to sustain, it had also taken an inevitable toll. In a series of essays written from prison he had wistfully imagined himself mingling with the London crowds beyond the prison walls, but once he was free again all those sights and sounds of outside life he had clung on to through two long, bitterly cold winters – the companionable crush of the theatre-bound coach, the smell of links, the 'mudshine' on the pavements, the awkward adjusting of 'shawls and smiles', the first jingle of music, the curtain, the opening words; London, in short, in all the heaving variety of the city that intoxicated Lamb – all filled him with an agoraphobic dread that he never entirely overcame.

'In sooth, I know not why I am so sad' – there would have been a time, in prison, when he would have given anything to hear that line and see the curtain rise on Shakespeare's Venice and Kean's Shylock and now he could no more have accepted Lord Byron's offer of his box than he could have gone back to his first garret cell in Surrey gaol. In the middle of February 1815, he had forced himself to see the new *enfant terrible*'s Richard III, but the only place he pined for was his old painted washroom, the only freedom he could actually enjoy – hidden away in his Maida Vale retreat, in the little white-and-green study, his 'box of lilies', he had made for himself – was that freedom of 'Fancy' that not even an attorney general 'could commit ... to custody'.

In a brutal way, too, events had left him behind, because while Leigh Hunt had never been a Bonapartist in the way that Hazlitt was, the bloodlust of the 'war-whoopers', the cant of the Tory press, the self-defeating madness of driving the French people into Bonaparte's arms, the horror of war and the prospect of another and stupider Bourbon tyranny succeeding to that of the 'Great Apostate from Liberty', left him stranded in a no-man's land of despair. In this Sunday's *Examiner* he wrote his usual sanely decent piece, but with dawn already breaking over the sodden and freezing armies in Belgium, and public opinion polarised between the Bonapartist ferocity of Hazlitt and Godwin and the baying of the bloodhounds, Hunt sounded not so much like a prophet crying in the wilderness as an escapist shut away in his Maida Vale hideaway.

He had come out of prison at the wrong time: '*Examiner* Hunt's' finger could point where it liked, the world was going its own way. The old campaigning Hunt, with his lightness of touch, and debonair spirit was not entirely silenced, however. As the printers finished setting the last page of Edition Number 390, and the newsboys, working on the one day of the week on which they could hope to see their families before nightfall, waited impatiently to begin their rounds, it would have been odd if they had not paused over a small item beneath the announcement that the Countess of Albemarle, George Keppel's mother, had given birth to another son – an item so at odds with the paper's avowed, high-minded policy of avoiding gossip and society news that it bears the imprint of Leigh Hunt's ironic sense of incongrui-ties: 'Capt. Bontein, of the Life Guards, son of Sir G.B. to the daughter of Sir E. Stanley,' it read. 'The parties rode out from Lady Bontein's to take an airing before dinner; they took post chaise and four at Barnet, and proceeded to Gretna Green, whither they were unsuccessfully pursued by Lady Stanley. The only objection to the match was, it is said, the age of the bride, who is under fourteen, and has a handsome fortune. The Parties have since been remarried in London.'

Huddled up with their horses in the freezing rain south of Brussels, Captain Bontein's friends in the Life Guards would enjoy that. It was, though, another item that would interest the navy operating off the French coast: one relating to Thomas Cochrane, the country's most famous sailor since Nelson. 'It is well known that many respectable persons have all along believed LORD COCHRANE to be perfectly free from any concern in the wretched fraud practised by De Berenger and others on the Stock Exchange,' The Examiner announced. 'This opinion, we are informed, will soon be shown to be the correct one ... and that his Lordship had not the slightest knowledge of their dirty schemes.'

6 a.m.

The Billy Ruffian

There was a touch of rain in the air and the breeze was fresh as the seventy-four-gun HMS *Bellerophon* shook a reef out of its top sails and fell in with *Myrmidon* and *Eridanus*. Within the shelter of Rochefort's harbour just over the horizon two French frigates lay at anchor, and if history and the British sailor were anything to go by, that was precisely where they were going to stay, safely bottled up in port by the Royal Navy until the war was over.

Blockading was not romantic or exciting work, it was not the stuff of reputations or the road to riches, but for the navy and ships such as the *Bellerophon* – the '*Billy Ruffian*' – it was what they had been doing for the last twenty years. The glamour of the service might belong to the frigate captains who had made household names of the *Speedy* or *Imperieuse*, but it was here on blockade duty off the coast of Europe, from the Baltic down to the Mediterranean, year after year, in all weathers, summer and winter, night and day, that those fighting and sailing skills had been honed that had strangled the continent's trade and won the war for Britain.

The Nelsonian man o' war was no more narrowly British than was Wellington's army – you could have found English, Scottish, Irish,

Americans, Canadians, Danes, Swedes, Spaniards, Portuguese, Puerto Ricans and Venetians fighting together in the same floating Babel – though it would have been an uphill task to persuade the British public of that. For a thousand years the sea had played a crucial role in the island's story, and a golden age of victories that left Britain in undisputed command of the oceans and of her own destiny had given the British tar and man of war a place in its heart no regiment or Tommy Atkins could rival.

For all the hatred of the press gangs, and the resentments of the merchant fleets robbed of manpower, the British loved the Royal Navy in a way that it had never loved the army. Over the past century the British soldier had fought and beat the French from Quebec to Pondicherry, but while victory at Blenheim or Ramillies or Minden might command an ode or add to the invincible conceit of John Bull, they were not triumphs that were bound up with the security, history and identity of an island race in the way that were the navy's.

It was not a mere matter of sentiment, either, because nobody looking out to sea at six o'clock this morning, to where the greatest East India fleet ever assembled lay spread across the Downs, could forget its role in the prosperity that had sustained Britain through two decades of war. For more than twenty years the navy had convoyed the world's trade across the face of the globe, and from Liverpool to Gravesend – from the *Isabella* and *Aimwell* just arrived from Surinam and Barbados with their cargoes of sugar, cotton, coffee, aloes, ginger and tamarind, to the *Heinrich* from Danzig, the *Frau Anna* from Stockholm, the *Jason* from Memel and the *Frederick* from Hamburg – the country's great ports and quaysides rang to the same commercial tune that the navy had made possible. 'The following account of one pound weight of manufactured cotton strikingly evinces the importance of that trade to Great Britain,' Exeter's subscribers to *The Alfred* could have read in the latest edition this Sunday; 'there was sent off to London, lately, a small piece of muslin, about one pound weight, the history of which is thus related; it was come from the East Indies to London; from London it went to Lancashire, where it was manufactured into yarn; from Manchester it came to Paisley, and there was veined; afterwards it was sent to Dumbarton, where it was hand sewed, and again brought to Paisley, whence it went to Glasgow and was finished, and from Glasgow it was sent per-coach to London.'

The British loved this drum-roll to their island's prosperity, loved the rattle of figures – the three years from picking to warehouse, the 5,000 miles by sea, the 920 miles by land, the 150 people employed in a single pound of cotton, the 2,000 per cent profit – and knew that this was how they had brought Bonaparte to his knees. Since the days of the Younger Pitt the country had been financing her continental allies, and as the Prussian, Russian and Austrian armies of the Seventh Coalition again marched against France on British gold, Britons could look out to sea and know that it was a war that their efforts and their industry would sustain as long as was necessary.

The *Robert Quayle* from St Domingo, carrying cotton, sugar, tea, coffee and mahogany; the *Unicorn* from Demerara with its rum and molasses; the *Sally* from Trinidad with its lime juice and indigo; the *Vestal* from New York with cotton and flaxseed, the *Integrity* from Charleston; they were all in Liverpool this Sunday. Before the day was out the *Jackson* would sail from Gravesend for Oporto and the *Minerva* for Gibraltar and the *Anna* for Riga and the *Acorn* for St Petersburg, and for as long as most people could recall it was the navy that had controlled these sea channels. It had kept open the Great Belt and the Baltic, it had supplied Britain's armies in Spain with its specie from South America and its grain; it had suppressed the coastal trade of Europe and turned the Mediterranean into a British lake. There had been reverses against the Americans – though they were being quietly massaged away – and there had been little to brag of since Trafalgar but for the public and sailor alike a British warship was the British character in action and the Royal Navy officer the incarnation of everything that made Britain innately superior to her enemies. Over the last few years the victories of Wellington's armies in Spain had gone some way to redressing the balance, but if the young Romantic, Thomas De Quincey, might thrill to the tragic heroics of the 23rd Dragoons at Talavera, it was in the virtues of the meritocratic, professional navy and not of the hunting field – resilience, discipline, self-reliance, skill, initiative, intelligence and patriotism – that an industrialising, entrepreneurial, thrusting, inventive, self-confident, stubbornly independent nation liked to see herself reflected.

It was a seductive idea, and one that would only grow and mutate with the century, and if there was no more truth in it than in most other national myths, the mere assumption of superiority had given the navy a psychological advantage that turned myth into a self-fulfilling prophecy. Over the last two decades the *Bellerophon* had played its part in some of the greatest victories of the war, and no veteran of the Nile or Trafalgar or the Glorious First of June – still less any French sailor skulking out of sight in Rochefort – would have had a moment's doubt of the outcome should the French squadron ever venture out from the safety of the Basque Roads.

There were fortunes to be made in the navy out of prize money too, and if Jane Austen's Sir Walter Elliot might lament it as the death knell of all rank and society, a commercial nation of shopkeepers knew what a wonderful lubricant it could be. During the course of the war the corruption of the Admiralty prize courts had been a standing grievance among fighting sailors, but a rich ship was a happy ship and the lure of the prize money had successfully woven patriotism and greed into a kind of symbiotic double-helix that had printed aggression and daring into the DNA of every ambitious officer.

In a culture and navy of this kind, simultaneously romantic and mercenary, it is probably no coincidence that so many of the navy's leading captains were Scottish, and Frederick Maitland of the *Bellerophon* was only ordinary in the sense that there were so many like him. At the age of almost thirty-eight, he was no longer the brilliant young frigate captain of the popular imagination, but with his thin clever face, long nose and high cheekbones, he might have been the archetype of the Nelsonian officer, the kind of sailor – and the kind of face – that would have again made Sir Walter and his barber despair of the ravages that long years at sea could inflict on a man's complexion.

With the Maitland appearance (the family were not known in Edinburgh society for their looks) came the aristocratic Maitland connections, though even a boy of his background still had to make his own way in Nelson's navy. From the seventeenth century the sons of the gentry had been entered into the service from a very early age, and while a junior officer like the young Wellington – Arthur *Wesley* as he then was – could happily trade commissions in and out of half a dozen regiments before he heard a shot fired in anger, the Frederick Maitlands of the navy had to learn and earn their promotions the hard way.

Maitland had first seen battle as a midshipman during the French Revolutionary Wars at the Glorious First of June, and the next dozen years were spent in almost continuous fighting up and down the French and Spanish coasts. In 1799, he had been chased down and captured in the cutter *Penelope*, but that had been the only setback in a charmed career that had brought him a rich haul of prizes, prize money, votes of thanks and ultimately, in March 1815, on Bonaparte's escape from Elba, the command of the old *Billy Ruffian*.

The war had been good to Maitland, but as he prepared to join Sir Henry Hotham's blockading squadron off the French coast he could not have dreamed that the best was yet to come. The fighting now belonged to the army and not the navy and there would have seemed little chance of either profit or excitement. On 24 May, however, the *Bellerophon* sailed from Cawsand Bay in Cornwall, and so it was that in the early hours of 18 June, in light winds and 'small rain', Captain Frederick Maitland found himself again in the Basque Roads, with La Rochelle and the Ile de Rey to the north and the great opening to the Gironde to the south. Between them lay the estuary of the Charente and Rochefort and the French squadron he had been despatched to watch. They were waters he knew well, and as the *Bellerophon* hove to for the captain of the *Ulysses* to come aboard, it would have been odd if his mind had not gone back to the last time he had been here, in the April of 1809. And odder still if he had not thought of another Scottish sailor, the most famous fighting captain of them all, '*Le Loup de Mer*', as the French called him, to whose help he had gone that day.

7 a.m.

Le Loup de Mer

On the south side of the Thames, at the junction of Southwark's Borough Road and Blackman Street, Thomas Cochrane was beginning the last forty-eight hours of his year-long sentence in one of the sadder curiosities of early nineteenth-century London. A few hundred yards to the north-west a great gallows beam high on the roof marked the entrance to Horsemonger Lane's Surrey gaol, but King's Bench prison dealt only in the small change of human misery and humiliation – in the debtors and bankrupts and their wives and children who lived here on the crumbling edges of society and on whatever their friends and families could provide to keep life and soul together.

A cell in the King's Bench – fifteen feet by ten and containing three beds – was the first room that Leigh Hunt could recall and its barrack-like corridors, filled with the laments 'of aged and unhappy parents' and weeping wives, his earliest introduction to the geography of London. Less than half a mile to the north, Dickens's Marshalsea might provide copy for a lifetime of shame, but if one was looking for a genuine microcosm of the world's greatest metropolis, a sink for all the deluded hopes, aspirations and ambitions that a voracious, commercial and imperial capital generated and disappointed, then the King's Bench and its floating and permanent population of debtors was the place.

It was not like Newgate to the north of the river, nor Horsemonger Lane, nor even the Marshalsea, and with its spacious parade and its speciously handsome Georgian buildings, its tap rooms, coffee house, marketplace and games of rackets, its atmosphere lay somewhere between an open prison, a refuge centre and a college for which the only entry qualifications were failure and ill-fortune. For the payment of a fee a debtor could enjoy the freedom of the prison 'Rules', an area of three square miles surrounding the gaol; but the immense spike-topped wall was a reminder that when night fell, and the last visitor had left and the only sounds were the cries of ailing babies, and the only view that of a blind wall just feet away, the King's Bench was still a prison.

Sometime in the middle hours of a March night three months earlier, when the watchman was at the farthest point of his prison rounds, a prisoner had paused in the window of his fourth-storey room with a length of rope looped around him and another shorter length in his hand. The fourth floor of the building was almost on a level with the top of the prison wall, and for a sailor in the prime of life a moment's work was enough to throw a running noose over a spike, and another to swing his six-foot-two-inch frame out of the window and, hand-over-hand, across the twelve-foot gap between sill and outer wall.

The prison wall was thirty-five feet high, and the narrow well beneath pitch-black, but once across he hauled himself on to the top and perched precariously between spikes while he secured the second rope to the ironwork. He had arranged with an old servant of his a safe house somewhere in the shadow of the prison wall below him, and had lowered himself nearly halfway down when his makeshift rope, smuggled into the prison in pieces, snapped and sent him crashing the last twenty feet to the ground.

The bruised and unconscious escapee was Thomas Cochrane, better known as Lord Cochrane, demagogue rabble-rouser, inventor, Member of Parliament, heir to the 9th Earl of Dundonald, and the most brilliant, ungovernable and imaginative naval captain the Revolutionary and Napoleonic Wars had produced. In the previous August, Cochrane had been sentenced to the stocks, a £1,000 fine and a year in the King's Bench on a charge of fraud, but his troubles with the authorities had really started – if they did not start with his birth – on an April day five years earlier when he had joined Frederick Maitland and the rest of Admiral Gambier's blockading force keeping an enemy fleet bound for the West Indies bottled up close to Rochefort in the inner Aix Road.

Cochrane knew these coastal waters and shore defences intimately, and with a record for courage and unorthodoxy that stretched back to the first years of the war, had been despatched by the Admiralty in the *Imperieuse* to mastermind a fireship attack on the French fleet. As a junior captain he knew well enough that his arrival would ruffle the feathers of the more senior captains in the fleet, but for once in his turbulent life he had the authority of the Admiralty behind him, and on the night of 11 June a mixed flotilla of fireships and bomb-vessels under his command had slipped off into the dark of a moonless night towards the coast and the double lines of the French fleet anchored under the guns of the Ile d'Aix.

Nobody who saw that attack ever forgot it – Cochrane had lit up a moonless night sky with a pyrotechnic exercise in the sublime that would have brought Sir William Hamilton and the whole of the Neapolitan School to watch – but to turn a French humiliation into a victory on a par with the Nile needed Admiral Gambier to follow up. The evangelical, Methodistical, psalm-singing, hypocritical, canting old woman – as one captain called him – had hated the idea of fireships from the first, and as he refused all urgings from Cochrane to follow up the attack and finish off a helpless and stranded enemy, a battle that had started off as a fight between the Royal Navy and the French turned into a war between the navy's most brilliant, outspoken and unforgiving sea captain and his own Admiralty.

The Battle of the Basque Roads was not over, as Gambier fervently hoped; it was just beginning, and it would be fought now in the newspapers, Parliament, pamphlets and the courts. For a country that had been forced to live off some pretty thin gruel since Trafalgar any victory was a relief, but as the implications of Gambier's despatches were mulled over, and a puzzled public wondered what Nelson would have done and Cochrane refused to be flattered, bullied, bribed or promoted into silence, the country and the navy divided along predictable political lines. 'Lord Gambier's plan,' the radical politician, Sir Francis Burdett said, 'seemed a desire to preserve the fleet – Cochrane's plan, to destroy the enemy's ... What if Nelson, at the Nile or Trafalgar, had acted on that principle.'

It was telling that the intervention came from Burdett, because ranged on Cochrane's side were the reformers, the radical press, young officers in the service such as Maitland and Jane Austen's brother Francis, and that amorphous body 'the people'; on Admiral Gambier's, the Tory Ministry, the Admiralty, the placemen, the senior captains who knew where their own interests lay, and most dangerous of all to his cause, Cochrane himself. Even before the Basque Roads he had made some powerful enemies in the Admiralty and Parliament by his outspoken attacks on naval abuses, and those very qualities of rule-breaking fearlessness and self-confidence that made him unrivalled at sea, simply rebounded on him in the world of institutional self-interest, sycophancy, cronyism, evidential procedures, court rulings and political chicanery in which his campaign against Gambier had mired him.

It was a campaign he could never win, but he was so used at sea to winning battles that could not be won, so lacking in the normal mechanisms of self-preservation, that he could not see what was going to happen even when Gambier resorted to a court martial to clear his name. The Admiralty moved quickly to despatch a hostile witness like

Maitland to Ireland before the trial started, but that was simply overkill because with a court packed with Gambier's friends and Cochrane's own angry, intemperate character to work on, the verdict was never in doubt. 'His Lordship's conduct on that occasion, as well as his general conduct and proceedings as Commander-in-Chief of the Channel Fleet,' the judge advocate read out in the great stern cabin of HMS *Gladiator* at Portsmouth, 'was marked by zeal, judgment, ability, and an anxious attention to the welfare of His Majesty's Service ... the said Admiral the Right Honourable Lord Gambier is hereby most honourably acquitted.'

For William Wilberforce – an evangelical ally of the God-fearing Gambier – the verdict was a clear manifestation of 'the Goodness of Him who has established your righteous cause', and yet if Wilberforce was right He was working in mysterious ways. In the same month that a court martial was exonerating Gambier at Portsmouth, the Walcheren disaster was exposing the incompetence and inadequacy of both government and Admiralty, and for the rest of the war the most brilliant captain Britain possessed was left fretting on half pay, his fertile, inventive mind consumed with experiments for gas warfare and sulphur ships or endless battles against the institutional corruption of an establishment that had no intention of forgetting the Basque Roads.

He was an odd mix, Cochrane: a Romantic without a 'particle of romance' in his body; a 'Sea Wolf' who eloped with his sixteen-year-old bride; a man of violence with a curiously quixotic streak to his nature; a chivalrous, gentlemanly exponent of 'shock and awe' before anyone had dreamed of the term; and a supreme exponent of amphibious warfare who was utterly at sea on land. From his earliest days in the service he had invariably made a point of choosing the wrong enemies to fight, and in these years after the Gambier trial – dangerous years of growing tension between the radicals and the government – he seems to have gone out of his way to broaden the field of attack, taking on anyone and everyone from the wretched proctor, marshal and general panjandrum of the Admiralty court in Malta to Wellington's powerful clan, the Wellesleys.

It is possible that, in spite of himself, Cochrane might still have got away with his campaign if he had not chosen his friends as unwisely as he chose his enemies. In the February of 1814 it even seemed as if there might at last be a way back into active service, but then occurred an event that, like some bizarre demonstration of chaos theory, would send Cochrane to the King's Bench and in doing so change the political contours of two continents.

Sometime after midnight on 21 February 1814, while France was still locked into the final, bloody endgame of the Napoleonic era, a man in a grey coat and the red uniform of the general staff was heard loudly knocking at the door of the Ship Inn at Dover. The landlord of the nearby Packet Boat came over to see what the commotion was, and the stranger announced himself as Lieutenant Colonel Du Bourg, aide-de-camp to Lord Cathcart, Britain's ambassador with the advancing allied armies to the Emperor Alexander's Russia.

He had just been landed by a French vessel, he said, and needed pen, paper and a horse and rider to take an urgent message to Admiral Foley at Deal. 'I have the honour to acquaint you,' he rapidly wrote to the admiral, 'that the L'Aigle from Calais, Pierre Duquin, Master, has this moment landed me near Dover, to proceed to the capital with despatches of the happiest nature ... my anxiety will allow me to say no more for your gratification than that the Allies obtained a final victory; that Bonaparte was overtaken by a party of Sacken's Cossacks, who immediately slayed him, and divided his body between them; General Platoff saved Paris from being reduced to ashes; the allied sovereigns are there, and the white cockade is universal; and immediate peace is certain.'

Foley could do nothing until the morning, and even then fog prevented the use of the Admiralty's semaphore system linking the coast with London, but by that time 'Du Bourg' and his chaise and four were well on their way to the capital and the news of Napoleon's death about to hit the city's stock exchange. On the previous Saturday the price of Omnium – the most volatile of government securities – had closed at 26¾, but within moments of the Exchange opening at ten it and all stock had begun to rise, faltering briefly before soaring again when another chaise and four, decked out with victory laurels, and occupied by three 'French' officers sporting the white Bourbon cockade, swept into the city to put an end to all doubts about Du Bourg's story.

There were large profits to be had for anyone who sold at 32 – immense margins for those who just a couple of weeks earlier had bought Omnium at 19⅛ – and by the time that the news came through that Bonaparte was alive and the price had slumped back to its morning 26½, the damage was done.

The Stock Exchange had immediately set up a committee to enquire into the hoax, and by the beginning of March the trail was leading towards Cochrane. For those supporters who never lost the faith this was all part of an overarching government plot to ruin him, and yet even for the neutral the long chain of associations, circumstantial evidence, personal and business connections and dealing patterns that placed him at the heart of the fraud left questions that needed answering.

Cochrane had certainly made money out of the hoax, and his worthless uncle, Andrew Cochrane-Johnstone – the corrupt and shameless ex-governor-slaver of Dominica – was up to his neck in it, but if Cochrane was innocent the circumstantial evidence was all that his enemies could possibly want. On the day that the conspirators had ridden up to London, Cochrane was at a factory in Cock Lane working on a new design of ship's convoy lamp, but a message from a servant had brought him back to his house in Green Street, where a man he knew as De Berenger and who had been masquerading as Du Bourg – a soldier of fortune and debtor living within the more liberal 'Rules' of the King's Bench – was there waiting for him.

Cochrane had his explanation for this, and why De Berenger was later found with his bank notes at the port of Leith, but the case ultimately came down to a question of the colour of the coat De Berenger had been wearing when he arrived. He had told Cochrane that he had to get out of the country to escape his creditors, and according to Cochrane's version, had turned up in the green uniform of a sharpshooter – a red uniform, a Hackney driver, William Crane, was ready to swear – to press his plea for help and, curiously, to ask for the loan of a change of clothes to throw the King's Bench officers off his scent.

It was the word of the coachman against Cochrane, but by the time that he was indicted for fraud and committed to trial at the Court of the King's Bench only Cochrane can have imagined innocence would prove any defence. He was so entirely sure of his case that, beyond his initial affidavit, he took no part in the proceedings, and was not even in court when the Lord Chief Justice, Edward Law – the same able, bruising, jury-hectoring 'bulldog' of the Tory government, Lord Ellenborough, who had tried the Hunts – began a trial that for 'partiality, misrepresentation, injustice, and oppression' would run the Gambier court martial close. 'You have before had the animal hunted home,' Ellenborough told the jury, referring to the discovery of Du Bourg's red uniform in the Thames, 'and now you have his skin ... De Berenger stripped himself at Lord Cochrane's. He pulled off his scarlet uniform there, and if the circumstances of it not being green did not excite Lord Cochrane's suspicion, what did he think of the star and the medal? It became him, as an officer and a gentleman, to communicate his suspicion of these circumstances. Did he not ask De Berenger where he had been in this masquerade dress? It was for the jury to say whether Lord Cochrane did not know where he had been. This was not the dress of a sharpshooter, but of a mountebank. He came before Lord Cochrane fully blazoned in the costume of his crime.'

It took the jury two-and-a-half hours to reach a guilty verdict, and on 20 June 1814, Cochrane and those defendants who had not fled the country appeared again before Ellenborough for sentencing. In the intervening days Cochrane and his lawyers had dredged up a number of witnesses ready to support his testimony, but true to form all new evidence was ruled inadmissible and a sentence of an hour in the pillory, a £1,000 fine and a year's imprisonment handed down. 'His appearance was … pitiable,' wrote Crabb Robinson in his diary that night. 'When the sentence was passed he stood without colour in his face, his eyes staring and without expression and it was with difficulty that he left the court like a man stupefied.'

It is impossible to be sure of Cochrane's absolute innocence, or the degree of his complicity, but his own *de haut en bas* disdain for the whole legal process made him again his own worst enemy. It was only at the sentencing that he made any attempt to distance himself from the hoaxers, and in standing or falling with men who were plainly guilty, in resting his case in the last resort – as he always had and always would – on an overweening sense of self that was equally impregnable to criticism or fact, the Romantic hero of the Byronic age took on the machinery of the state with all the self-destructive consequences that inevitably followed.

The Establishment did not just want to send him down, it wanted him humiliated, and if it was too frightened to put the people's champion in the stocks there were subtler methods at their disposal. 'I will never permit a service, hitherto of unblemished honour, to be disgraced by the continuance of Lord Cochrane,' the Prince Regent told a dinner of naval officers at Portsmouth, 'I shall … strip him of the Order of the Bath.' He was, perhaps for the only time in his life, as good as his word. Cochrane's name was removed from the Navy List and at midnight, on 11 August 1814, in an arcane and vindictive ceremony of symbolic disgrace, beneath the great fan-vaulted ceiling of Westminster Abbey's Henry VII chapel, his coat of arms and banner were removed by Bath King of Arms from the walls, and his banner of knighthood – the reward for his heroics in the Basque Roads – kicked out of the chapel and down the steps 'according to the ancient form'.

Gambier's victory was complete. Cochrane was expelled from the navy, he was expelled from the Commons by a vote of 144 to 44, and although the voters of Westminster, the most numerous, independent and famously uncontrollable of all the parliamentary constituencies, returned him unopposed as their member at the subsequent election, he was a ruined man. His escape from gaol – the news of it went round London on the same day that news from Elba reached the capital – was only one more, sad codicil to this. It was an act of theatre, desperation, publicity and folly in equal measures. A 300-guinea reward was offered for his capture and a poster of fatuous inaccuracy posted: 'Escaped from the King's Bench prison, on Monday the 6th day of March, instant, Lord Cochrane. He is about five feet eleven inches in height, thin and narrow-chested, with sandy hair and full eyes, red whiskers and eyebrows.'

It was little wonder that with this description, the towering, broadly built Cochrane was sighted from the City to the Channel Isles, but this was no ordinary escape. It was the publication of his grievances he wanted and not simply his freedom. Two weeks after slipping over the King's Bench wall he appeared in the clerk's room in Parliament to claim his right to speak in the Commons as the elected member for Westminster. William Jones, the Marshal of the King's Bench – another target of Cochrane's campaigning hatred – was sent for to re-arrest him, and after a scuffle with his officers, Cochrane was overpowered and dragged back to prison. This time, though, it was not to his two comfortable rooms on the top floor of the Bench's State House but to a subterranean and airless 'strong room', fourteen feet square, without windows, fire, table or bed, and smelling of some cross between slaughter-house dump and barracks latrine. Within weeks it had taken a dangerous toll on his health, with symptoms of what appeared to be putrid fever or typhus developing. The last thing that the authorities wanted was a martyr of Cochrane's stature, and after twenty-six days he was moved to another cell to see out the final weeks of his sentence.

There was, though, one last and very Cochrane-like complication. His release, scheduled for 20 June 1815, was dependent on the payment of the £1,000 fine, and this he refused to do. His friends had urged him, subscriptions would have settled it in a trice, but Cochrane would not budge. One of the jurors at the hoax trial, uneasy at his complicity in the verdict, even offered to pay the fine but as Cochrane told another jury it was 'justice he wanted and not mercy'. And on the morning of Sunday 18 June, as Maitland's *Bellerophon* patrolled Cochrane's old haunts off the Aix Road, and the great standard-bearer of the hated Wellesley clan, the Duke of Wellington, prepared to give battle, and consols fell, and the City nervously waited on the next rumour from Belgium, and an obdurate Cochrane languished in the King's Bench, justice in England was an endangered ideal.

8 a.m.

The 'Article'

On the same page of *The Examiner* that carried the news of Lord Cochrane's imminent justification was a small item bringing the latest intelligence from the front. There had been no information coming out of Paris since the previous Monday, and while it was pretty certain that Bonaparte must by now have joined his army, anything else was guesswork. 'It is very difficult for people who are not military to make any particular guesses,' Leigh Hunt wrote with a becoming show of humility, reserving his barb for the end, 'and soldiers are no doubt in the habit of making fine jokes of the speculations of Editors in this way. It is generally supposed however, that he will endeavour to strike a blow in the Low Countries, where the people are decidedly averse to their new masters; and ... should the Duke of WELLINGTON come in contact with him, we shall have a better opportunity of judging of his Grace's genius for war than has yet been offered.'

It was a small dig but nicely judged – who had Wellington ever beaten, his enemies wanted to know? – and Hunt was not the only man this morning wondering the same, nor George Keppel the only soldier thinking of prize fights. It had always irked Wellington that Bonaparte dismissed him as a mere 'sepoy general', and from Hunt and his friend

Haydon in London, sparring over their respective champions, to the army in Brussels there was a genuine sense of anticipation that here, finally, on the field of Waterloo, 'When Greek meets Greek,' as Sir Augustus Frazer told his wife, are 'now the two great captains fairly met.'

It would have been inconceivable to his old soldiers that they might have to fight under another general and unimaginable that they could lose under 'Old Nosey'. In the weeks before Wellington arrived in Brussels the young Prince of Orange had been in command of the army, and a 'hundred times a day', the old Peninsula-hand William Wheeler had told his family, the question is asked, 'Where is Wellington, surely we shall not be led to battle by that boy.'

'I never remember anything that caused such joy,' Wheeler wrote again when a general order announced that 'Silly Billy' was surrendering 'the Command of the Army into the more able hands of His Grace the Duke of Wellington'. Throughout the day soldiers of the 51st were rushing up to him 'almost frantic' with the news, and that night, as they sat over their hollands and tobacco, singing and dancing and 'reminding each other of the glorious deeds done in the Peninsula', they drank in gin 'to the health of their old commander' and told themselves that if every Frenchman was a Boney they would still give them a good thrashing.

On the morning of the 18th, William Wheeler still had his hollands, still had his tobacco, and was still talking about the Peninsula, and Wellington, for one, knew that if he was going to win the battle it was the Wheelers who were going to win it for him. A few weeks earlier Wellington had met the Whig politician and gossip Thomas Creevey in the Parc in Brussels, and Creevey, an old political sparring partner from the days when the duke was still no more than an ex-sepoy general, had famously asked him what he reckoned would happen.

"'By God! I think Blücher and myself can do the thing!'"

"'Do you calculate on any desertions in Bonaparte's army?'"

"Not upon a man, from the Colonel to the private ... We may pick up a marshal or two, perhaps, but not worth a damn ..."

Just then a British infantryman came in sight, peering about at the Parc and its statuary.

"There," said Wellington, pointing to the small scarlet figure, "There, it all depends upon that article whether we do the business or not. Give me enough of it, and I am sure.'"

Wellington had not got the 'article' in anything like the quantity he wanted, but along the length of the allied line, carefully eked out to stiffen the resolve of less experienced units, were the old Peninsula men who had taken him from Portugal to Toulouse. Even for soldiers who could remember the preludes to Vittoria and Salamanca the night had been terrible, but for a canny old Walcheren and Peninsula campaigner like Wheeler, fully recovered now from the bad leg wound that had ended his war at the Nivelle, there was always 'an angle' to be exploited – a handy box of Spanish dollars to be dug up, a ham or brandy to be filched, an arrangement over an apple tree to come to with the French – or, if all else failed, an endless supply of phlegmatic, good-humoured patience to call on.

He had struck lucky the day before, when on the two days' march from Grammont to Waterloo, he had picked up a purse dropped as a squadron of Belgian heavy cavalry, fleeing from Quatre Bras, had thundered through Nivelles. There were not many left of the battalion who had marched into France with Wellington just over a year before, but the few of them still there in his company had banded together to share their plunder, and the 'Godsend' had already come in handy, buying them bread and cheese from a local peasant and enough brandy and hollands to leave them, 'in the expression of one of my old comrades', as he told his family, 'wet and comfortable', and fraternally consoled by the thought that at least the French were in the same boat.

It is unlikely that William Wheeler asked himself what he was doing there, not even when the gin and brandy had worn off and only the tobacco his family disapproved of kept his benumbed and shivering body and soul together, but it was certainly a question that his opposite number across the valley would have wanted an answer to. It was bad enough for the French soldier to have been driven out of Spain by aristocratic amateurs of the George Keppel stamp, but for a citizen soldier brought up on the heady doctrines of liberty and equality, there was something degrading – something, even, that smacked of betrayal – about a hardened, professional old sweat like Wheeler and a species of discipline and animal courage that owed more to drink and the lash than to patriotism or *gloire*.

The charge would not have remotely worried either Wheeler or Wellington – any notion that his men had volunteered out of 'fine military feeling' was 'all stuff', Wellington insisted – but it would have been more irritating still that the British soldier took an inverted pride in the very brutality that no self-respecting Frenchman would have tolerated. The average British redcoat might not have volunteered out of any high patriotic ideals, but that did not stop him defining himself in opposition to everything that was foreign, or putting up with gallows, the lash and the firing squad in the same way his countrymen at home put up with the most barbaric penal system in Europe.

The Jacobin's 'liberty' and John Bull's 'freedom' had never been the same thing – the freeborn Englishman's right to be hanged for stealing a sheep was the price he paid for a country without a police or the overweening presence of the state – but there was something else at work in the William Wheelers of Wellington's army that French indignation missed. For all his talk of 'the scum of the earth' Wellington knew better than anyone that that was only half a truth, and in the loyalties that had bound his troops together in Spain, in the extraordinary alchemy that could turn the detritus of the assizes and prisons into the finest army Britain had ever had, abstract notions of patriotism took on a solid actuality that existed nowhere else in national life. 'As much as I desire to see my dear native land, my home and all dear relations, old playmates and neighbours,' Wheeler had written home in 1814, after a wound had taken him away from the 51st, 'I would much rather rejoin my Regiment again and take my chance with it. Then, when this long protracted war is over, if fortune should favour me I should have the proud satisfaction of landing on my native shores with many a brave and gallant comrade, with whom I have braved the dangers of many a hard-fought battle. This is the first time of my being absent from my Regiment since I entered into it and I hope it will not be long before I should hear the sound of its soul stirring bugles again.'

For the last six years the regiment had been his family and country, and if Wheeler probably would not have troubled himself to say why he fought, he knew the answer was not the abject subservience of which the French accused him. 'When I look around me and see so many strange faces,' he movingly wrote of his return from hospital to the 51st and to England nine months before, 'I am a wonder to myself, scarcely four years has rolled over, ere, at this place I embarked with about 900 of my comrades. Where are they now? I could not muster one company out of the whole number. The battle field, fatigue, privations and sickness has made sad havoc in the ranks of as fine a set of young fellows as ever belonged to the service.'

It was not the fear of the lash that had wreaked this havoc or left the 'Diehards' of the 57th lying like a pack of cards where they had fallen on the field of Albuera four years earlier. It was not any external discipline that fuelled the 'vengeance and grief' of the 79th after the death of their Colonel Philip Cameron at Fuentes d'Onor. They were not Scottish 'hirelings' in the 92nd who had taken such crippling casualties in the bloody defence of Quatre Bras two days before. It would not be treason to their own country that would leave the Irishmen of the 27th of Foot dead within their perfect square before the day was out, and no one in the army needed telling that. In the anonymous memoir of a lowland Scot of the 71st at Waterloo can be heard another and more bitter note, but in the voice of William Wheeler, in its inimitable mix of tolerance, curiosity and disdain, in its unsentimental affections and clear-eyed scepticism, in its infinite capacity for putting up with incompetence and misery – the drenching rains of Waterloo, waking in Spain to find your head frozen to the ground – we can hear the voice that links the men of Waterloo in a tradition of dogged, grumbling, ironic endurance to the soldiers of Inkerman and to the trenches of the Great War.

And at eight o'clock in the morning, as Wheeler's brigade quit their cornfield and took up their positions on the high ground above the chateau of Hougoumont, and all down the line Wellington's 'article', the British infantryman, with his contradictory qualities and vices, his courage and brutality, his love of fighting and invincible contempt for foreigners, his petty venality, sporadic viciousness and his kindness, his drunkenness and sober resolution, his iron discipline, wildness and impiousness, cleaned his weapon and got ready for battle, it was this tradition that was taking shape. Very occasionally that article has a name, saved by chance or heroics from anonymity – Wheeler of the 51st; William Hooper of the 40th who had just hours to live; the unbloodied recruit Bartram vomiting with fear; the thirty-seven-year-old Norman Macdonald of Harris 'shivering like an aspen' on the ridge by La Haye Sainte; Shaw the Lifeguardsman; Graham of Hougoumont fame; Ewart of the Scots Greys – but he was, as the soldier-poet Edmund Blunden, who would fight with his descendants just miles from the slopes of Waterloo in another war, wrote, 'called Legion, or nothing'. He was Scottish, he was Irish, he was English, he was Welsh; he had been recruited from the islands and the cities, from the plough and from the loom; he had been tricked out and bought, like Coleridge's gentle shepherd; he had been plucked from Newgate and the transport ships; he had woken from a drunken stupor to find himself a soldier; he had fallen for the spurious glamour of a recruiting poster; he had been dispossessed of his croft; he had been promised land; he had been bribed out of the militia; he had volunteered.

And as he waited, something was about to happen to him and to the whole of Britain. The day before Sir Augustus Frazer had asked what the real name of this place was and now a new word was about to be given to the language, a new dynamic forged in the shifting triangular relationship of government, army and people, a heightened sense of British history, prestige and destiny born. And at the heart of it were the Wheelers, the outcasts and casualties of society who made up the core of Wellington's 'infamous army'. 'Think what they are thinking of us in England,' Wellington told them, and it was not only England. As Wheeler took up his new position north of Hougoumont, the Bath mail-coach from London would be just arriving, bringing the last letter he had written to his family from Grammont five days before, to add to all the letters of his they had carefully kept since he had joined the army six years before. And across the whole of the British Isles, wives, parents, children, brothers and sisters of every class waited on the same news. They waited in Dublin and Drogheda – to take just one regiment at random, the 73rd of Foot, a Highland regiment only six years earlier – they waited in Ballyboy and Ballyseedy, in Trallee, Tyrone, Tipperary, Lismore and Leitrim; in Glasgow, Paisley, Perth, Peebles, Annan, Ayr, Dumfries, Inverness, Edinburgh and the Isle of Mull; in Betchworth, Bewdley, Birmingham, Blackfriars and Banstead, in Walsall, Worcester, Warwick, Wells, Wolverhampton, Wadhurst and Westminster, in Ashbourne, St Albans, Smarden, Bromyard, Meopham, Uppingham, Hereford, Northampton, Tower Hamlets, Lincoln, Frome, Isleworth, Colchester, Boston, Tamworth, York, Bingley, Oxford, Shepton Mallet and a hundred more cities, towns, villages and farms across Britain and Ireland. For the last time in Wellington's career, the scum of the earth was about to rise to the surface.

9 a.m.

Carrot and Stick

The Duke of Wellington might have harboured his suspicions about the levelling tendency of Methodism among the scum of the earth who made up his army, but if the Reverend Edmund Grindrod's Altrincham Methodist Sunday School was anything to go by, he had little to fear. If you had walked past the school building earlier you would have heard the sound of hymns, but at nine o'clock in the morning, with the Superintendant Mr John Barrow's final exhortation to the children still seven interminable hours away, hardly a murmur escaped the schoolroom to ruffle the Sabbath peace.

In the world beyond the classroom walls, Altrincham was still the bustling, 'cheerful' market town that had delighted the infant Thomas De Quincey – the square full on market day of fruit and flowers and 'bonny young women' 'tripping *coquettishly*' about – but here there was an order and rhythm to the day that no child was ever allowed to disturb. At eight thirty in the morning each teacher would take the school register for the different classes, and as a child answered to his or her name, make a neat slanting mark from left to right, completing the 'x' at the afternoon roll call with a corresponding mark in the opposite direction: Charles Leicester, William Leicester, John Leicester – the

Leicesters were all strict in their attendance, and on their way to the reward of a first hymnal – Christopher Briggs, Mary Hewitt, George Worsley, Ellen Roger, little Macaijah Harrington … something just over two hundred and fifty in all, boys and girls in roughly equal numbers from the age of seven upwards, crowded into the one cramped schoolroom.

There had been a Sunday school in the town since 1783, when another Leicester – the Wesleyan Oswald Leicester, a prosperous grocer and mayor of Altrincham for that year – rented for his son Oswald a small upper room above a cottage in Thorley Moor Lane to teach the town's children. Within a year or two that room had become too small for their growing numbers, and soon after the school had moved to a site at the corner of Norman Place and Regent Road where, under the shadow of the four-storey-high Kinder's Mill, Oswald senior built his son a new schoolroom.

The Leicesters were a successful and upwardly mobile Altrincham family – the different branches hovered somewhere, socially and religiously, between the Church of England and dissent – but many of the children were there because the mills were there, and the mills were there for those same reasons of geography that had underpinned the whole course of Britain's Industrial Revolution. The ancient market town of Altrincham was unusual in the fact that it was remote from the usual sources of power in the Pennines, but there was enough water in the streams that came off Hale Moss and Bowdon Hill to drive three or four mills, and situated only miles from Manchester – and linked since 1766 by the Bridgewater Canal and the Mersey to the Liverpool docks and the open sea – Altrincham was perfectly placed to take advantage of the raw cotton that came from the West Indies into the port of Liverpool.

For thousands of children across the north-west of England, mills such as these would be their lives – from half-past five or six in the morning until eight at night, with all that meant for their health and life expectancy, for their physical strength and stature, for the erosion of family ties – and yet if Reverend Grindrod's pupils wanted any warning of an even darker future it was there across the road in the empty shell of Kinder's Mill. The factory had been there since 1784 but it had been closed now for eight years, and a community like Altrincham's, its livelihood closely tied to the fluctuating demands of the textile market, was going to be no more immune to the economic effects of peace than was Eury MacLeod's Caolas Scalpaigh.

On 18 June, the *Isabella* from Surinam, the *Aimwell* from Barbados, the *Robert Quayle* from San Domingo, the *Unicorn* from Demerara, the *Integrity* from Charleston, were all unloading their cotton at Liverpool, but this was the Sabbath, and if the Battle of Waterloo might not have been won on the playing fields of Altrincham it was here that the battle for the souls of Britain's poor would be fought. Two-hundred-odd miles to the south on the banks of the Thames, the young Thomas Fremantle was talking cricket and skipping 'Lyricks' to celebrate the taking of Naples, but here beside the Bridgewater Canal on the Lord's Day there would be no skipping anything, no lounging in the Parade with officers from the Castle, no company or fun, no ogling Miss Goodall, no writing letters to uncles – the Reverend Grindrod would no more have allowed writing on the Sabbath than he would have allowed cricket – but only the intimidated murmur of the under-teachers, the silence of 250 children and the answering silence of the mills.

There were five classes within the one school room, taught by young teachers and monitors picked from among the older children, and ranging from a 'trial class' for the newest pupils, up through Spelling Book, Reading, Testament and Bible. The teachers were instructed to pay particular attention to spelling and reading, but the avowed 'object' of the school was 'eternal salvation' not education and the first duty of the teacher to set an example of Godliness, order, submissiveness, and punctuality. 'The teachers are expected to submit to the direction of the Superintendant,' the Rules for the Management of the Altrincham

Methodist Sunday School, spelled out, 'to speak as quietly as they can ... to observe well whether their Pupils are clean, and free from any infectious Disease or Eruption; to prevent them talking with each other ... and oblige them to sit in an upright posture ... to shew an example of serious behaviour, and profound reverence for the Lord's Day, Word, and Ordinance.'

If the Reverend Grindrod imagined he could teach a child to read and shackle his mind for ever he was badly mistaken – a school like his was as likely to produce a Chartist as another Sunday school teacher – but its whole ethos was one in which religion was both carrot and stick for that dismal form of social conservatism and moral coercion to which early nineteenth-century Methodism lent itself. It might have been different before the threat of French Jacobinism, infidelity and Revolutionary violence had frightened Methodism into the enemy camp, but if the men who made up the school committee, small traders and craftsmen in the main – William Worsley, constable; Mr Jonathan Potter, worsted manufacturer; Mr Joshua Ashcroft, grocer – had ever seen the world differently they knew better now. 'What is the People?' a passionate Hazlitt demanded of the men of power. 'Millions of men like you, with hearts beating in their bosoms, with thoughts stirring in their minds, with the blood circulating in their veins, with wants and appetites, and passions and anxious cares, and affections for others and a respect for themselves, and a right to freedom, and a will to be free.' And here, and in hundreds of schools like it, the first steps were being taken to stifle these instincts in them before they had ever had time to develop.

This was partly a matter of theology – Hannah More's unbending conviction that children were of 'a corrupt nature and evil disposition' ran deep in evangelical circles – but it was also partly a real fear of social disorder and one fed off the other until the two impulses were virtually indistinguishable. There is no doubt that men like Edmund Grindrod would have seen severity first and foremost as a religious duty, but William Wilberforce's Society for the Suppression of Vice, with its suspicions of the working classes and their 'disgusting' and 'unsubdued passions' had no more effective lieutenant than the Sunday school teacher.

'The Scholars must come to school clean washed and combed,' read Grindrod's instructions for the management at Altrincham, instructions that might equally well serve as a blueprint for the orderly, mechanised, submissive ideal of every mill-owner's dreams; 'they must not go out, if they can possibly avoid it, during School hours ... Not one word must be spoken in School hours to any but the Teachers ... Girls [are] not to wear their patterns or bonnets in school ... books [are] not to be removed on any pretext ... no cursing, swearing, gaming, quarrelling, wilful lying, calling by names, using indecent language ...'

Altrincham's was, on paper at least, by no means a harsh regime compared with many Anglican schools – there is something peculiarly touching in the injunction to teachers 'to exercise much patience towards those who may be dull and stupid' – but it was a police state and if there were children absent this Sunday the two appointed 'Visitors', Mr William Worsley and Mr William Potts, would make it their business to visit the homes in the week ahead. With the school numbers growing steadily with each quarter the committee urgently needed more Visitors, but the two men did what they could, checking up on their teachers' morals, reporting on Sabbath absenteeism, and visiting the sick of seven and up 'for the purpose of pious advice and prayer; and to administer temporal relief in cases of necessity'.

It would be a hard call whether Wilberforce and his Society for the Suppression of Vice had most to learn in the way of moral espionage from the Methodists or the Methodists from Wilberforce, but in both cases their motives were again the same blurred mix of religious conviction and social control. At the core of all evangelical faith – Anglican, or Methodist – was the absolute conviction that the miseries and rewards of this world were of no consequence beside the bliss and torments of the next, and if it was always easier to tell that to the poor than the rich, heaven and hell remained wonderfully effective tools at the sick-bed of a seven-year-old with nothing more to look forward to than a short life in the mills.

At what point duty shaded into pleasure in the work of men like William Potts and William Worsley, and the pious monitoring of souls into the love and exercise of power, was something that had exercised Sydney Smith, but Anglican and Methodist alike could at least point to the best authority. The Established Church had long taught the poor that their 'more lowly path,' as Wilberforce put it, 'has been allotted to them by the hand of God', and Methodism had not just inherited the Tory John Wesley's social conservatism but all of the unattractive theology that served it so well. 'Break their wills betimes,' Wesley had warned his followers – and the Reverend Edmund Grindrod, the loyal supporter of Jabez Bunting, was not the man to ignore an injunction of this kind; 'Begin this work before they can run alone, before they can speak plain, perhaps before they can speak at all. Whatever pains it costs, break the will if you would not damn the child. Let a child from a year old be taught to fear the rod and to cry softly; from that age make him do as he is bid, if you whip him ten times running to effect it. Break his will now, and his soul shall live, and he will probably bless you to all eternity.'

And so, too, in the meantime would the mill-owners of Altrincham and masters across the country – 'I have left most of my works in Lancashire under the management of Methodists,' the first Sir Robert Peel had written nearly thirty years before, 'and they serve me excellently well' – and a generation of war with a Jacobin and infidel France had only cemented the compact. While it was hardly surprising that an Anglican establishment tied to the status quo and the landed interest saw the poor as 'the enemy', in schools like Altrincham, where from the moment the children had bowed and curtseyed their way into school in the morning, to the moment they had bowed and curtseyed their way out at the end of their final moral scolding, the poor were doing their and the factory owners' work for them.

There had been nervous suspicions in some Tory circles at the rise of the Sunday schools in which Wilberforce and Hannah More were such leading figures, but this was no *trahison des clercs*, but its opposite. There were certainly ways in which the school reflected the supportive and improving ethos of the Methodist communities, and yet when all that is recognised there is still something heartbreaking in the fact that here at Altrincham, Sunday in Sunday out, from nine in the morning in winter, eight thirty in summer, a pool of twenty-three teachers, none of them paid, none of them any different from the children they taught, many of them scarcely any older, were willingly sacrificing their one day of freedom a week to collude in the industrial and political stifling of their own class.

They were powerful sanctions they had at their disposal, too, heaven and hell, and vivid and imminent for a small, sinful child in Altrincham. The next world was never far away – the Leicester children had already lost a sister – and no scholar sitting through Mr John Barrow's dark warnings would ever be allowed to forget it. In the midst of life they were in death and if any girl leaving the school that week to begin her life in service – Betty Bray, Hannah Gibbon, Mary Pearson – was in any doubt where '*cocquettishness*' would lead her then there were examples enough to hand. Before they had answered to their names for the last time that afternoon, and the teacher had added her mark to complete her 'x', another young Methodist servant girl, who had sat over the same lessons as they had and climbed in the same way from Spelling Class to Bible, would be ending another day in her Newgate cell.

Nine of her brothers and sisters had already died, and yet only this morning, faced with the gallows and her Maker, she was still stubbornly refusing to take Communion. Where had lewdness and deceit led her? What foul lies still, in the darkness of her cell, was Satan spinning? 'Believe me,' warned her Methodist visitor, addressing himself to all the

Betty Brays and Mary Pearsons and Hannah Gibbons across the country faced with the Tempter, 'Newgate is a dreadful place, confined in narrow cells, where the light of day is only admitted to light the wretched criminal to the knowledge that it is day; the heavy doors, and massy bolts and bars, strike terror into the beholders ... O, My beloved friends! Pray heartily unto God that you may never enter into that abode of wretchedness and despair.'

10 a.m.

The Sinews of War

There was possibly no man happier to be on the battlefield that morning than Welsh Ensign Rees Howell Gronow of the Guards. For almost everyone in the allied army the morning of the 18th was one of unremitting cold and misery, but for the gloriously dandified and irrepressible miniature, 'No grow' Gronow, it was a day chosen by 'some providential accident' beyond the 'wisdom of man', a Sunday morning of such glorious sunshine and clarity of vision that it might have been designed for the ultimate act of Sabbath-breaking that Christian Europe was planning.

The rain had at last stopped, but if Gronow's irrepressible good humour was largely a matter of temperament, it was at least in part because this Sunday morning he was supposed to be with his regiment in London. When the Guards embarked for the Low Countries in May the 1st Battalion had remained behind, and a frustrated Gronow, a twenty-year-old veteran of the Peninsula and one of the finest pistol shots in England, was left to kick his heels on ceremonial duties while the fate of Europe was being decided on the other side of the Channel. 'Early in June I had the honour of dining with Colonel Darling, the deputy adjutant,' Gronow recalled, 'and I was there introduced to Sir

Thomas Picton, as a countryman and neighbour of his brother, Mr Turberville of Evenney Abbey, in Glamorganshire. He was very gracious, and, on his two aides-de-camp – Major Tyler and my friend Chambers, of the Guards – lamenting that I was obliged to remain at home, Sir Thomas said: "Is the lad really anxious to go out?" Chambers answered that it was the height of my ambition. Sir Thomas inquired if all the appointments on his staff were filled up; and then added, with a grim smile, "If Tyler is killed, which is not at all unlikely, I do not know why I should not take my young countryman: he may go over with me if he can get leave.'"

If the idea of a 'gracious' Sir Thomas Picton would have been new to most people – a 'rough, foul-mouthed devil' was Wellington's pithy verdict on the man who had commanded the famous 3rd Division in Spain – there was a well-hidden streak of kindness in him and he was as good as his word. There seemed to be no chance of Gronow getting leave from his regiment to join the army in Brussels, but he reckoned that if he managed things smoothly he could be across and back again in time to mount guard at St James's before he was missed.

The whole plan, of course, depended on an 'untimely end' for one or more of his friends, but then at that age, as he engagingly put it, '*on ne doute de rien*', and 'so I set about thinking how I should manage to get my outfit, in order to appear at Brussels in a manner worthy of the aide-de-camp of the great general'. As his 'funds' were at a characteristically 'low ebb' at the time, Gronow negotiated a loan from 'those staunch friends of the hard-up soldier' Cox and Greenwood's, and armed with their £200, turned it 'by some wonderful accident' at a St James's Square gambling house into £800, and thus well equipped with 'the sinews of war', splashed out on a pair of first-rate horses from Tattersalls and embarked for Ostend and the seat of war with his groom.

He could have made himself another tidy profit if he had had the time and funds – in the London clubs they were offering three-to-one on an allied victory – but by the 11th he was down at Ramsgate and five days later with Picton and his suite at Brussels. They had only arrived on the morning of the Duchess of Richmond's ball, and Gronow had barely time to put in an essentially decorative appearance at Quatre Bras before caution and his old friend Chambers suggested that he should sell the aide-de-camp's horse he had picked up at Tattersalls and resume the life of an honest infantryman before he found himself in an even bigger scrape.

It was probably a wise move – only a supreme optimist like Gronow could have thought Sir Thomas Picton's side was the best place to be in battle – and even a frosty welcome from the Guards' colonel seemed a small price to pay for the pleasures of such a perfect Sunday morning. The Guards had been positioned on the right of the British centre, and from where Gronow now found himself he had the whole of the battle-field spread out in front of him, with the allied troops stretched out on either side in 'a continuous wall of human beings' and the 'long impos-ing lines of the enemy distinctly visible' across the shallow valley only a thousand yards away.

It was the first and last time anyone that day would see Wellington's 'ballroom' and 'ball' in their entirety before the one disappeared into smoke and the other dissolved into a hundred thousand fragmentary and contradictory impressions. Wellington had drawn his troops up on the reverse slope of a low but pronounced ridge bisected by the main Brussels–Charleroi road. From one end of the line to the other was a distance of about two miles. Along it ran a lane, deeply sunken in parts and bordered by hedges, which led to Ohain in the east and to Braine l'Alleud in the west. In front of this lane at the far left of the allied posi-tion stood the buildings of Papelotte; at the centre, and lying on the west side of the Brussels road some three hundred yards below the Ohain crossroads, the farm of La Haye Sainte; and at the right of the allied army, below and in advance of the ridge, the walled chateau, outbuildings, garden, wood and orchard of Hougoumont.

Across the valley, covered in its tall summer crops, which sloped gently down from the Ohain road and then rose again towards the inn of La Belle Alliance on the Brussels road less than a mile away, were the French. Their line too stretched in a mirror image from Papelotte on their far right to the open ground to the south of Hougoumont on their left. Behind them, in the centre, lay the village of Plancenoit and almost two miles to the east, in the direction of Wavre, the Bois de Paris. 'On the opposite heights we could perceive large dark moving masses of something impossible to distinguish individually,' wrote Edmund Wheatley of the King's German Legion, standing in solid square to the rear of La Haye Sainte and to the left of Gronow, 'where the edge of the ground bound the horizon, shoals of these gloomy bodies glided down, disjointing then contracting, like fields of animated clouds sweeping over the plains, like melted lava from a volcano, boding ruin and destruction to whatever dared impede its course. It had a fairy look and border'd on the supernatural.'

In the French army were 69,000 men, including 14,000 cavalry, and 250 guns; on the allied side 67,000 men, just 24,000 of whom were British, with 11,000 cavalry and just over 150 guns. Within four square miles, then, were 140,000 men and 400 guns, and for the moment they were silent. The rain had turned the ground between the two armies into a quagmire, neutering the effective use of artillery or cavalry until it dried, and stretching out the long wait for battle deep into the morning. Already, though, as the two armies waited, the Waterloo ball was fragmenting again into its thousand shifting perspectives. There, on the far left of the French line, opposite where the young George Keppel stood thinking of his father's story and the immortal words of the Game Chicken, were clearly visible Jérôme Bonaparte and his suite. And there, farther to the right, a small, remote figure, surrounded by his staff, mounted on a white horse. 'How often,' thought Captain Mercer of the horse artillery, as the roars of '*Vive l'Empereur*' rolled across the valley towards the allied ridge, had he 'longed to see

Napoleon, that mighty man of war – that astonishing genius who has filled the world with renown.'

Now he had his wish, but Keppel was not the only one wishing that it was *fit*. Close to Wheatley stood a 'swelled-faced, ignorant booby, raw from England, staring with haggard and pallid cheek on the swarm of foes over against him. One could perceive,' Wheatley remembered, 'the torture of his feelings by the hectic quivering of his muscles, as if fear and cold were contending for the natural colour of the cheek.' Farther back in reserve a young and unblooded private, Bartram of the 40th, wet and cold after a night bivouacking in the forest of Soignes, was too terrified to move while elsewhere fear had already given way to a soldier's superstitious fatalism. The Duke of Brunswick's premonitions had proved right and Thomas Picton, dressed in his old blue coat and black hat, his broken ribs bandaged from a musket ball at Quatre Bras, was not the only one who knew he was going to die. 'Tom, you are an old soldier, and have escaped often,' a new, young recruit, an Edinburgh lad in the 71st, was saying, 'I am sure I am to fall ... I am certain ... All I ask is that you tell my parents when you get home that I ask God's pardon for the evil I have done and the grief I have given them. Be sure to tell I died praying for their blessing and pardon.'

How many were praying, God knows, but if they were, they were praying alone. There were a few harmless Methodists among the Guards, who the duke tolerated without much liking, but they were the exception. It was a Sunday, and yet it could have been any day of the week for all the difference that made. 'I have often heard the remark,' William Wheeler once told his family, 'that a Chaplain is of no more use than a town pump without a handle,' and as the Reverend Stonestreet, Chaplain of the Guards, busied himself back in Brussels cashing a cheque for £40 there were few at the front likely to have disagreed.

Prayers, though, there were. Of thanks: 'For the second time I go to take to the field,' Captain John Blackman of the Guards, another old

Westminster boy who had fought his way up through Spain, had written home, 'and I pray once again for that Divine Protection hitherto so bountifully & so undeservedly bestowed upon me; and you may rest assured the wholesome instruction I received in my youth from yourself and my *very dear* Mother will ever remain *implanted* in my breast.' For a wife, in the case of Augustus Frazer, writing a last letter home at three that morning, his mind 'tranquil and composed'. Of gratitude – for such a glorious day to fight – if it was Gronow. For a parent's forgiveness; even, in some obscure way – Yeats a century before Yeats – for a different kind of forgiveness or understanding. 'It is an awful situation to be in,' Wheatley mused, a British officer among 'heavy, selfish' soldiers of the King's German Legion for whom he felt nothing and fellow countrymen he did not know, and faced with an enemy he did not hate, 'to stand with a sharp-edged instrument at one's side, waiting for the signal to drag it out of its peaceful innocent house to snap the thread of existence of those we never saw, never spoke to, never offended. On the opposite ascent stand hundreds of young men like myself ... and yet with all my soul I wished them dead as the earth they trampled on and anticipated their total annihilation.'

Nine miles away to the north, as the armies waited, the citizens of an edgy, frightened Brussels were taking the caricatures and satires against Bonaparte out of their windows and readying themselves for another change of rule. In her Antwerp room, farther again to the north, Magdalene De Lancey, nerves stretched to breaking, was listening while a Captain Mitchell broke the news that there was to be another battle. In her old chamber in the Laboureur Inn, the black-plumed and uniformed Brunswickers stood guard over the corpse of their chief, while far over to the east, on the French–Swiss border, Byron's friend and the source of *The Examiner*'s French intelligence, John Cam Hobhouse, was wondering what was happening to his brother in the 69th. He did not know him as well as he should have done and felt guilty about that. He had gone to see him on his way to

Paris, where he had rushed when he first heard of the escape of his hero Bonaparte. His brother had shown him the grapeshot mark in his cap, with its two neat holes, entrance and exit, collected at the disastrous assault on Bergen-op-Zoom the year before. 'It will be lower down next time,' he had told him and he had been right. As Hobhouse stood at the Morez border post, this Sunday morning, waiting to cross into Switzerland, and struggled to square family and political feelings, his brother, shot through the neck, lay as dead as the Duke of Brunswick in a Quatre Bras grave. It was 'strange', thought Private Dixon Vallance of the 79th, a battalion that had already been brutally mauled on the 16th, 'that two of the most powerful and civilised nations, ranked foremost in every department of knowledge, science and art, found no other way of settling their differences, than the old and barbarous method of going to war and killing each other'.

He might as well have been in Leigh Hunt's box of lilies. It had been too late for thoughts like that from the moment that Vienna had declared Bonaparte the enemy of mankind. 'A ball' suddenly 'whizzed in the air' and Wheatley looked at his watch. 'It was just eleven o'clock, Sunday morning,' and as 'a stunning noise' shook the air and 'a shocking havoc commenced', Wheatley found himself thinking that his fiancée, 'Eliza, would just be going into church at Wallingford'.

11 a.m.

The Sabbath

At just about the same time that Edmund Wheatley was taking out his watch and thinking of Eliza, a man in his mid-fifties, with a mild, almost winsome sweetness of expression, and something of the frail, oddly stooped and birdlike air of the permanent valetudinarian, was making his slow way up the hill to Taplow church. He had only arrived from town late the previous evening, and as he paused to look about him in the bright morning sunshine, the 'dust and bustle of the city' forgotten, the Thames gleaming in the valley far below the ancient Norman church and its still more ancient Saxon burial mound, he turned to his children and called on them 'to rejoice in the visible goodness of *his* God'.

William Wilberforce and his family were going to worship, and if his was perhaps an insensitive celebration from a man whose Society for the Suppression of Vice had dedicated so much of its energies to ensuring that the lower orders would not enjoy their Sundays, men, women and children across the country were doing the same. In his private chapel in Carlton House, the fount of royal mercy was at prayer with his brother, the Duke of Cumberland, and in churches and chapels and meeting houses and open fields up and down Britain, Anglicans and Episcopalians, Methodists, Congregationalists and Unitarians, Moderates and High-Flyers, Secessionists, Presbyterians and Reformed Presbyterians, Old Licht Burgher and Old Anti-Licht Burghers, New Licht Burghers and New Anti-Licht Burghers, Quakers, Roman Catholics and every conceivable shade of Dissenter were coming stubbornly together to worship their God in their way.

There is nothing quite like a Sabbath to bring out the divisions and fissures in a Christian nation and Sunday 18 June was no exception. In the cathedral at Antwerp this morning Thomas Musgrave – a young Cambridge junior fellow and future Archbishop of York – was eavesdropping on the ladies' confessions and thanking God that he had been born a Protestant, but beyond a deep antipathy to Roman Catholicism that linked Church and Chapel in a common bond, the British Sunday, in all its theological, social, cultural, emotional and political variety, was as much a celebration of difference as it was of national unity.

After the long latitudinarian slumber of the eighteenth century, religion was on the march and nowhere more so than in the remote village of Kilmany in northern Fife. 'In my last I attempted to awaken the heart. In my present I shall attempt to give direction to the awakened' – the minister's accent was a 'broad and vulgar' Scots, the language 'negligent and coarse', but none of this had ever mattered in the impassioned rush of words and emotion that for the last four turbulent years had spilled down like 'fragments of burning mountains' from the Kilmany pulpit. 'For you will observe' – the periods would roll on, the heavily lidded, almost somnolent eyes light up with a strange 'watery glare', the arms flail the air, the feet stamp out the rhythm of the sentences like some half-demented weaver, 'that a man may long feel uneasy, and anxious for deliverance, and yet be at a loss how to go about it … He may feel haunted by remorse and a strong overpowering sentiment that all is not right about him – but the darkness of nature is over him and he cannot command light to arise in the midst of it – and he remains in gloomy and obstinate alienation from God – with no success in his attempts at the exercise of faith – no comfort in his prayers – no progress in his seeking after the face of a reconciled Father.'

The name of the minister was Thomas Chalmers – preacher, social reformer, ecclesiastical wrecking ball, and a man whose life and career might stand as a paradigm of the age itself. Chalmers had been born at Anstruther on the east coast of Scotland thirty-five years before, and after an education at St Andrews which had taken him closer to atheism than to Calvin, had been ordained into the Church of Scotland at a time when its dominant 'Moderates' party had ossified into little more than Henry Dundas's Tory interest 'at prayer'.

As a young man of wide secular interests, more interested in science and philosophy than theology, Chalmers had found a natural home among the Moderates and might well have stayed there without the event that four years earlier had changed his life and with it the future of the Church of Scotland. In his early years at Kilmany he had approached his ministry in much the same spirit that any unenthusiastic Moderate would have done, but in the spring of 1811 something happened to him, and an inextricable mesh of emotional, physical and spiritual factors combined to produce in him one of those sudden and total conversion experiences that were so beloved of evangelical tract writers. 'On the fast day,' a minister's widow from the nearby village of Dairsie celebrated it in the classic conversion language of the time, 'we had a new miracle of Divine grace, in a Mr Chalmers of Kilmany, a great philosopher, but once an enemy avowedly to the peculiar doctrines of the gospel. For a year back the Lord has been teaching him by the rod … and now he comes forward to preach the faith which he once destroyed, and I trust we glorify God in him.'

It would be impertinent even to think of judging the nature of Chalmers's conversion, and if it is always tempting to understand it in human rather than theological terms – blighted love, family tragedy, disappointed ambition, physical illness and mental stress would all seem to have played their part – its impact was immediate and profound. In a notorious pamphlet Chalmers had once insisted that a parish minister could do all that had to be done in two days a week, but from the date of the 'miracle' he was a man reborn, overseeing parish and Sunday schools, Bible Society and Mission meetings in a programme of pastoral visitations, moral and secular instruction, practical charity, Bible lectures and preaching for which seven days in a week had never proved enough.

At the heart of his pastoral mission was the pulpit, though even those who knew him best could never understand quite what it was that would make Thomas Chalmers the most famous preacher of his age. There was nothing very remarkable in his conversation around a dinner table or even in his printed sermons, but raise him high above a congregation in a pulpit, the fount of moral authority where all the warring elements of his complex, passionate, dominant character came into alignment, and he could empty the streets of Glasgow or pack a London church so full that he could only climb in himself by a window. Did they think, he implored his Kilmany congregation this Sunday morning, that because they had not yet found Christ, there was nothing to do? Did those who heard Isaiah do nothing because salvation was not yet at hand? Did the 'publicans and harlots and soldiers and men of avarice' who listened to John preaching continue in sin because Christ was not yet come? No, 'even before salvation had actually come and before righteousness was actually revealed – there was a part for these people to take, and by taking this part they prepared themselves for greater things which were to follow and put themselves in a likelier way for receiving the benefit of them, than if they had delivered themselves up to idleness and refused to do anything'.

It was not an intellectually challenging sermon that he was giving this Sunday morning, but then this was not a show of theological pyrotechnics, but the final exhortations of a pastor saying farewell to the parish where he had discovered his faith. In his earlier, careless years in Kilmany he had naturally looked beyond its narrow boundaries to the political, literary and religious worlds of Edinburgh, Glasgow and London, and even after conversion a deep conviction of miserable worthlessness had never quite stifled a sense of his own abilities or an ambition that the narrow world of a remote rural parish was never likely to satisfy.

There was nothing ignoble in his ambition – it was, after all, God's work out there – and if God's will and Chalmers's often seemed conveniently close he was not the first or the last nineteenth-century evangelical to come to the same cosy accommodation. He might have been more reluctant to leave the parish if Kilmany's gentry had embraced his communitarianism with greater zeal, but entrenched interests die hard and when late the previous summer his growing fame as a preacher attracted the attention of the Tron church in Glasgow, there seemed nothing in Fife to stop him hearing in the summons the unmistakable 'Call of Providence'.

There could have been no greater challenge or contrast than that facing Chalmers as he said goodbye to Kilmany, behind him a homogenous rural parish without Dissenters or Catholics, and before him a dynamic, heaving world of violent extremes, of cotton mills, dye works, iron foundries and merchant princes; of miserable, overcrowded tenements, squalor, unemployment, ignorance, pollution and disease. On the eve of the French wars Glasgow had numbered something over forty thousand inhabitants, but by 1815 that figure had almost trebled to create a metropolis that had outgrown its political and religious institutions, a city of Irish Catholics, frustrated radicals, dispossessed agricultural labourers and aggressive Dissenters to whom the established Church of Scotland had nothing to say and no relevance.

For the established Churches of Scotland and England, sunk in the long snooze of the eighteenth century and tied by education and interest to the propertied classes, here was the challenge of the future. It is no coincidence that at the same time that Chalmers was assuming his new ministry the newly ordained John Keble was beginning his down in a Cotswold village, because that same deep evangelical current that would take Chalmers to Glasgow and stir the Churches out of their latitudinarian torpor was flowing into every aspect of national life in a way that it had not done since the Commonwealth and the reign of the saints.

This evangelical movement was not a very attractive impulse – a conviction of the utter depravity of unredeemed man is not a happy base for social regeneration – but if the tree is to be known by its fruits then there is no escaping its power. Within the Churches themselves it would soon lose its initial transforming vitality, but one of the great paradoxes of evangelicalism – as of Chalmers's own long career in public life – is that a socially conservative faith so firmly rooted in the futility of merit and good works should have its greatest impact in so many areas of practical philanthropy on which it left its indelible mark.

Prison reform, education, asylums, pauperism, factory hours, drink, Sabbath observance, the abolition of slavery – if there was little that was gloomy in the nineteenth century that evangelicalism was not answerable for then it would equally play its part in almost everything that was good in the public life of the country. Thomas Chalmers was under no illusion as to the immense size of the task facing him in Glasgow, but if there were any doubts this Sunday as he looked down on his Kilmany parishioners – was there one soul there that he had saved? Was Kilmany any closer, after all the years of striving, to the 'Godly Commonwealth' of the old Reformation dream? – the life of the evangelical Christian was one of endless struggle and Chalmers was ready for the fight.

It would be a fight, too, against lukewarm indifference and entrenched class interest on the one hand and bigotry on the other. This Sunday morning, as the congregation of a small Methodist chapel near London's Red Lion Square prayed for justice for one of their own, the Reverend Mr Cotton, the Newgate Ordinary, was praying for her confession. At the same time that Thomas Chalmers was heading for

Glasgow with its great mass of Catholic immigrants, a Roman Catholic priest in the Scottish Highlands, Father John Lamont, denounced by a neighbouring Protestant minister for celebrating a Catholic marriage, was awaiting trial at the next Inverness sessions. And as Thomas Chalmers was awakening the hearts of his Kilmany parishioners to Christian love, an angry Calvinist mob further north on the east coast was gathering in the churchyard to dig up the body of a recently buried suicide. On such a Sunday – in such a divided, suspicious Britain – what could a minister of the Establishment have to offer to the dissenting poor of Glasgow? What could a Presbyterian have to say to the city's teeming Irish Catholics? What could the transforming message of the gospel mean to those dying in the slums of Glasgow, like William Wheeler's soldiers, 'with despair and horrid oaths' on their lips? What price national regeneration when the 'fount of royal mercy' that twenty-two men and women in Newgate's condemned cells were waiting on – Shelley's 'mud from a muddy stream' – dribbled as sluggishly as it did in Carlton House?

He was ready though. And so too, five hundred miles to the south, as he made his way between the mouldering graves and burial mound of Taplow's St Nicholas church, was William Wilberforce. Five years earlier his *View of Practical Religion* had been the book that had opened Chalmers to the gift of grace and Wilberforce had travelled the same conversion road himself. And twenty years after his own conversion he was still fighting. He had spent that week battling to push a Slave Registration bill through Parliament, only to founder on the same specious arguments, the same entrenched selfishness, the same plantation coteries as always. There would, though, be other bills, and God's work would finally triumph, and Britain be made worthy of the place in God's dispensation that had been chosen for her. 'In the midst of crooked and perverse nations ye shine as lights of the world' was Mr Moodie of Edinburgh's text for the day from Philippians, and in Glasgow this Sunday, was not Thomas Campbell, just returned from

Africa with his three fellow ministers of the London Missionary Society, preaching and collecting for the African missions? And on a morning such as this, bright again after the rain, what better proof could one have of God's infinite mercies? 'Perhaps at this very moment,' Wilberforce added, turning to his children, 'when we are walking thus in peace together to the House of God, our brave fellows may be fighting hard in Belgium. Oh how grateful we should be for all God's goodness to us!'

12 noon

Ah, You Don't Know Macdonell

From the moment that Wellington chose the ridge at Mont-Saint-Jean to fight his battle, the chateau and outbuildings of Hougoumont were destined to play a crucial role. It is possible that history and myth have exaggerated its strategic significance, but situated as it was, below and in advance of the British right wing, Hougoumont might have been equally designed to ease or aggravate the fears that Wellington had always had for the safety of his right flank.

Wellington was probably giving Bonaparte more credit for finesse than was his due in fact, because as far as Bonaparte was concerned any flank attack would be launched as nothing but a diversion. On the day before the battle a French advance guard had probed as far as the chateau, but Bonaparte's battle plan – in so far as he thought one was needed to defeat an inferior army and an inferior general before he ate that night in Brussels – was to force Wellington to draw troops away from the allied centre to reinforce his right before he smashed his way through the middle.

With his right flank anchored on the village of Braine l'Alleud, a thousand yards to the north and west of Hougoumont, and a division placed around it, Wellington was taking no chances though, and the chateau and its outbuildings formed a key part of his defences. From the north, or allied, side a sunken lane ran at an angle down from the ridge to the chateau gate, which opened in turn on to a walled court-yard, enclosed on the northern and western sides by cowsheds and barn, and dominated on the south side by the handsome facade of the chateau itself.

Immediately to the right of the chateau was another massive gate, leading through to a second courtyard at the rear of the main building, with more cowsheds and stables along its western range, and the gardener's house closing it in at its southern end. On the eastern side of the chateau and farm buildings was a large walled garden and orchard, and beyond the whole complex to the south, a wooded park, bounded by hedges and ditches, stretched out towards the left wing of the French lines.

It was just as well that Wellington had reinforced these buildings because battles have a way of developing a logic of their own, and from the opening shots of the day Hougoumont took on a significance for both sides beyond its strategic value. The division on the far left of the French line was under the command of Napoleon's youngest brother Jérôme, but if he had understood the nature of his orders there was not much sign of it, and an attack that was begun as a diversionary feint was allowed to develop into a battle within a battle that would play a major part in the final outcome.

It would do more than that, as well, because every religion needs its holy places and in Hougoumont the nineteenth-century cult of British military heroism was about to gain one of its bloodiest shrines. On the evening of the 17th, Wellington had deployed four light companies of Guards to secure the buildings and grounds, and at twelve o'clock, as the first of the French skirmishers, fanned out in front of Jérôme's advancing column, reached the southern edge of the wood, he had something like a thousand men – a mix of dark-green-uniformed German Jägers, a battalion of Nassau troops and the Guards – standing between the enemy and strategic control of the ground in front of the allied right.

The numbers were in an important sense misleading – the sunken lane, 'the hollow way', would allow Wellington to go on reinforcing and resupplying the chateau throughout the day without weakening his centre – but as the Nassauers who had taken a mauling at Quatre Bras broke and fled, the real battle for Hougoumont began. The sheer weight of French numbers took them as far as the garden wall before they were finally driven back, but with the artillery of both sides weighing in, and British shrapnel and howitzers lacerating man and tree indiscriminately, the wood had already changed hands twice more by the time an even more acute threat to Hougoumont began to develop.

The hours spent overnight and through the long morning wait, throwing up firing platforms, cutting loopholes and barricading gates, had paid dividends, but the overwhelming numerical superiority in artillery had given the French control of ground on either side of the chateau. It was clear even to Prince Jérôme that another frontal assault on the south side would only cost more lives, and sometime between noon and one, about an hour after the opening cannonade, he sent his reinforcements forward along both flanks, driving the heavily outnumbered defenders out of the orchard on the east and sweeping around through the tall crops of the flat ground to the west until they found themselves in the sunken lane and at the north gate.

On the right of the advance, the attack was halted in ferocious fighting in the hollow way, but it was on the battle for the north gate, the supply line for the allied reinforcements and ammunition, that the mastery of the chateau rested. When the French arrived Colonel James Macdonell's two companies of Guards were outside the gate, and there was a desperate scramble to get inside the courtyard and bar the gate shut before the French could pour in and overwhelm the chateau's battered defences.

'Ah, you don't know Macdonell' had been Wellington's laconic response when the Prussian Baron von Muffling had queried his chances of clinging on to Hougoumont, and Macdonell did not let him down. With every moment the threat on the other side of the gate was growing, and when a huge ex-sapper called Legros – '*l'Enfonceur*', 'the Smasher' – succeeded in axing a way through, the battle for Hougoumont, the battle for the allied right, the battle itself, momentarily shrank to the hidden confines of a courtyard enclosed by barn and cowsheds, and to a murderous, brawling, hacking, race to secure the gate again before the rest of the attackers could stream in.

From the windows of the chateau and the cowshed on the northern flank, from the summits of the garrets, from the depths of the cellars, through air holes and cracks in the masonry – a bloody farmyard rat hunt – the fire poured in on the French as the massive figure of James Macdonell battled his way back towards the gate. There might have been a hundred attackers already inside the courtyard at this moment, but the real danger lay with those still outside and with the French pushing one way, and Macdonell and a handful of Coldstreams the other, the great heavy wooden gates of the north door were somehow forced shut and barred.

Hougoumont had been saved – 'the success of the Battle of Waterloo depended on the closing of the gates of Hougoumont,' declared an unusually theatrical Wellington – and from the chateau steps and the wicket gate into the garden, to the covered well and cowsheds on its northern side, Legros and his company lay dead. On the other side of the gates there was one last abortive attempt to scale the courtyard wall, but as the killing within slackened and the isolated besiegers outside in their turn became the besieged, only a solitary French drummer boy, carried inside the chateau by an English private to save his life, survived to show how close run a thing it had been.

In the orchard to the east of the courtyard, now back again in allied hands, the bodies of Lord Saltoun's Guards, Germans and

Wellington: 'the Genius of the Storm'. 'By God! I don't think
it would have been done if I had not been there!'

Napoleon Bonaparte: 'that mighty man of war – the astonishing genius who has filled the world with renown'. Even as Wellington's army was fighting at Waterloo, London crowds were queuing to see Lefebvre's portrait.

Marshal 'Forward': 'I should not do justice to my own feelings or to Marshal Blücher and the Prussian army,' wrote Wellington after the battle, 'if I did not attribute the successful result of this day to the cordial and timely assistance I received from them.'

A romantic heroine for the Victorian age: Magdalene De Lancey had been married only weeks when she joined her husband in Brussels just days before the battle.

Sir William Howe De Lancey, Wellington's chief of staff and one of the first men the duke asked for at the outbreak of war.

Mary and Charles Lamb. Nobody has ever been quite sure which of them was looking after which, but not even the mad-house or death would separate them.

'That singular compound of malice, candour, cowardice, genius, purity, vice, democracy and conceit' that was the essayist, Bonapartist and follower of the 'Fancy', William Hazlitt. Hazlitt was drunk for a month after the news of his hero's defeat at Waterloo.

J. H. Leigh 'Examiner' Hunt: poet, essayist, journalist and hero of the younger generation of Romantics, he had only just been released from prison himself at the time of Bonaparte's escape from Elba.

Benjamin Haydon, painter, diarist and paranoid suicide. 'Poor Haydon,' exclaimed Elizabeth Barrett after his death. 'Think what an agony life was to him to be thus constituted. Tell me if Laocoon's anguish was not an infant's sleep compared to this.'

Dr Thomas Chalmers, evangelical churchman, social reformer, ecclesiastical wrecking-ball and one of the great preachers of the age.

Thomas Cochrane, naval hero, radical, liberator and perennial thorn in the side of Admiralty and Government. Cochrane spent the day of Waterloo in the King's Bench prison.

The North Gate, Hougoumont: 'The success of the Battle of Waterloo,'
Wellington would later insist, 'depended on the closing of the gates of Hougoumont.'

Life-Guardsman Shaw, pugilist, swordsman and popular hero.
His last moments took their place among the legends of Waterloo.

Colonel Macdonell: 'the bravest man in the army'. 'Ah, but you don't know Macdonell,' Wellington remarked when doubts were expressed that Hougoumont could be held.

Edmund Wheatley, natural-born fighter and philosopher: a self-portrait. 'It is an awful situation,' Wheatley wrote, 'to stand with a sharp-edged instrument waiting for the signal to snap the thread of existence of those we never saw, never spoke to, never offended.'

French attackers lay jumbled together. In the hollow way behind, the French dead and dying marked the farthest limit of Jérôme's offensive as, across to the west, French Tirailleurs dissolved into the long corn. It was not the end of the attacks on Hougoumont – they would continue all through the day, squandering lives with a wanton and useless profligacy – but it was as near as it would ever come to falling. The north door was again in allied hands, the sunken road again an English thoroughfare, and Wellington free to think about the rest of his battle.

The indomitable James Macdonell, the younger brother of Alexander Macdonell of Glengarry, the violent and pantomime Highland chieftain of Walter Scott's dreaming and Raeburn's portrait … Harry Wyndham, a younger son of the Earl of Egremont … Ensign Gooch … Harvey … Corporal James Graham from County Monaghan, the 'bravest man in England' as he was known – apart from Colonel Macdonell, none of these could expect to find their way into Wellington's despatch, but these were the names, the men who had closed the north door, that would resonate down the century and out of which a mythology of nationhood was forged.

And Hougoumont itself. The tall, ripening fields of Waterloo, cut down in their swathes by cannonball and cavalry, might serve their turn as an easy poetic metaphor, but in the physical destruction of Hougoumont, in the blasted trees of its park and the lacerated branches of the orchard, an anthropomorphised, wounded nature seemed to have shared in the suffering and sacrifice of its defenders. 'The dead and the wounded positively covered the whole area of the orchard,' wrote an awed Gronow, 'not less than two thousand men had fallen there. The apple-trees presented a singular appearance; shattered branches were seen hanging about their mother trunks in such profusion that one might almost suppose the stiff-growing and stunted tree had been converted into a willow: every tree was riddled and smashed in a manner which told that the showers of shot had been incessant. On this spot I lost some of my dearest and bravest friends, and the country had to mourn many of its most heroic sons slain here.' A corner of a foreign field had become forever England.

1 p.m.

Never Such a Period as This

One of the first things that any stranger coming into London from the countryside would have noticed was that nobody noticed him. It would have been pretty well impossible to pass through an English village unremarked, but as the young American visitor George Ticknor told his father, London was an exhilaratingly anonymous place, a city – a new Rome, a new Babylon, a 'Nation' in itself the essayist, and addict, Thomas De Quincey insisted – of a million men and women, too poor, too rich, too wretched, too modest, too busy or too preoccupied with their own lives to take much notice of anyone else's.

At just about the same time as Ticknor was making his way to the publisher John Murray's in Albemarle Street, and Henry Crabb Robinson was threading a path towards the Wordsworths' lodgings in Marylebone, the Quaker banker, philanthropist and translator of Homer, Charles Lloyd, was walking to the Bedford Coffee House in Covent Garden. He had spent that morning at the meeting house in Westminster where Priscilla Gurney had spoken, and for an affectionate family man who was never at ease away from his wife in Birmingham – 'I wish thou wert with me ... I am not formed to dwell alone' he told her – he was feeling unusually 'quiet' and at 'home' among the Gurneys and the Hanburys and the Barclays and the Allens of London's tight-knit, intermarried Quaker community.

If Sunday 18 June seems a curious day to feel unusually 'quiet' – and Bonaparte's tumultuous 'Hundred Days' the last thing that anyone but a Quaker could describe as a 'time of much unction and great dominion of the truth' – it perhaps goes some way to explaining the absence of any real moral opposition to the renewal of war. In the weeks before the campaign opened there had been any amount of anger in radical circles, but the one voice that seems curiously muted among all the hyperbole of Byron and Hazlitt or the self-interested indignation of Liverpool merchants was the one voice that could legitimately command the moral high ground: that of the Quaker community.

It had not always been the case, and certainly not so with the Lloyd family of Birmingham. The Lloyds had originally come to England from mid-Wales in the time of Charles II, and within a generation a family that had paid for their religious convictions with ten years in a fetid Welshpool gaol had become one of the country's leading manufacturers, making their fortunes and reputation in the iron industry before turning, in the mid-1760s, to the banking business that still carries their name.

In 1815 'Charles Lloyd the Banker', as he was commonly known – his son 'Charles Lloyd the Poet', the nervy, depressive protégé of Coleridge had been among Lamb's guests the previous evening – was sixty-seven years old, a businessman of energy, culture, probity and talent. From the bank's foundation the Quakers' reputation for honesty had given the Lloyds a natural advantage, and in the fifty years since Sampson Lloyd had set up his bank with the great 'Shakespeare and Newton' of the Birmingham button trade, John Taylor, the family had continued to prosper, placing the Lloyds squarely at the heart of the economic, cultural, scientific, philosophical, religious and philanthropic lives of Britain's most dynamic, creative manufacturing centre.

It was a long way from the heroic resistance of the Welsh Lloyds and the foul straw bedding of Welshpool gaol, and in the gradual accommodation of Quaker ideals and separateness to a more accepting world something had been lost. In many ways the late eighteenth and early nineteenth centuries were a golden age of Quaker philanthropy, but for all the dedication of such men as Fowell Buxton or Charles Lloyd himself to the abolitionist cause, the gradual transition from outsider to insider, compounded by twenty years of war, had made it increasingly difficult for the Quakers' prosperous business community to square the circle of principle and profit.

They could go on addressing each other as 'thee' and 'thou' and intermarry – the Gurneys, the Frys, the Barclays, the Hanburys – but they could not be in the world and not of it in a great manufacturing centre like Birmingham that made everything from the slave owner's shackles to the army's guns. The Lloyds' fortunes in the iron industry had been made in the manufacture of nails by a technique smuggled out of Sweden, and yet even among the Friends it was hard to see what possible moral distinction separated the arms manufacturer from the banker who lubricated the town's trade or helped finance the government's war. 'I am convinced by my feelings and my reason that the manufacture of arms implies no approbation of offensive war,' one sword manufacturer, Samuel Galton protested, when Birmingham's Quaker community, alarmed at the charges of hypocrisy levelled against them, called him to public account for his family's business; 'Will any person for a moment suppose that as a manufacturer it is my object to encourage the principle or practice of war, or that I propose to myself any other end than that which all other commercial persons propose; the acquisition of property? … Is the farmer who sows barley, the brewer who makes it into a beverage, the merchant who imports rum, responsible for the intemperance, the disease, the vice, and misery which may ensue from their abuse?'

In another and stricter generation the answer might well have been 'yes', but for the Quaker who subscribed to government loans or happily paid the land or malt tax that were levied for the payment of the army, life was not so simple. The censures and laws of the Society of Friends were just as strict against the practice of war as slavery, Galton reminded his accusers, and if they were going to carry 'speculative principles into strict and rigid practice' then they had better abstain not just from the consumption of West Indian commodities – from rum, tobacco, rice, cotton, indigo, all of them the products 'and the very ground of slavery' – but 'from all commodities which are taxed ... for you may be well assured that every morsel of bread you eat and every cup of beer you drink has furnished the resources for carrying on this war, which you so justly censure'.

This was not an easy challenge to meet, especially in a community increasingly inclined to accept earthly prosperity as a token of divine favour, and perhaps in this summer of 1815, the muted response of the Society to the resumption of war is not the surprise it ought to be. It was probably no coincidence that the 'Church and Throne' mob who burned the Unitarian Joseph Priestley's books in 1791 had spared the Quaker Lloyds, and twenty-odd years later – twenty years of total war that had absorbed the energies of the whole nation – the Friends' disapproval of killing scarcely seemed to rise above a kind of inward spiritual self-absorption and a '*noli me tangere*' detachment from the outside world.

There was nothing complacent about Charles Lloyd, none of the moral smugness that creeps into the Quaker reformer Elizabeth Fry's journal for these months, but there was no more sense in his letters to his wife of horizons beyond the self-contained world of the Friends. As a good Quaker he hated the 'carnage' of war and as a good banker he deplored the crippling cost of renewed hostilities, but even though he had shared the coach down from Birmingham with an 'agreeable' gentleman of sixty who had been imprisoned in France for eleven years and his handsome young wife – 'at least I thought she was his wife as he called her my dear and she had a ring on her finger' – this Sunday in London, war and France seemed a long way away. 'I found a most kind reception at my nephew Hanbury's,' he wrote home chattily, as if no news could compete with the movements of their Quaker friends or with the comfort of his Gower Street accommodation: 'His second son Robert … went with me to Westminster meeting this morning, where I met several of my Friends – Anne Buxton & Priscilla Gurney were there; the latter preached a short feeling sermon … My Nephew Robert tells me that the young man … who was so violently in love with Sarah Buxton was a very nice youth, and had acquired a large fortune, he had been refused by her before he went abroad, but still indulged hopes – on his return he resumed his addresses, and wrote to her, she answered the letter, so as not to deprive him of all hopes, tho' very distantly, he wrote again and then a positive denial – this affected him extremely, and he was soon after taken ill, but unfortunately said nothing could restore him, but Sarah's favour, and when delirious he called on her, & at length he earnestly requested to see her, but he was dead 3 hours before her arrival – it is a very moving tale. My Nephew Robert says he believed Catherine Gurney is turned a Catholic but this I think must be a mistake …'

If the heroic Quaker age of Penn and Fox and Lloyd of Dolobran was well and truly over, a mile or so to the north-west of the Bedford Coffee House this Sunday morning a new heroic age was waiting to be born. Over the last few days Benjamin Haydon had been working feverishly on the canvas of *Christ's Entry into Jerusalem* that was going to raise British art to a new high, and if he had stopped now – midway through painting the arm of his Centurion – it was only because the thought of what might be happening in Flanders made it impossible for either Haydon or his model, Sammons, to concentrate on anything else.

Sammons was a corporal in the 2nd Life Guards and, like the young Gronow, had been left behind when his regiment embarked for Belgium. There had been real doubts among the rest of the army out there whether the Life Guards would prove anything more than 'decorative' when it came to a real fight, but even in the murky demi-monde of London, where a 'Piccadilly Butcher' was as likely to be found with a visiting Irish bishop in the Haymarket's White Lion Tavern as on more orthodox ceremonial duties, it would have taken a brave man to tell Sammons that. 'Sammons was a favourite model, a living Ilissus' – the great River God figured in the Parthenon's West Pediment – Haydon wrote of him, 'a soldier in every sense of the word. He would have brought a million safe and sound from Portsmouth to the King's Mint, but he popped his hand into King Joseph's coaches at Vittoria and brought away a silver pepper pot. He was an old satyr, very like Socrates in face, faithful to me, his colonel, and his King; but let a pretty girl come in the way and the Lord have mercy on her.'

Captain Bontein might have preferred the idea of Gretna Green and his fourteen-year-old heiress to the Low Countries, but Sammons had been like a caged animal since his regiment had sailed. It had seemed inconceivable to him that the army could think of fighting without him, and if it was not bad enough to be left behind when there were boys going who had never seen active service, it was worse still when for all he knew Haydon's other models – Jack Shaw, Corporal Dakin, the model for the drunken groom in his *Macbeth*, and, 'finest of all, six feet four inches, a perfect Achilles', Private Hodgson might be charging the enemy at this very moment.

It was almost impossible, in the usual course of events, to distract Benjamin Haydon from his art – not even the death of his father had dragged him from his *Judgement of Solomon* – but between Sammons and his own fevered excitement there was no going on. In 1814 he had been among the first of that great exodus of the rich, the curious and the indigent who had flocked across the Channel at the end of the long war with France, but even the excitement of those heady Paris weeks with David Wilkie, the thrill of seeing with his own starved eyes the great Masters in the Louvre he had only known in prints – the prickling fear of tramping those streets and squares where the tempestuous history of the last twenty years had been written in blood – the Lilliputian awe as he had tiptoed through the very apartments where the Great Ogre himself, the 'Apollyon of Revelations' the 'wonderful Napoleon who had snatched the crown from the hands of the Pope to put it on his own head', had eaten and slept and snuffed out candles and pulled bell ropes, was nothing to the sense now of living through great events.

'In the history of the world never was there such a period as this,' declared Haydon, and he thanked God he was there to share in its glory and its drama. As a young boy growing up in Plymouth he had slashed and carved his way through poppy fields of imaginary Frenchmen, and for the last three months he had been in a fever of excitement, dreaming of this day and of an England raised to new pinnacles in the arts of war and peace by the triple triumphs of Wellington, Nelson and Benjamin Haydon.

No one had a greater sense of his destiny than Haydon, no one so bitter a hatred of all those who would thwart it, and with God's help the canvas he had on stretchers in his Marlborough Street studio this Sunday was the work that would add lustre to the name that the sword would win for Britain. In the years since he had first come up to London there had been many more rebuffs than triumphs, but every setback was an angry spur to Haydon, every rejection only another proof that the whole corrupt, jealous cabal of British art – Academicians, teachers, critics, connoisseurs, patrons, 'the learned despots of dinner parties', foreigners, the royals, anyone and everyone who had ever questioned his genius – had to be swept away as Christ had driven the money-lenders out of the Temple.

With his massive domed head and piercing eyes he certainly looked the part – and played and sounded it too – and if Benjamin Haydon could only have painted half as well as he wrote his life and British art would have been very different. There was no diarist of the period who could match the vividness and immediacy of Haydon, but if he was a David Wilkie with a pen in hand, a born genre painter in words, full of narrative and detail, of personalities and grotesques, of acute observation and caricaturist spite, of brilliantly arranged tableaux vivants, he might just as well have been trained in a plaster cast studio the moment he took up his brushes and addressed himself to 'High Art'.

It was a living torture, in fact, to be Benjamin Haydon, to see enemies in every room and suspect every friend, to be so sure of his destiny and so frustrated by the world – 'tell me,' one friend would say 'if Laocoon's anguish was not an infant's sleep' to Haydon's misery – and yet for all the dogmatic intemperance and towering egotism, he was a man of high thoughts and noble impulses, of generous and chivalrous feelings, of gratitude and reverence and hope and prayer, always in love, always in debt, and not always in the wrong. For most of his life he had been half-mad and for some of it completely so, but in those moments when the clouds of paranoia and hysterical self-assertion parted, he would glimpse truths that others could not see and, like some nineteenth-century garret Galahad – living for weeks at a time only on potatoes so that he 'would not cloud' his 'mind with the fumes of indigestion' – be vouchsafed visions of the Grail.

He was one of the first and boldest to recognise and trumpet the greatness and artistic truth of the Elgin Marbles, had championed them in the face of derision and dilettante sneers, day after day had gone to the shed in Park Lane where they mouldered forgotten to draw and take casts and learn from them, and there was no sacrifice or hardship he would not suffer to make his own work worthy of their example. In the previous year he had come close to starving and blinding himself whilst painting the *Judgement of Solomon*, and no disappointment could ever stop him believing that the next canvas, the next vision, the next head he started would, with the grace of God, be the one to scatter his enemies and raise English history painting to its proper place among the nations.

There were periods of deep despair, days when even he could see the gap between the conception and the deed, between what he had glimpsed in his imagination and what his poor hand would perform, but in this first year of Christian triumph over the forces of atheism, of the defeat of Apollyon and the entry of Emperor Alexander into Paris, he had at last found his subject. 'Designing my *Entry into Jerusalem*,' he had written in his journal on 3 February, a month before Bonaparte's escape – that word *my* a wholly unconscious but wonderfully Haydon-esque ambiguity – 'In the left-hand corner I will have a penitent girl, pale, lovely, shrinking, entreating pardon of her Saviour, protected by her mother … who is clasping her in an agony of apprehension, yet with a gleam of hope through her tears … Christ shall have regarded this penitent girl with intense and tender compassion, pointing to Heaven with his hand. I thank God for this conception, and pray him to grant I may execute it with exquisiteness.'

It was a large canvas, not the 400 by 200 feet of his megalomaniac fantasies, but as big as his pocket and his studio would take: fifteen feet by thirteen and showing Christ's triumphal entry into Jerusalem on Palm Sunday. He would have the figure of Christ on His ass at the centre of the painting, with His right hand raised in benediction, the left arm extended in a gesture of restrained acknowledgement and His head – and somewhere at the back of Haydon's mind was the pricking knowledge of the trouble he had with heads – framed in a halo of brilliant white light that would cast its glow across the dense crowd parting to greet Him.

A Samaritan woman, spreading out a cloak for the ass to walk upon, would gaze up into the divine face from the bottom right. Beside her another woman would kneel with bowed head. Opposite them, his body curiously twisted, his massive right arm curved to mirror the line of the woman's cloak, would be his Centurion. Behind them he would paint a sea of faces – Wordsworth, Keats, Hazlitt, Voltaire – poets, critic and sneerer – awed onlookers together at Christ's and his own triumphal entry into their rightful inheritance. 'I am full of aspiration and glowing elasticity of imagination ... O God Almighty! I bless Thee for this with all my heart,' he was writing a week later, and with each succeeding day his sense of divine afflatus grew. 'This week has really been a week of great delight,' he recorded again at the end of April; 'Never have I had such irresistible and perpetual urgings of future greatness. I have been like a man with air-balloons under his arm-pits, and ether in his soul. While I was painting, walking, or thinking, beaming flashes of energy followed and impressed me. O God! grant they may not be presumptuous feelings. Grant they may be the fiery anticipation of a great soul born to realise them. They came over me, and shot across, and shook me, till I lifted up my heart, and thanked God.'

Through those early weeks of the Hundred Days he had worked on the Samaritan woman 'with the passionate self-seclusion of the ascetic, holding intercourse only with my art and my great Creator'. He had, too, taken the opportunity of Wordsworth's visit to London to take a cast of the great man's head for his portrait in the crowd. 'He bore it like a philosopher,' Haydon recorded in his journal for 13 April; 'John Scott was to meet him at breakfast, and just as he came in the plaster was put on. Wordsworth was sitting in the other room in my dressing-gown, with his hands folded, sedate, solemn, and still. I stepped in to Scott and told him as a curiosity to take a peep, that he might say the first sight he ever had of so great a poet was in this stage towards immortality.'

Immortality, though, was going to have to wait. He would show that fine head bowed in awe before his Saviour, a moving contrast with the critical 'investigative' look he would give to that 'singular compound of malice, candour, cowardice, genius, purity, vice, democracy and conceit' that was William Hazlitt. The Centurion too, for the time being, would have to wait. His 'patron', Sir George Beaumont, was coming to the studio the next day, and would enjoy watching him working on the sleeve. Beaumont was talking again of buying a picture from him, but that was Beaumont all over. He would make these offers and then pull back. He had done so with his *Macbeth*. Offer him a mighty work and Lady Beaumont would want something that would fit over her mantelpiece instead. Such, in England, was the fate of the history painter. But with God's help, here was the painting that would make the Beaumonts, and the Payne Knights, and the Lawrences and the Northcotes see what they had among them. 'O God,' he prayed, 'let me not know again the horrors of being harassed, not that I fear or shrink from any horror on earth that I must meet in my path, but that I wish to put forth my powers unburthened & unchecked to their full capacity. Thou knowest I have not yet done this, because I have always been obliged to leave things incomplete from necessity. But O God, if it be thy will that I just be further tried in trouble, I submit; grant me only health & confidence in thee. Let me only attain my great object at last. In thee with all my Soul I trust.'

The day was clearing, and his small, airless studio, 'stinking with the effluvium of paint' and crammed with his sketches and studies of the marbles, overpoweringly oppressive. If Haydon could not paint he would sit at the feet of genius. He would visit the Wordsworths in their lodgings.

2 p.m.

Ha, Ha

As the recumbent figure of Corporal Sammons lay waiting the finishing touches intended to bring him immortality, the short and violent life of another of Haydon's models was moving from fact into legend. The fighting for Hougoumont would continue for hours yet, but by two o'clock the point of crisis had shifted from the right to the centre, and it was here, behind and to the west of La Haye Sainte that Corporals Shaw and Dakin and Private Hodgson of Lord Edward Somerset's Household Brigade, stood waiting the command to charge.

Of all the men who fought at Waterloo, Corporal Jack Shaw's was the single name that Regency England would certainly have known before the battle started. In the eyes of Benjamin Haydon, Hodgson was the finest specimen of all his models, but it was in the figure of the prize-fighter Jack Shaw – six feet and half an inch in height, 210 pounds in weight, round face, grey eyes, fair complexion – that the brutal, bare-knuckle world of the Game Chicken, Tom Cribb and the freed American slave 'Blackie' Molyneux, reached its bloody and logical apotheosis on the field of Waterloo.

Jack Shaw had been born in 1789 into a respectable farming family near the village of Cossal in Nottinghamshire. As a young boy he had gone to Trowell school before dutifully serving his apprenticeship to a local wheelwright, but for any recruiting corporal at the Nottingham Goose Fair on the look-out for likely victims, a strong and hardened eighteen-year-old with a taste for excitement and the fists of a born fighter like Shaw would have been as easy a goose to pluck as anything that the assizes or prisons could put before him. 'THE OLD SAUCY SEVENTH ... Commanded by that Gallant and Well Known Hero, Lieut. General HENRY LORD PAGET,' ran one typical recruiting cavalry regiment poster:

> YOUNG Fellows whose hearts beat high to tread the paths of
> Glory, could not have a better opportunity than now offers.
> Come forward then and Enrol yourselves in a Regiment that
> stands unrivalled, and where the kind treatment the Men ever
> experienced is well known throughout the whole Kingdom.
>
> Each Young Hero on being approved, will receive the largest
> Bounty allowed by Government. A few smart Young Lads, will
> be taken at Sixteen Years of Age, 5 Feet 2 Inches, but they must
> be active, and well limbed ...
>
> NB. This Regiment is mounted on Blood Horses, and being
> lately returned from SPAIN, and the Horses Young, the Men
> will not be allowed to HUNT during the next Season, more
> than once a week.

Adventure, the swagger of a uniform, the chance to fight – these were powerful inducements to a boy whose whole life had been lived out against the distant background of war with Revolutionary and Napoleonic France. Shaw had already made a local name for himself as a boxer before the Goose Fair, and after an early street brawl in Piccadilly with three Londoners who had made the mistake of mocking his uniform, he was taken up by the regiment's officers and schooled at the Little St Martin's Lane Fives Court and in the Bond Street rooms where the young Byron sparred and fenced under the tutelage of Gentleman John Jackson and Henry Angelo.

Here was the louche, accommodating and curiously classless world that provided the model for the young George Keppel's Westminster; a world shading at one end into a duelling, gaming, whoring demi-monde of money-lenders and pimps and blazing at the other into the full glare of the prize ring. As a nineteen-year-old Henry Angelo had stopped off at the Surgeons' Hall on his way to Dolly's Chop House to watch the public dissection of Martha Ray's murderer, and thirty-six years later his Bond Street rooms and the Newgate gallows remained two sides of the same coin: two of the great London institutions servicing in their different ways that same, insatiable voyeuristic taste for brutality and violence that underlay the surface 'tinsel' of Thomas Lawrence's Regency England.

It was against this England that Wilberforce had directed all his moral fervour, the England of 'the Fancy', gambling and the London under-world, of fair booths, pickpockets and Morocco men; of the mermaids, philosophical pigs, cannibal heads, performing dwarfs and giantesses of Bartholomew Fair, the disappearing, anarchic England of the eighteenth century. 'Reader have you seen a fight?' asked Hazlitt, magically conjuring up the esoterica and moral intricacies of a culture in which Englishmen liked to imagine violence and some exclusively English code of honour and fair play eternally sharing the same ring; 'If not, you have a pleasure to come, at least if it's a fight like that between the Gas-man [Tom Hickman] and Bill Neate. The crowd was very great when we arrived on the spot; open carriages were coming up, with streamers flying and music playing, and the country people were pouring in over hedge and ditch in all directions to see their hero beat or be beaten.'

There had been heavy betting on the fight – five-to-four on the 'Gas' – but it was the Gas-man's bragging as to what he was going to do to

Neate that had offended Hazlitt's sense of decorum. 'Why?' demanded Hazlitt, should he roll back his sleeve to brandish the right arm he called 'his grave-digger'? Why 'should he go up to his antagonist, the first time he ever saw him at the Fives Court, and measuring him from head to foot with a glance of contempt, as Achilles surveyed Hector, say to him, "What, are you Bill Neate? I'll knock more blood out of that great carcase of thine, this day fortnight, than you ever knock'd out of a bullock's!" It was not manly, 'twas not fighter like ... [and] the less said about it the better. Modesty should become the FANCY as its shadow. The best men were always the best behaved. Jem Belcher, the Game Chicken, (before whom the Gas-man could not have lived) were civil, silent men. So is Cribb, so is Tom Belcher, the most elegant of sparrers and not a man for everyone to take by the nose.'

This is an evocation of England and Englishness – of plain, manly courage tempered by modesty that, suitably gentrified and Christianised, Rugby School's Tom Brown would have fitted into happily – and in Lifeguardsman Shaw it had found its prototype. In his first sparring sessions he had seemed little more than a clumsy country lad, but discipline and practice with the sword and dumbbells had given him wrists and shoulders of steel that soon made him more than a match for anyone put in the ring. 'His height, length, weight and strength,' the sporting journalist Pierce Egan wrote of him, 'united with a heart which knew no fear, rendered Shaw a truly formidable antagonist ... In a sort of trial set-to at Mr Jackson's rooms, with Captain Barclay, who, it is urged, never shrunk from punishment ... received such a convincing blow on his mouth from the paw of the Lifeguardsman ... that a dentist was absolutely necessary to replace matters in status quo.'

The sparring and set-tos at Jackson's and the Fives Court were 'friendlies' fought with gloves, but the transition to bare-knuckles proved no difficulty for Shaw. In these early days he had seen off Molyneux as well as the renowned Barclay, and after savagely disposing of another fighter called Burrows, had returned from the Peninsula to the all-England orbit of Cribb and Oliver with a bout against Ned Painter in front of a crowd of 25,000 on Hounslow Heath.

The fight lasted just twenty-eight minutes, ended with Painter an insensible and bloodied pulp, and netted Shaw a purse of fifty guineas, but there would be no challenge for the Championship of England. By the time the contest was reported in the *Morning Post* the first of Wellington's reinforcements were already on their way to Belgium, and within weeks Shaw, Dakin and the Life Guards had joined them, distinguishing themselves on the withdrawal from Quatre Bras to the ridge of Mont-Saint-Jean by a coolness that not everyone had expected of them.

There might have been no chance to test himself against Oliver or Cribb, but Waterloo was a battle designed for a prize-fighter of Shaw's calibre. For an officer like Harry Smith who took a rare and un-amateurish interest in his profession, there was something retrogressive in the brute simplicity of Waterloo, but in a battle so utterly devoid of finesse, variety, tactics or movement – a stand-to 'milling' of 'hard pounding' in which the only qualities required were courage, strength and endurance – then the Jack Shaws of the army came into their own.

They were needed, too, because at two o'clock in the afternoon, along the Ohain road to the east of the La Haye Sainte, the battle was being lost. Almost exactly an hour earlier Bonaparte had unleashed the first of the Comte d'Erlon's divisions on the farmhouse at the centre of the allied line, and when at half-past one a second wave followed it up the slopes to the beat of the *pas de charge* and the continuous roar of '*Vive l'Empereur*', the whole allied centre along the sunken road was in danger of being overwhelmed.

It was at this second great crisis of the battle – with La Haye Sainte surrounded, Picton killed while rallying his men, whole battalions decimated, the second line committed, Cuirassiers on the ridge, the Highlanders wavering, the Ohain road to the left in enemy hands – that for the first time Uxbridge's cavalry were called into action. During the earliest stages of the fighting they had been drawn up in the rear of La Haye Sainte as if they were still back at Knightsbridge, and as the order came to mount, the 'ball' that was Waterloo for a moment stood still. From right to left, stretched out on either side of the Brussels road in their finest summer condition, were over two thousand of the most magnificent horses in Europe, nineteen squadrons in all, of more than a hundred sabres each; to the left of the road, Sir William Ponsonby's Union Brigade made up of the Royal Dragoons, the Scots Greys and the Inniskillings, and to the right of it Lord Edward Somerset's Household Brigade of the Royal Horse Guards and the 1st and 2nd Life Guards.

It was for this moment that an eighteen-year-old boy who 'had heard of battles and ... long'd to follow to the field Some warlike lord', had joined up at the Nottingham Goose Fair eight years before. In London he had laid out three men for objecting to the colour of his coat, and now, in the uniform of the 2nd Life Guards – red jacket, white cross belts, red stripe down grey trousers, and a wonderful confection of a plumed and crested helmet designed by the Prince Regent – Corporal Shaw and a wall of horses half-a-mile long advanced at a walk and then a trot up the reverse slope of the ridge towards the unsuspecting French.

That brief, illusory moment of stasis was over. Between Uxbridge's brigades and the 14,000 infantry and supporting cavalry of d'Erlon's corps were the retreating allied troops, and as they parted to allow their cavalry to pass through, one of the great classics of heroism, triumph, fury, indiscipline and disaster began to unfold. 'No one but a soldier,' the infantryman Edmund Wheatley insisted, 'can describe the thrill one instantly feels' at the sound of the word 'Charge' – and no one but Job could say what that felt like for man and horse. 'Hast thou given the Horse strength' – the verses would be inscribed above the grave of William Verner's Waterloo charger, Constantia – 'Hast thou clothed his neck with thunder? The quiver rattleth against him, the glittering spear and the shield. He swalloweth the ground with fierceness and rage: neither believeth he that it is the sound of the trumpet. He saith among the trumpets, *Ha, Ha*: and he smelleth the battle afar off, the thunder of the Captains, and the shouting.'

It would have been enough to have thrown the most experienced French cavalry, and discipline had never been the British cavalry's forte. At the left of the line, Corporal Dickson of the Scots Greys 'felt a strange thrill run through' him, and as his 'noble beast' Rattler 'sprang forward, neighing and snorting, and leapt' the holly hedge flanking the Ohain road, any last vestige of control or order disappeared. 'All of us were greatly excited,' Dickson recalled, 'and began crying "Hurrah, Ninety-Second! Scotland for ever!" … for we heard the Highland pipers playing among the smoke … and a moment more were among them … and as we passed through them … many of the Highlanders grasped our stirrups, and in the fiercest excitement dashed with us into the fight.'

After twenty years without seeing action the Greys were waiting for this day, and as Uxbridge's brigades hacked and trampled their way through the French attackers and whole battalions fled, surrendered or simply disintegrated in front of them, excitement, ill-discipline, and the impetus of their own charge took them farther and farther down the muddy slopes and upwards again towards the French guns and the waiting French lancers.

It was a matter only of minutes – less than half the time it had taken to thrash Ned Painter – and even as triumph threatened to turn into disaster, and the exhausted men and horses of Uxbridge's cavalry found themselves mired in the mud at the foot of the slope at the mercy of the French guns and lancers, Shaw could still be seen cutting and slashing his way to an immortality that poor Haydon could never give him. According to one witness, he had been drinking heavily before the charge, and as the battle dissolved again into a thousand frenzied separate encounters, and Haydon's 'Achilles' split the bald and white-haired head of an elderly officer in two, and the model for his drunken groom, foaming at the mouth, divided the heads of two Cuirassiers, all those years of the dumbbells and sword drill, of the Fives Court milling and the bare-knuckle ring, of a life consecrated to fighting, spilt out in an orgy of violence that no one who saw it forgot.

No one knows how many men Shaw killed – one downward swing of his arm and a face fell off 'like a bit of apple' – and no one could be quite sure how he died. In Gronow's account he was killed by the sword thrust of a French colonel while fighting at the side of the formidable Captain Kelly, but myth required something more than a single adversary for the Champion Elect of All England. 'In the melee he found himself isolated, and surrounded by *ten* of the enemy's horsemen,' Captain Knollys would write – numbers taking on an almost symbolic, classical roundness, as explicit and spurious as any 300 Spartans; 'whirling his good blade swiftly around, he for a time keeps his foes at bay. At length his sword breaks in his hand; but Shaw will not give in, he tears his helmet from his head, and tries to use it as a cestus. The Cuirassiers now close in upon him, and the heroic Guardsman is struck to the earth, and they ride off exulting in the thought that they have at length avenged the hecatomb of Frenchmen who have fallen victim to Shaw's slaughtering hand.'

Bleeding from a myriad wounds, the dying Shaw dragged himself towards La Haye Sainte and somehow propped himself against a wall among the beaten enemy. To the left and south of him the shattered remnants of the Scots Greys – led, when his arms had been shot off, by Colonel Hamilton gripping the reins in his mouth – struggled to make their way back to the safety of the ridge and the allied lines. In the hollow Sir William Ponsonby, commander of the Union Brigade, lay dead but the second great crisis of the day was over.

And 'Ye who despise the FANCY', Hazlitt defiantly wrote of the climax of the great Gas-man–Neate fight, when both men were 'smeared with gore, stunned, senseless, the breath beaten out of their bodies' and 'eyes filled with blood' and 'noses streamed with blood' and mouths 'gaped blood', and the only thing that kept Bill Neate standing was English courage, 'Ye, who despise the FANCY, do something to shew as much *pluck* as this before you assume a superiority which you could have never given a single proof of by any one action in the whole course of your life.'

It was an odd irony that it should be Hazlitt who provided England with its perfect metaphor – Neate versus the Gas-man; English guts against French arrogance – but if Shaw might have missed his chance against Tom Cribb, he had got his fight. And 'on that great day of milling', as Tom Moore put it, 'when blood lay in lakes, When Kings held the bottle and Europe the stakes', John Bull and his children had found themselves a new hero.

3 p.m.

The Walking Dead

There can have been nowhere in England where Sundays dawned as reluctantly or bitterly as they did in the condemned cells of London's Newgate gaol. For twenty-one men and women the nights might at least bring the hope of oblivion, but as the small, pale square of light high in their cell walls slowly gathered strength, and the heavy peal of church bells – five, six, seven and, grimmest of all, eight – tolled away their lives, all the horror that sleep had kept at bay would return. 'Confused by his dreams, he starts from his uneasy bed in momentary uncertainty,' one young journalist wrote of those interminable nights and of that moment of recognition when the feverish hopes of dreams gave way to stony reality: 'It is but momentary. Every object in the narrow cell is too frightfully real to admit of doubt or mistake. He is the condemned felon again … and soon he will be dead.'

It had already been a long Sunday at the 'Bottom of the Masters', where a young servant girl of twenty-two called Eliza Fenning was waiting to know whether she was to hang or be reprieved. By the afternoon of 18 June she had already been in Newgate for more than two months, and her 'nightmare', as she thought and spoke of these weeks, had begun even before that, on a Tuesday in March – the Tuesday of

Easter Week – in the household of a law-stationer called Robert Turner at 68 Chancery Lane.

It was appropriate that her 'public life' should begin in Chancery Lane, at the heart of London's legal system set on destroying her, but nothing in her first twenty-two years had ever suggested that it might be where she would end her days. Eliza Fenning – she only used her full name, Elizabeth, in her final letter to her mother – had been born on the island of Dominica in 1793, the daughter of an 'industrious' and 'respectable' Irish Protestant woman from Cork and of a 'steady, honest and sober' Suffolk man who, in twenty years with the 15th of Foot, had risen to the rank of sergeant and the position of Master of the Band.

There were nine other children born to William Fenning and his wife – all dead by 1815, the last two buried in the churchyard of St George the Martyr in Bloomsbury – but Eliza was made of more robust stuff. In the early years of the nineteenth century, cholera and 'Yellow Jack' made the West Indies a notorious graveyard for the European, but while her father's regiment was ravaged by disease and her brothers and sisters dropped tamely away, the young Eliza thrived on a world of rich and exotic colour, sounds and textures that she would never forget.

During her Newgate ordeal every minutest biographical detail – the Irish mother, the soldier father, the lushly, proto Bertha-esque suggestiveness of her Caribbean childhood, her London Dissenters' school, even the rush candle that set fire to her infant cot – would take on a dangerously protean life of its own; but probably nothing counted to her fate quite like her appearance. The only authentic picture that survives of her does not give much away (the first image used on ballad sheets made do with a portrait of the Duke of York's mistress), but at the age of twenty-two she was clearly a woman of greater charms and intelligence than was good for a servant girl, with a learning, intelligence and fastidiousness that was a credit to her sober Methodist upbringing, and a piquancy and figure – if Robert Cruikshank's Newgate sketch is any guide – that was anything but.

It perhaps says everything that needs saying about her faintly erotic blend of Methodistical piety and worldly allure – 'highly interesting' was the seasoned Newgate-watcher's verdict on her – that it took her heavily pregnant new mistress in Chancery Lane less than a month to rumble the danger a young woman like that might be in her household. 'I am the wife of Mr Robert Gregson Turner, who is a law-stationer in Chancery-lane, in partnership with his father, Mr. Orlibar Turner,' Charlotte Turner had begun her own version of the events that within two months would turn a servant girl of blameless character into a convicted poisoner fighting for her life. There had been an 'incident' only weeks after she had come into service with them, she told the court, when she had seen the prisoner emerging from their apprentices' room 'partly undressed' – and with hindsight Eliza Fenning's fate was already sealed. For the next month, the young woman's attitude had continued to displease her mistress, but then sometime near the beginning of March there had been a change and Eliza had asked if she could make some dumplings at which she said she was 'a capital hand'. Over the next three weeks the request was repeated frequently, and on Monday 20 March, Charlotte Turner had reluctantly agreed, telling her that she might as well make some for the family the next day after she had made a meat pie for the apprentices.

The jury, if they were listening that is – the country beyond the walls of the Old Bailey certainly was – must have learned more about the making of dumplings than they can have either expected or wanted to know, but the gist of the case was clear. The apprentices ate at two in the afternoon and the family at three, Charlotte Turner explained, and she had barely had time to serve her husband, Robert, and his father, Orlibar, their dumplings and try a small piece for herself before an 'excruciating pain' – 'an extreme violent pain, which increased every minute' – followed by retching and a swelling of the tongue, head and chest, drove her upstairs where she lay prostrate in bed for the next six hours.

Robert and his father had also been taken ill, and by the time 'Mr Marshall, the surgeon', was called, Eliza lay similarly doubled up 'in agonies below stairs'. The wonderfully Dickensian Orlibar Turner had spent the afternoon between the parlour and the backyard retching uncontrollably, but by the time that same evening that William Fenning turned up to see his daughter, Turner was recovered enough – and suspicious enough – to order the maid, Sarah Peer, to tell the father that Eliza was out on 'a message for her mistress'.

The family's first unshakeable conviction that night, was that they had been poisoned, the second that it was arsenic, the third that it was the dumplings, and the next morning Orlibar Turner went into the kitchen to inspect the remains of their Tuesday lunch. He put some water into the pan in which Eliza had mixed the dumplings, and stirring it up with a spoon 'to form a liquid of the whole', allowed it to settle for a moment or two before carefully tilting it to reveal at the bottom a distinct residue of 'white powder'.

There was no doubt in his mind that it was arsenic, and none either in the mind of the surgeon, Marshall, when he returned that morning to see his patients. He had been sure enough the previous evening that their symptoms were those of arsenic poisoning, and when he repeated Orlibar's experiment, washing the dish in warm water, allowing it to subside and then decanting off the liquid, there – in all its damning, rigorously achieved, scientific purity – was the 'half-teaspoon of white powder' that they had been looking for. 'I washed it the second time,' he later declared, and 'decidedly found it to be arsenic. Arsenic cut with a knife will produce the appearance of blackness on the knife; I have no doubt of it. There was not a grain of arsenic in the yeast: I examined the flour-tub; there was no arsenic there.'

There was obviously genuine horror in the discovery – the thought of 'poison' and an unknown poisoner in their midst was an insidious fear for any household – and in the young and newly arrived Eliza Fenning, the unprotected daughter of an upholsterer and ex-soldier, family, apprentices and maid had found their perfect scapegoat. By the time that Marshall had finished with the dumpling dish Eliza was sicker than any of them, but that did not stop the Turners sending for an officer from Hatton Garden to stand guard, and the next day, Maundy Thursday – she was too ill to be moved any earlier – Eliza was taken into custody, charged and transported in an open carriage across London to the New Clerkenwell prison. 'I now lay ill at the infirmary sick ward,' she wrote to a man called Edward on 29 March – a man to whom she clearly considered herself engaged; 'My mother attends me three times a day, and brings me everything I can wish for; but, Edward, I never shall be right or happy again, to think I ever was in prison.'

The shame was real enough – the shame of a girl brought up by respectable, hard-working and God-fearing parents – but it is clear that she had still not fully realised the danger she was in. On 30 March she was again brought before the magistrate, and faced with the choice of a £20 bail that she could never hope to raise or immediate committal to Newgate, chose to stand trial and clear herself at the coming sessions, due to open in just over a week.

It gave her little time to prepare a defence, especially a defence against accusers as deeply embedded in the legal world as the Turners, but with only the £5 that her parents had scratched together, time would have done her little good. For the princely sum of two guineas the Fennings had managed to secure Eliza the unenthusiastic services of a barrister called Alley, but with the rest of the money disappearing in Newgate 'gratuities' there remained nothing – money, interest, credibility – to stand between her and those retributive winds of 'justice' that howled through the cold, disease-breeding cells of England's most infamous prison.

No one could have walked beneath the grim exterior of Nathaniel Dance's gaol with its massive, blind, yard-thick walls, and its notorious Debtor's Gate from which the condemned emerged for the last time, and expected any shelter for its inmates from Thomas Moore's protective 'thicket of the laws'. Within the prison walls there were areas that not even the governor or a turnkey would have dared to enter alone, and of all of them the women's yard was notoriously the worst, a savage and overcrowded hell of drunkenness, filth, degradation and despair.

For a few, illusory days at the beginning of April, Eliza Fenning must at least have had the hope of public justification to keep her from slipping beneath the mire, but that can have lasted no longer than the opening of her trial on the 11th. In the first third of the nineteenth century the Old Bailey was at the best of times the bloodiest court in England, and the Recorder for London in 1815 was the loathsome Sir John Silvester – a man notorious in an age of mediocre Tory placemen for a callousness and corruption that made no scruple of demanding a wife's favours as the price of a husband's reprieve.

There was possibly something about Eliza Fenning – perhaps her combination of prettiness (which he certainly noticed) and unavailability – that goaded the old lecher into particular irritability, but she probably received no better or worse a trial than any of the other prisoners hauled up to learn their fates. There is nothing but the sessions reports to gather any sense of the fairness or not of the other verdicts handed down that session, and yet in the transcripts of Eliza Fenning's trial – the official, carefully edited version on which any subsequent appeal would be based and the full script of the court shorthand writer – there survives so disturbing an insight into the battery-farm 'justice' handed down at the Old Bailey that it would echo down Home Office minutes and abolitionist debate for the best part of another eighty years.

Even before proceedings had opened, there was a built-in bias against the prisoner in a capital trial – and no one knew quite how many capital offences there were on the books, but certainly well over two hundred – because at that time and for another twenty years there was no summing up permitted to the defence. In the case of Eliza Fenning this might have made no difference as her two-guinea counsel had already left the court, and long before that anyway the overt prejudice of the judge and the carefully rehearsed and choreographed evidence of the prosecution's witnesses had made the jury's verdict a virtual formality.

The earlier row with Charlotte Turner, the prisoner's 'disarranged' dress, her brooding 'sulkiness', her repeated requests to make dumplings, their odd and heavy appearance, the impossibility of anyone else having touched them, her utter indifference to her employers' suffering, her knowledge of where the rat poison was kept, her ability to read and write, and finally, the residue of white powder and Marshall's blackened knife: one by one, family, apprentice, maid and surgeon stood up to give their damning evidence that pointed in only one direction.

There is no way of knowing with absolute certainty whether Eliza Fenning was innocent or guilty but the one unarguable fact is that there was too much doubt to convict. There may have been a superficial – even suspicious – coherence to the witnesses' depositions, but in a case that ultimately depended on opportunity and motive even two guineas should have been enough to secure an acquittal.

If every spat between servant and mistress, as one observer noted, had ended in a poisoning no one in Georgian London would have been safe, and still no one seems to have asked how likely it was that the young woman of 'integrity, sobriety, cheerfulness and humanity' a string of character witnesses described could have plotted so appalling a mass murder. It might have been conceivable if the prosecution had evoked a crime of passion, but their case was that on the basis of a single, trivial scolding from Charlotte Turner back in January, she had stolen the poison from her master's office, secreted it away for more than a fortnight in a room she shared with her fellow servant, and then systematically and ruthlessly worked on her mistress to secure herself the opportunity to settle an old score.

It was not as if she was the only one with access to poison or dumplings, or that any of the prosecution witnesses were unimpeachable – Charlotte Turner's version of events was demonstrably inaccurate,

Sarah Peer was self-confessedly no friend to the prisoner, the apprentice Gadsden who spoke against her seems to have had his advances repelled, Marshall would not have known arsenic if it came labelled in a bottle – but between Alley's indolence and the Recorder's hostility Eliza Fenning's hopes slowly guttered away. It did not even seem to have troubled anyone that a young woman of her intelligence should have so thoroughly poisoned herself, but perhaps by that time an experienced Old Bailey hand like Alley could see the way the wind was blowing, and that nothing more was to be gained by coming between Sir John Silvester and his assize dinner.

Silvester had certainly already done all he could to influence the outcome – allowing or discounting evidence as it suited the prosecution case, denying Eliza the witnesses she asked for, silencing her father before he could even speak – and as the prisoner's last hopeless plea of innocence echoed around the court room all that was left was to instruct the jury.

'Gentleman, you have now heard the evidence given on this trial,' Silvester concluded his heavily weighted summary: 'And the case lies in a very narrow compass ... The prisoner, when taxed with poisoning the dumplings threw the blame first on the milk, next on the yeast, and then on the sauce; but it has been proved most satisfactorily, that none of these contained it, and that it was in the dumplings alone, which no person but the prisoner had made. Gentleman, if poison had been given even to a dog, one would suppose that even common humanity would have prompted us to assist it in its agonies: here is a case of a master and mistress being both poisoned, and no assistance was offered. Gentleman, I have now stated all the facts as they have arisen, and I leave the case in your hands, being fully persuaded that, whatever your verdict may be, you will conscientiously discharge your duty both to your God and to your country.'

In the London of 1815, a nervous, combustible city stirred by undercurrents of disaffection and suspicions of Jacobinism, Sir John Silvester could afford his confidence, because as he looked at the jurymen – gentlemen, mercer, saddler, vintner, coal merchant, and one man so deaf he had heard nothing of the trial – he might have been looking at the Turners' natural allies. There had been absolutely no proof offered that Eliza Fenning had so much as seen the poison that the Turners kept in an office drawer, or that the arsenic was in the dumplings or – for that matter – that any crime had been committed at all, but within five to ten minutes the jury were back with the inevitable verdict of guilty.

The foreman had even prefixed it with an apologetic explanation that they would have been even quicker if they had not had to go over it all with the deaf Edward Beasley, but for Eliza Fenning it came like a bolt out of the blue. In the days before the trial she had genuinely looked forward to the chance of clearing her name, but now for the first time she collapsed, and had to be 'carried from the bar convulsed with agony, and uttering frightful screams'.

There was, though, one last public charade to go through before Silvester was done with her, and on the 15th of April, at the end of the sessions, she was brought back to court with the nine other convicted prisoners for sentencing. She would at least have recognised the women in the dock from the women's side in Newgate, but as one by one the sentences were handed down and another forger, horse stealer, burglar, returnee, child rapist or sodomite was sentenced to the gallows, the young, particularly fastidious, twenty-two-year-old Methodist-taught servant girl must have realised for the first time just how deep the pit was into which she had sunk.

That had been two months ago – two months since, as she told her parents, she had been numbered among the walking dead – and all she could do now was wait and pray. The blaspheming rapist William Oldfield had been told by Silvester to expect no mercy this side of the grave, but except for him and the fifty-eight-year-old sodomite

Abraham Adams – the invisible, unmentionable spectre at the Recorder's feast – all could still cling on to hope as they waited to learn whether the fount of royal mercy that flowed from the vast and improbable bulk of the Prince Regent had marked them for the gallows or for Sydney.[1]

It might take weeks or even months to discover whether 'the Prince Regent in Council' would confirm or commute a sentence – weeks of wildly fluctuating hope and terror for the condemned – and as May had turned into June and Bonaparte quitted Paris to join his army, Eliza Fenning had still been waiting to know her fate. 'As to exercise, where can I take it?' she asked plaintively – she would seem to have had a London accent from the one unedited letter of hers that survives: 'excepting I am to intermix with those who are lost to every principle … I believe I had better leave this dreadful place to go to a better world, than to be sent to another country with such desperate wretches. Mary Ann Clark [under sentence of death for stealing in a dwelling house] is the person I sleep with, and she is the only one that has the least feeling, but we have not any other prisoners as yet with us. As we are the four that are under sentence, Mr Cotton does not think it proper to place any person with us.'

As the weeks passed, her relationship with the evangelical champion of property and the law, the Prison Ordinary the Reverend Cotton, had deteriorated into open hostility and her letters chart the slow, inexorable guttering of her spirits. There were still days of hope and religious resignation, but this Sunday morning she had refused communion from him and in between the exalted Methodistical outbursts ran a more bitter and authentic realisation of the system that had her in its grasp. 'Be careful of Mr Cotton,' she wrote desperately to the reformed rapist Oldfield, who had undergone a classic death-cell 'conversion', her letter bleakly headed from 'the Bottom of Master's side' and addressed to 'Oldfield, condemned cell': 'Some one has made evil report to him about me; and I fear it has done me much harm.'

There can have been nothing unusual in these swings of mood, the alternating days of despondency and defiance, the creeping paranoia, the fits of weeping, the self-dramatisation – these were the natural operations of fear, humiliation and alienation on human beings already at the furthest pitch of emotional endurance – but what is unusual is that the record of it survives. The names of those felons condemned alongside her – Beard, Cambridge, Sweetman, Elizabeth Young – had disappeared from public consciousness long before this Sunday, but in these weeks around 18 June, while Cotton harried and bullied her for a confession of guilt and she waited for the fount of royal mercy to trickle into life, something was stirring outside the walls of Newgate that would turn the conviction of Eliza Fenning into a battleground of nineteenth-century legal and political life.

In the climate of the time the battle would inevitably take on a party colouring, but beyond the influence of government newspapers the pressure to re-examine the case against Eliza Fenning was gathering momentum. There was strong professional disquiet at the brutal conduct of the trial, and as the focus shifted to the crucial evidence of the surgeon, and a chemist repeated his experiments to demonstrate that, if the prosecution were to be believed, there must have been enough arsenic in Mrs Turner's quarter of a dumpling alone to have killed 120 people, the integrity of witnesses, process and conviction all stood arraigned in the same dock.

Never before had a criminal case been subjected to such close and critical scrutiny – not a single deposition or discrepancy in evidence, not a bullying intervention of Silvester's or failure of Alley's, not a lie of Mrs Turner and Sarah Peer or an 'expert' claim went unchallenged – and if Eliza Fenning had not done it, then, as Leigh Hunt's *Examiner* asked, who had? In the early weeks in prison she had asked the same dangerous question herself, and if she was no closer to an answer this Sunday than she had ever been the terrible paradox of her position was that in the mere act of asking – in the threat it posed to the Turner household and the challenge it threw down to the authority of Silvester and his court – Eliza had transformed herself from a helpless victim of legal indifference into a nuisance that needed crushing. 'Some one,' as she wrote, 'must be guilty, and I still hope it will [be] strictly inquired into.' Perhaps, at times, she believed that herself. But after two long months in Newgate, she would have been familiar enough with the system to know that the man who would do the inquiring and take her case to the 'Prince Regent in Council' would be Sir John Silvester himself.

4 p.m.

The Finger of Providence

It is a moot point whether there was a more dangerous place to be this Sunday than among the entourage of the Duke of Wellington. The duke had told one over-enthusiastic artilleryman that commanders-in-chief had better things to do than go firing at each other, but if Bonaparte had reciprocated in kind then the gunners of the Grande Batterie parked on the opposing slope of the valley to the east of the Brussels–Charleroi road had not been listening.

From the opening shots of the battle the duke had been 'everywhere to be found', 'encouraging, directing, animating … the Genius of the storm, who, borne upon its wings, directed its thunder where to break'. In the days before the campaign opened at Quatre Bras, Bonaparte had run rings around his opponent, but with the start of battle – as Sir Augustus Frazer had confidently predicted – the roles were reversed, and the more remote a memory the Bonaparte of his dazzling victory at Lodi appeared the more decisive and masterly Wellington became.

No genius of the storm ever cut a more soberly understated figure than Wellington in his boots, white nankeen trousers, white stock, plain blue coat and cocked hat, and it might have been as well if his entourage had followed suit. In the early stages of the battle he had ordered his generals to disperse for safety, but even after the wastage of four hours of fighting, the glittering cavalcade of aides and plumed and beribboned foreign ministers and hangers-on that accompanied him – the whole *Troupe dorée*, as Lord Uxbridge called them – still provided an irresistible target to any French gunner worth his powder.

It was all right for Wellington – 'the finger of Providence', as he claimed, was most certainly upon him that day – but for those of his staff who stood next to him it was another story. By the end of the day there would be scarcely one of them who had gone unscathed, and at four o'clock they found themselves again in the heat of the battle, close to the lone elm tree, the Waterloo pilgrim's answer to the 'true cross' of the medieval relics market, that stood in the south-west angle of the crossing of the Ohain and the main Brussels roads and marked the duke's central command position.

Two crises had been averted, but as Wellington looked through his spyglass at the field spread out below him, things did again, in Captain Mercer's words, 'indeed look very bad'. On the slopes beneath La Haye Sainte and over to the left of the road the great cavalry actions that had begun with the charge of the Union and Heavy Brigades had gradually petered out. Around the three pivotal defensive points in front of the allied ridge, though – Papelotte at the eastern extremity of the line, most perilously La Haye Sainte in the centre, and Hougoumont to the right – the fighting was continuing with the same ferocity as ever, draining away allied manpower which Wellington could ill afford. In the no-man's land between the two armies the French Tirailleurs held sway. In the far distance units of the still unused and massive French reserve – forty-six of Bonaparte's 103 battalions, including twenty-two of the Imperial Guard – could be seen moving in the direction of the hoped-for Prussian advance. But for Wellington and his staff, as they shuffled their dwindling pack and plugged gaps and watched preparations unfold for the next massed cavalry attack, night was beginning to look a very long way off.

What happened next seemed in retrospect to have occurred in that suspended time that gives to moments of sudden violence their curious air of slow motion. After the attack of the Scots Greys had temporarily silenced the Grande Batterie, it was again in full voice as a prelude to the first of Marshal Ney's great cavalry charges. Wellington had his glass to his eye. On horseback at his side was his newly married quartermaster-general and childhood friend Sir William De Lancey. They were talking and as Wellington broke off to dismiss a warning shout from a nearby soldier with a nonchalant 'never mind', 'a ball came bounding along *en ricochet* ... and striking [Sir William] on the back, sent him many yards over the head of his horse. He fell on his face,' the duke later told Samuel Rogers, 'and bounded upwards and fell again. All the staff dismounted and ran to him, and when I came up he said, "Pray tell them to leave me and let me die in peace."'

The ricocheting ball had struck him a glancing blow on the back near his right shoulder, ripping eight ribs from the spine, piercing the lung with the shattered fragments of bone, but drawing no blood and leaving no visible sign of injury. As the duke knelt at his side, holding his hand, it was clear, though, that there was nothing to be done. 'The Duke bade him farewell, and endeavoured to draw away the Staff, who oppressed him; they wanted to take leave of him, and wondered at his calmness. He was left, as they imagined, to die.'

As the sound of the French guns ominously ceased a cousin of De Lancey's called Barclay ran to his side. Across the valley, a long, rippling line of enemy cavalry, 'ever advancing ... like a stormy wave of the sea when it catches the sunlight', told why the cannon had fallen quiet. Barclay begged De Lancey to let him move him before they were engulfed in the tide but De Lancey asked only to be left where he was. It was impossible he could live, he told him, and bearers would be more use looking after others. 'But as he spoke with ease,' and there was no sign of blood, Barclay 'took the opinion of a surgeon, who thought he might live, and got some soldiers to carry him in a blanket to a barn at the side of the road, a little to the rear'.

There the wound was dressed, and Barclay, anxious to rejoin the battle, ordered him to be taken farther back before the barn fell into enemy hands. Before he left, De Lancey drew him closer to him. He wanted to speak of his wife, Magdalene. Only three days earlier they had stood together on their balcony overlooking the Parc as the sound of the fifes faded into the night and now, again, the war seemed to recede from his consciousness as completely as if they were together in her Antwerp room with the windows shut tight against the distant rumble of cannon. 'Nothing else seemed to occupy his mind. He desired Barclay to write to [her] … to say everything kind, and to endeavour to soften this business, and to break it to [her] as gently as he could. He then said he might move him, as if he fancied it was to be his last effort.'

They had been married just ten weeks. Just two months ago they had been walking together along the cliffs on her family's Dunglass estate, where Sir James had rowed James Hutton below the rock formations of Siccar Point and seen the immeasurable vistas of geological time opening up before him. For a few brief days in Brussels, closeted in their apartment, going out only when they knew they could be alone, their minds ruthlessly shut to thoughts of what lay ahead, love had pushed the notion away. But now, alone in the cottage at Mont-Saint-Jean to which De Lancey had been carried, the bleaker lesson of Siccar Point lay starkly before him. Wellington might talk of the hand of God and the finger of Providence, but where in the universe that Herschel's astronomy and the unimaginable aeons of Hutton's geology had conjured into being did man fit? What price that 'bank and shoal of time' on which he feebly huddled? There would be no easy comforts as De Lancey waited to die, close to the inn where he had reserved a table for that night, in a cottage where no one knew who he was or even that he was alive, with the knowledge that he was leaving behind a young wife in a foreign land. No comfort of any sort.

5 p.m.

Portraits, Portraits, Portraits

On the south side of London's Strand, midway between the City to the east and the government offices of Whitehall to the west, rose the neo-classical facade of the most ambitious piece of public building of the eighteenth century. There had been a palace of some kind on this site since Tudor times, and for the last twenty years Sir William Chambers's Somerset House had been at the heart of Britain's war effort against France, the home of the Navy Board and the administrative and clerical centre for the immense industrial and economic machine that built, maintained and fed Britain's fleets.

There was possibly no building in the capital that was simultaneously so un-English in its feel and so 'British' in what it said as Somerset House. In the seventeenth century the restored and Frenchified Stuart monarchy had harboured building ambitions well above its temporary status in the nation's life, and when eighteenth-century London finally did build to impress the world and itself with a sense of Britain's greatness it was not a royal palace it raised but a set of government offices brought together for convenience and efficiency.

The site was not an easy one to build on, sloping steeply down to the Thames as it did – and the river front, in a miniature parable of the national effort, still remained unfinished – but from the start display had been as important as utility. The pride of place in Chambers's building belonged to the Navy Board itself, but on the northern, or Strand side, of the great court around which Somerset House was arranged, the premises of the country's three great cultural institutions – the Royal Society, the Royal Society of Antiquaries and the Royal Academy – consciously and proudly linked the fruits of peace to the triumphs of war.

Here was Benjamin Haydon's vision in stone – Britain as great in the arts as she was in battle – and so it was perhaps appropriate that late on this Sunday afternoon in June an Academician in his late sixties might have been seen walking in under the arch through which twenty years earlier William Pitt had so often ridden on horseback to visit his naval Comptroller of Works. Off the coast of France the *Bellerophon* and the rest of Hotham's blockading fleet were a reminder that the work of the Navy Board and the Victualling Board was never done, but for the last two months of the summer, Somerset House had belonged to the Royal Academy and to the tens of thousands of visitors who flocked in off the Strand to pay their 1/- to see its annual exhibition.

For one reason or another it had been a frustrating sort of day for Joseph Farington – he had been forced to miss church in the morning at St James's Piccadilly, which he hated doing – but from the moment he turned in under the archway of Somerset House and right into Chambers's imposing vestibule, he was at home. Farington had never been very much more than a jobbing topographical painter himself, but for more than thirty years now the Academy had been his life, and its cabals and elections, its hanging committees, private shows and dinners, its artistic rivalries, finances, business, intrigues and politics the lifeblood of one of Regency London's most inexhaustible diarists and fixers.

He had only been abroad twice – once in 1793 to make topographical drawings of the fortifications at Valenciennes and once at the Treaty of Amiens with Benjamin West, Henry Fuseli and other Academicians – but while younger artists like Haydon and Wilkie could not wait for the peace in 1814 so they could travel, the Lancashire-born Farington was English to the bone. As a young painter he had studied under Richard Wilson, who had made his own name in Italy, but the Thames and the Lakes were about the farthest poles of Farington's artistic range, modest and old-fashioned watercolours of the river at Eton or Reading about the limit of his ambitions, and the Royal Academy all an elderly widower could now want of life.

Age and health had limited his active involvement in its committees of late, but this was the final Sunday of the exhibition, and with no one there but the porter, the former Lifeguardsman Samuel Strawger, it was a good chance for one last visit. It was generally agreed in the press that this year's exhibition was well up to the standard of recent years, and yet in some ways it must have been a bittersweet exercise in nostalgia to be here this Sunday, to see all the portraits and busts commissioned the previous year, to see preserved in paint long after the actuality had faded, all the euphoria and hopes and confidence and pride of the Summer of Sovereigns of 1814, when a whole generation that had never known peace thought that the war with Bonaparte was over for good.

It was exactly a year to the day – 18 June 1814 – that the City had held a banquet for the Prince Regent, the Emperor of all the Russias and the King of Prussia to celebrate victory, and here still were the heroes of the hour as if everything that they had celebrated was not at that moment under threat. In the inner room visitors could see a design of the Guildhall decorations for that banquet, and stacked high to the ceilings, frame to frame, were reminder after reminder of that year: portraits of the politicians and soldiers – Metternich, Platov, Picton, Vivian, Beresford and Hill – who thought they had done with war; paintings of officers' favourite chargers that thought they had heard their last trumpet; of naval officers who hoped they had cut out their last prize; of Wellington holding the Sword of State at the Thanksgiving

Service for Peace; of Louis 'le Désiré' on board a British man o' war on his way to reclaim his throne; of the celebrations on the Serpentine. And majestically, fraudulently, presiding over them all, resplendent in his military uniform, in the premier position on the east wall opposite the door, Sir Thomas Lawrence's portrait of the Prince Regent himself. 'One of the most admirable pictures, either as a likeness or a painting,' the *Morning Post* had assured its readers seven weeks earlier, on the eve of the exhibition's opening, 'is a portrait of the Prince Regent ... The characteristic benevolence of countenance, and that animation that speaks superior mental intelligence and discernment, are inimitably displayed and notwithstanding the numerous excellent portraits which we have seen of this illustrious personage, we can recollect no one which more deserves the title of *chef d'oeuvre*, than the one in question. The scarlet regimental costume imparts a brilliancy to the general effect of the picture, superior to any other that could have been shown.'

This was a golden age of British painting within and without the Academy orbit – Turner, Constable, Lawrence, Blake, Cotman, the precocious young Bonington in the wings – but there was no doubt who the star of this exhibition was. Haydon's influential patron Sir George Beaumont was not at all sure that Lawrence had not gone back rather than progressed since the last show, but he had never been generous about him, and if he was right that there was still that air of 'tinsel' about his work, something of trickery in all the painterly surface brilliance that was not quite honest, then was that not exactly the quality that made him the great interpreter of his age?

Nothing could be more appropriate, in fact, than that the Prince Regent and that supreme royal cosmetician and master of surface appearances, Sir Thomas Lawrence, should hold pride of place, because if a visitor had wanted to see Regency Britain shorn of all disturbing realities, then at the price of a shilling's entrance and a shilling for the catalogue he could do a lot worse than spend an afternoon at the exhibition. The Academy had decided early in its life to charge an entry fee in order to keep out the wrong sort of person, and if the right sort of person wanted his vanity or patriotism massaged, if he had wanted his own image and that of his countrymen and countrywomen reflected back at him as he would like to see them, then here was the place to be.

If he wanted to see Britain in all its physical beauty and variety, then here was the landscape, with all the historic associations that had seduced George Ticknor; if he wanted to see the men who had proved Britain's martial prowess then here were their likenesses; if he wanted to see children in all their romantic innocence untainted by the Reverend Grindrod's doctrines of sinfulness then here they were romping with their mothers; if he wanted to be reassured of the country's social stability then here was its gentry with their dogs and horses; and if he wanted his conscience and sense of fellow feeling agreeably stirred then here too could be found what he was looking for. 'The *Distraining for Rent* will be the point of attraction for every feeling visitor of the Exhibition,' the *Morning Chronicle* told its readers on the eve of the exhibition's opening. 'Never before has Mr Wilkie addressed himself so powerfully to the emotions of the breast. No eye can dwell on the picture, without having the sympathies of the soul aroused – so true, so faithful, and so affecting, are all the dramatic personae of this domestic scene. KEAN, with all the aid of language, added to his expressive features and burning passions, never spoke more feelingly home to the heart, than Wilkie has done in this tale of everyday occurrence.'

If the soul did not waken to the plight of David Wilkie's family, faced with eviction, then there was Westall's *Drowned Fisherman* or William Collins's *The Reluctant Departure* to evoke just the right degree of sympathy for the poor. At the private view at the end of April the Tory Sir George Beaumont had complained angrily at the 'politics' of Wilkie's painting, but in the summer of 1815 – a summer when the Duke of Sutherland's agent, Patrick Sellar, was waiting trial for murder, and the burned and demolished cottages and wrecked lives of the Strathnaver crofters might have showed a bolder child of the manse than the long, thin, cautious David Wilkie what real evictions looked like – the orchestrated emotions and harmonious treatment of *Distraining for Rent* were not designed to frighten anyone. 'The colouring of this picture is equal, if not superior,' to anything he had done before, one critic, enraptured with the particularly fine characterisation of the toothless old crone, insisted, only wishing that the cradle in the foreground, 'most exquisitely painted in a perspective point of view ... had not so new an appearance, in fact that is a fault with some of the other furniture – it is too fine for the family here represented. When we look at the bason and stand in the right-hand corner of the picture, we are induced to say, Mr Wilkie forgets that the furniture of Kensington is not adapted for a rustic cottage.'

It was not as if Wilkie was alone in his evasions – no one, shilling programme in hand, admiring *The Reluctant Departure* need give a thought to the misery of the emigrants waiting in Glasgow slums for their passage to Canada that Sunday – and wherever Farington looked he would have found the same discreetly comforting reassurance. Across the south of England this Sunday young mothers and their bastard children were being shunted on from parish to parish, but here was an art in which poverty, inequalities and tragedy – a country work-house, a drowned fisherman, a punished schoolchild, an evicted tenant – could be safely contained and enjoyed within the humorous or senti-mentalising conventions of genre painting.

Idle Boys ... *Infant Gleaner* ... *A lady presenting to a cottager an edition of the Sacred Scriptures, given by the Bible Society* ... *The Poor house, Fitzhead, Somersetshire* ... it says it all that such subjects could hang alongside Miss Geddis's *Children of Quality*, or *Portraits of the Grandchildren of Sir G. Osborne, Bart*, and only reinforce rather than undermine the social order. It is possible that the odd liberal-minded visitor might wonder how many men and women had been hanged so that the Sir John Silvester portrait might also hang, but he might as well have expected to see Géricault's basket of severed heads or Goya's horrors of war as anything that intruded a note of ugly reality into the self-confident Britain that in portrait after portrait stared down on him from the Academy's walls.

'Portraits! Portraits!! Portraits!!!' protested one critic of the obsession of the age – portraits of wives and children, portraits of grandchildren, portraits of politicians and statesmen, of gentlemen, self-portraits, group portraits, family portraits, domestic, public and royal portraits, portraits of favourite spaniels and broodmares, portraits of hound packs, portraits of ponies, portraits of mules – but he might as well have held his peace. Benjamin Haydon might complain that portraiture was a debasing of the real business of High Art, but the Academy was a market as well as an exhibition, and this is what Britain wanted and was willing to pay for and pay to see: its own image in its day of triumph reflected back at it as if it could go on unchanged for ever.

And if that triumph now hung in the balance – across the Channel, Sir Thomas Picton, full of robust life in Beechey's portrait here at the Academy, lay dead with a neat hole from a musket ball through his hat – a visitor to London this Sunday might be forgiven for thinking they were right. In Albemarle Street, in the famous room over John Murray's bookshop, George Ticknor had spent an agreeable day of literary gossip with 'Classic Hallam', Elmsley, Boswell – the son of Johnson's James Boswell – and the vicious editor of the *Quarterly*, William Gifford, as if there was nothing in the world to disturb their Tory certainties. The Prince Regent was on his way back from Windsor, where he had gone after morning service at Carlton House. His daughter, Princess Charlotte, whose portrait was also in the exhibition, would have returned from her exercise in the park, unaware that her loved uncle, the Duke of Brunswick, was dead. In her Arlington Street house, the Marchioness of Salisbury was preparing to receive her 'usual' 700 'distinguished Fashionables'. In Grosvenor Square, Lady Hampden was expecting another large party; in Curzon Street a dowager countess awaited a more select group. Haydon – represented in the exhibition only by his portrait – would be back in front of his *Christ's Entry into Jerusalem* fretting over his Centurion. Crabb Robinson would be walking home down the New River after taking tea with the poet Anne Barbauld. Lamb would soon be on his way to Samuel Rogers's house in Piccadilly. So, too, would Wordsworth and Byron. 'The seventh day this, the Jubilee of man,' Byron had written of such a London Sunday, and of all the myriad obscure lives that intersected,

> London! right well thou know'st the day of prayer,
> Then thy spruce citizen, wash'd artisan,
> And smug apprentice gulp their weekly air …
> Some o'er thy Thamis row the ribbon'd fair,
> Others along the safer turnpike fly,
> Some Richmond Hill ascend, some scud to Ware,
> And many to the steep of Highgate hie.

Here was Farington's England – the England of the Thames and Greenwich Park, the England that had nothing to do with war, the England of a permanent Sunday afternoon. It was time, though, that he was home. He usually liked to eat at around seven or so, though tonight he was dining alone and could please himself. As he made his way down the staircase and out into the Strand, the doors of the Academy closed on the last Sunday of the exhibition. Within the week only the shilling catalogue would remain to show how Britain saw itself on the day of Waterloo. For the moment, however, as the early evening light came through the skylight in the ceiling of the great room, and the old Lifeguardsman Samuel Strawger had the place to himself, the illusion could hold. And if old Strawger had turned from Lawrence's portrait of Wellington to his great full length of old Marshal Blücher – '*Marschall Vorwärts*' – standing square and defiant against the billowing smoke of battle, one hand resting on his sword, the other pointing to his right, then at this very moment he would not have been the only one doing so.

6 p.m.

Vorwärts

On the evening of 18 June 1815, Marshal Gebhard von Blücher, hero of Leipzig and commander of the Prussian forces, was seventy-two years old and very sore. Two days earlier he had been lying half-conscious under his dead horse on the field of Ligny, and only the quick reactions of his aide-de-camp and large applications of alcohol – brandy externally for his battered old body, and a vile brew of garlic, gin and rhubarb for his much-abused innards – had saved the smoked and pickled old war horse for another day.

If Sergeant Cotton was right that the trumpets would never sound for the dead of Quatre Bras as they should, the dead and wounded of Ligny had fared still worse. In British mythology the defence at Quatre Bras is always the crucial prelude to the ultimate victory of Waterloo, but the Anglo-Dutch action at the crossroads was never more than a sideshow against the left of Bonaparte's army, while the real battle, a raging inferno that cost the Prussians 30,000 in dead, wounded and deserters, was being fought and lost a few miles to the east at Ligny.

Two long days after the battle, two days of alternating summer heat and cold and driving rain, the Prussian wounded still lay among the bloated and mutilated corpses of the dead, helpless prey to Belgian peasants who hated them quite as much as they did the French. For the defeated Prussians the obvious line of retreat would have taken them eastwards towards Liège and safety, but when instead they determined to fall back on Wavre to the north – 'the decisive moment of the century', Wellington later called it – contact was crucially maintained between the two allied armies and the campaign saved.

Not everyone in the Prussian army was happy with the decision – Blücher's able chief of staff, Gneisenau, did not trust Wellington or the British to stand their ground – but whatever his tactical shortcomings there was no stauncher ally than Blücher. He had rejoined his army at Wavre early on the morning of the 17th, and by the end of the day, with the scattered units of his Ligny army once more a fighting force and the fresh troops of General von Bülow's corps just three miles to the southeast of the town, Blücher was at last in a position to give Wellington the assurance he needed: two corps of Prussian troops, he promised, Bülow's IVth and Pirch's IInd – some 60,000 men in all – would be marching at daybreak to his support.

There were still serious hazards facing the allies – Bonaparte had despatched 30,000 men under Marshal Grouchy in a dilatory pursuit of the Prussians after Ligny – and between Blücher's widely spread army and Wellington's position was a difficult march of seventeen miles. The news of Blücher's intentions had reached Wellington sometime in the early hours of the 18th though, and from the middle of the day, when a messenger had brought him intelligence that von Bülow's corps were nearing the battlefield, one increasingly anxious eye had been fixed on the woods to the east of Papelotte beyond the far left of the British lines.

He had not been the only one looking in that direction, either, because on the far side of the valley, at around one o'clock, Bonaparte and his generals had also been peering through their spyglasses, wondering whether the movement they caught in the far distance was Grouchy's French or the van of a Prussian army. If any of them had thought about it dispassionately they would have known that it could not possibly have been Grouchy, but whether they were Prussians or not they were still three or four hours away from playing any decisive part in the fighting, and a battle that had begun that morning with the odds ninety-to-ten in Bonaparte's favour he still confidently reckoned to be no worse than sixty-forty.

The Battle of Waterloo was a close-run thing, Wellington would famously say when it was all safely over, but the truth is that it was always going to be. Wellington had never been a gambler in the same way that Bonaparte was, and yet in choosing to fight his battle where he did he was making the same sort of calculations as his opposite number, reckoning that he could hold his ridge until the Prussians arrived just as Bonaparte thought he could wrap up the British before Blücher's reinforcements could swing the balance the allies' way.

And at just about six o'clock in the evening, as twenty-two-year-old Edmund Wheatley of the King's German Legion was standing in square on the high ground to the north of La Haye Sainte, no one still could have said which of them was right. For the last seven hours Wheatley had been musing in a vague sort of way over Southey's anti-war poem 'The Battle of Blenheim', but if he was still wondering what he was doing fighting Frenchmen he neither knew nor hated, his powder-blackened mouth and face would suggest that he had overcome his scruples as comfortably as everyone else in the regiment.

In every respect in fact, save for the Southey, a commission 'without purchase' in the King's German Legion – not a fashionable or lovable formation, particularly their infantry – was exactly where you might expect to find the young man with the staring eyes and stolid features that look out of Edmund Wheatley's self-portrait. Within the army he would always be on the right side of the social gulf that separated the man from the officer, but in the world beyond it – the world of his beloved Eliza Brookes, the girl he had thought of on her way to church as the battle opened – clearly neither Wheatley's appearance nor the social status of a man too respectable for the ranks and too poor even for a commission into the 'Peasants' made him a particularly eligible prospect.

'Not an individual related to you approves of me,' he had complained to Eliza, 'you are forbidden to write to or hear from me', but whether that was a cause or consequence of his joining the King's German Legion he had become very good at doing what he did. At the end of his first battle he had retched helplessly at the sight of the butchery, and yet from the very start he seems to have been as immune to personal fear – even the first 'hissing plaintive whistling' of musket balls around the ears – as he was to the brutality of army life in a more than usually brutal regiment.

He never much liked his German fellow officers or the rag-bag mix of nationalities and petty crooks under him, but even that had its compensations. 'Impelled by curiosity as well as humanity,' he had written while still an ensign, of a bundle wrapped in a cloak which he had come across among the dead and wounded outside Bayonne, 'on turning it up I washed away the blood and gore from the features ... and discovered the countenance of Lieutenant Kohler of my regiment. My promotion instantly suggested itself and thoughts of my own danger. I walked up to Captain Bacmeister and, bowing, said in the midst of the shot: "Allow me to introduce Lieutenant E. Wheatley to your notice." And I actually received his congratulations. Can there be any thirst for glory when actions like this take place on the fields of havock? Ambition's made of sterner stuff. Interest is the impulse in these our modern wars. Paulus Emilius threw his spoils into the public treasury. I throw mine into my private pocket.'

He might not have had much time for glory – 'Ten thousand slain you say and more? What did they kill each other for?' – but for all his philosophising a good fight was another thing. The battalion had only joined Wellington in time to hear the distant cannonades of Quatre Bras, and robbed of his fun there he had had no intention of missing out on the battle he knew was coming. 'About two o'clock the Grenadier company was ordered to headquarters with orders to clear the road all the way back to Brussels,' he wrote of 17 June; 'Captain Notting ordered me to leave him with thirteen men ... and join our company at Brussels at night, which I had resolved not to do ... as I was confident a grand battle would take place and I had never been absent in the least skirmish since I first campaign'd.'

Wheatley was there, this Sunday, because, like Gronow, he wanted to be, and the more furious the fighting, the greater 'the ardor of the fight' within him. The first man killed near him had been standing just five *files* away, but by six o'clock 'when a passe-parole ran down the line not to be disheartened, as the Prussians were coming up to our left', it was long since anyone had time to count the dead and dying that lay thick either in or around their square.

For the last two hours they had undergone a ferocious onslaught, as Ney flung wave after wave of cavalry up the slope, turning the whole reverse plateau behind the Ohain road into a desperate checkerboard of red squares and swirling, milling cavalry. 'About four P.M. the enemy's artillery in front of us ceased firing all of a sudden and we saw large masses of cavalry advance,' recalled Gronow; 'not a man present who survived could have forgotten in after life the awful grandeur of that charge. You discovered at a distance what appeared to be an overwhelming, long moving line, which, ever advancing, glittered like a stormy wave of the sea when it catches the sunlight. On they came until they got near enough, whilst the very earth seemed to vibrate beneath the thundering tramp of the mounted host ... In an almost incredible short period they were within twenty yards of us, shouting "*Vive l'Empereur!*" The word of command, "Prepare to receive cavalry", had been given, every man in the front ranks knelt, and a wall bristling with steel, held together by steady hands, presented itself to the infuriated Cuirassiers.'

'Nothing could equal the splendour and terror of the scene,' echoed Wheatley, in square with the King's German Legion, face unrecognisable, firing shoulder turned to jelly, the field around him thick with heaps of bodies and mutilated struggling animals, as Cuirassiers charged and shied, and cursed and reared, and time and time again broke against the hedges of steel. 'Charge after charge succeeded in constant succession. The clashing of swords, the clattering of musketry, the hissing of balls, and shouts and clamour ... as if Hell and the Devil were in evil contention.'

In the memories of survivors it was always the French cavalry and above all the Cuirassiers who held visual pride of place – the undulating lines, the gleam of sunlight on steel, the stricken horses, the private jousts, the flashing sabres, the posturing, gesturing and wheeling, the sheer raw immediacy of the fighting – but far more devastating was the artillery fire that punctuated the attacks. The French had failed in coordinating their cavalry and horse artillery to wreak the havoc that they might have done, but as a mesmerised Ensign Leeke watched a ball from the cannon's mouth tracing its lethal parabola towards his square, he had only time to wonder at the 'exact rapidity of a cannonball' and count to two before 'it struck the front face of the square. It did not strike the four men in the rear of whom I was standing, but the poor fellows on their right. It was fired with some elevation, and struck the front man about the knees, and coming to the ground under the feet of the rear man of the four, whom it severely wounded, it rose and passing within an inch or two of the Colour pole, went over the rear face of the square without doing further injury.'

'About four o'clock I was ordered to the colours,' recalled Sergeant Lawrence of the 40th, a West Country veteran of Spain and the disastrous River Plate campaign. There had already been fourteen sergeants killed or wounded in charge of the colours, and he had not been there a quarter of an hour, before a cannon shot had taken off the head of the captain standing next to him, spattering him from head to foot with the poor man's blood. One of his company who was close by at the time cried out, '"Hullo, there goes my best friend," which caused a lieutenant, who quickly stepped forward to take his place, to say to the man, "Never mind, I will be as good a friend to you as the captain." The man replied, "I hope not, sir," the officer having not rightly understood his meaning.'

Wheatley and his men were right to cheer the news of the Prussians – with the benefit of hindsight, the battle was effectively lost and won when Blücher kept his promise – but within the exhausted British lines it would still precipitate the last major crisis of the battle. The first Prussians had begun to emerge from the cover of Frischermont Wood anything from two to three hours earlier, but with the line of their advance taking them in a south-westerly direction towards the French right and rear rather than in the westerly direction Wellington had bargained on, he was left still with that same gap between Blücher's men and his badly weakened centre that had been there to exploit all day.

Wellington had always seen the main French threat in terms of his right wing – both before the battle and deep into the day – and even so late in the action his dispositions dangerously reflected that fear. Behind Hougoumont he had enough reserves to repel a last futile attempt to take the chateau and threaten his flank, but with the impetus of the Prussian advance faltering in the ferocious fighting for Plancenoit two miles to the south, the battle was still there to be gained if the French could break through the badly thinned allied centre.

The British would be still holding Hougoumont and still fighting there now if it were necessary – the carnage around buildings and orchard would show just how many lives it cost the French – but at the centre of the lines the beleaguered and isolated garrison of La Haye Sainte had been holding on by a thread all afternoon. Within the burning and devastated farm buildings the men were down to their last rounds of ammunition, and at some time shortly after six – and after repeated desperate calls for assistance had gone unanswered – it finally fell as the French swarmed in over its walls and its last forty-three surviving defenders fought their way out in a final, savage frenzy of slaughter.

It had taken them almost seven hours, but the French had at last got what they needed, and with La Haye Sainte and its walls and vantage points now in their hands, Wellington's position was more perilous by the moment. From the start of the battle La Haye Sainte had been receiving the full attention of the Grande Batterie, and now that the farm was in French control, with their sharpshooters on its roofs sweeping the exposed allied centre with their fire and their Tirailleurs swarming over the hollow, its guns could be brought up to support the final breakthrough that had been threatening since Uxbridge's charge had earlier thwarted it.

It was at this moment in the battle that, rather like the tableau vivant that memories made of De Lancey's wounding, the wider action seemed to pause to give a single incident an almost symbolic significance in people's recollections. For the last few hours Edmund Wheatley had been standing in square with his KGL troops behind and above La Haye Sainte, and as the French pressed forward an order came for the battalion to deploy into line and advance. There were French cavalry in support of their infantry and, as everyone in the battalion knew, it was a command that could only end in tragedy. Earlier in the day the Prince of Orange – 'screaming like a newborn infant, "Form into line!, Form into line!"' – had very nearly wiped them out and their luck was not going to hold a second time. 'Would it not be advisable to advance in square, and not form line till close to the enemy's infantry?' the KGL's Colonel Ompteda asked.

'God damn it!' an ADC shouted back. 'My order is to order you to deploy immediately.' As General Alten came up, Ompteda repeated his worry: would it not, at least, be wise to advance with cavalry cover? he asked, pointing to the French Cuirassiers.

Just then the Prince of Orange galloped up, and 'Silly Billy' was not a man to learn by his mistakes. 'I must still repeat my order to attack in line with the bayonet,' he insisted, 'and I will listen to no further arguments.'

'Then I will,' Ompteda replied and mounted his horse.

Quietly asking his battalion commander von Lisingen 'to save his two nephews', Ompteda ordered his men into line 'with a strong injunction to walk forward' until he gave the word. 'I saw that the French had their muskets pointed at the Colonel,' another officer in the battalion recalled, 'but they did not fire', the officers striking up the men's barrels with their swords, 'astonished at the extraordinarily calm approach of the solitary horseman whose white plume showed him an officer of the highest rank'. When they had got within sixty yards, Ompteda gave the order to charge, and as the bugle sounded and they surged forward huzzaing, the last words Wheatley heard from Ompteda as he ran past him were: 'That's right Wheatley.'

'No one but a soldier can describe the thrill one instantly feels in such an awful moment,' wrote the young lieutenant; 'I found myself in contact with a French officer but ere we could decide, he fell by an unknown hand. I then ran at a drummer, but he leaped over a ditch through a hedge in which he stuck fast. I heard a cry of, "The Cavalry! The Cavalry!" But so eager was I that I did not mind it at the moment, and when on the eve of dragging the Frenchman back (his iron-bound hat having saved him from a cut) I recollect no more. On recovering my senses, I look'd up and found myself, bareheaded, in a clay ditch with a violent head-ache. Close by me lay Colonel Ompteda on his back, his head stretched back with his mouth open, and a hole in his throat.'

Across Wheatley's leg, pinning him down, was a French arm, and for a moment he was too confused to realise where he was. Lifting himself up a little, he looked over the rim of the ditch and found he was behind the enemy's positions, and playing dead, held his breath until a tug at his epaulettes and a '*Voici un autre b*' signalled the end of his battle. 'A thought struck me – he would turn me round to rifle my pockets. So starting up, I leaped up the ditch; but a swimming seized me and I was half on the ground when the fellow thrust his hand in my collar, grinning, "*Ou va's tu, chien*?" I begged of him to let me pick up my cap and he dragged me into the house.'

It may have been the end of Wheatley's battle, but it was not the end of his day. Inside the ruins of La Haye Sainte nothing remained but the rafters and props, and flung together on the brick floor the bodies of Baring's German infantry and French Tirailleurs. As he was dragged down through the French lines to the rear – captor and captive crouching together in a ditch by the main chaussée to escape the answering cannonade of the allied guns – Wheatley looked over the edge and back up the ridge above La Haye Sainte to where he had fought. 'I could see our Cavalry behaving gallantly,' he recalled, 'and felt a national pride at sight of our little squares, enveloped in a light mist, surrounded by innumerable Foes. The ground on which I had stood since the morning was bare and I felt a chill on supposing the whole of my Comrades had sunk under the French sword.'

They had. Ompteda had been right. The French cavalry had fallen on their flank and rear, slaughtering them. '*Allons! Marche!*' a guard jabbed him in the arm, pushing him along the road south through the French lines towards Genappe. Behind Wheatley the battle was entering its last, brutal phase. As they tramped back through the human wreckage of war – the ditches beside the road crammed with corpses and filled with the groans of the wounded and the dying – Bonaparte was playing his last card. Smoke covered the battlefield, but from Hougoumont on their left to La Haye Sainte on the right the sounds of drums and the roar of voices filled the air. The Imperial Guard – still fresh – were marching towards the shattered units of Wellington's exhausted army.

7 p.m.

Noblesse Oblige

Colonel Thomas Nicholl was old-fashioned enough to have long since finished his dinner. Down in town smarter men might be edging the time of the meal back, but a retired colonel and a JP with slaves in the West Indies and a fine old, seven-bay pile, topped with shaped gables, near Hendon called Copt Hall, probably felt secure enough of his place in the world to hold on to his own ways.

He would not have been a soldier, though, if his thoughts had not been elsewhere this Sunday because on the other side of the Channel he might have seen the story of a great part of his life mapped out along the ridge of Mont-Saint-Jean. Nicholl had been commissioned into the 33rd of Foot – Wellington's own regiment – in 1772, and had sailed as an ensign to America on the outbreak of the War of Independence, serving with the 33rd from the First Siege of Charleston in 1776 right through to Guilford Court House in 1781, before transferring as lieutenant and captain into the 70th in the May of that year.

The 33rd had already had a bad time of it at Quatre Bras but it was for the soldiers of the 44th that he would have been most anxious. Nicholl had been unfortunate in his time with the 70th if it was fighting he wanted, and after serving in that historic graveyard of the British

Army, the West Indies, had done nothing more exciting than garrison duties in Gibraltar and Jersey, steadily rising by purchase during one of the most dismal periods in the history of the army, before transferring to the command of the newly formed 2nd Battalion of the 44th in 1803.

The 2nd Battalion of the regiment – the East Essex – had been raised in Ireland after the collapse of the Treaty of Amiens and if regimental form was anything to go by, colonel and men might well have been relieved to find themselves on garrison duties. During the course of the previous sixty years the 44th had established its claim to be the most disaster-prone unit in the army, but under Nicholl's brief command the regiment that had been decimated at Prestonpans by Highlanders, slaughtered at Monongamela by Indians, and turkey-shot by backwoodsmen at New Orleans two weeks after the peace treaty with the United States had been signed, had, perhaps mercifully, got no farther than routine duties on English soil.

The worst was still to come – the regiment would be wiped out to a man on the disastrous retreat from Kabul – but if ever a regimental tradition offered a testimony to the enduring spirit of the British soldier in the face of his generals it is that of the 44th. In the hundred-and-thirty-odd years of its history it found itself under the command of some of the most unfortunate leaders ever to send troops into battle, and yet time and again the men and junior officers who had been mauled in one campaign would be there to take their chance in the next, the survivors from Scotland turn up to die under General Braddock in America, the men fighting under Lord Raglan who had slogged up the slopes of Alma reappear to win Inkerman, the battalion who had been beaten at Bergen-op-Zoom in the last disastrous operation of 1814 under Sir Thomas Graham come back under Wellington at Quatre Bras and Waterloo to fight as if they had never known what defeat was.

It seems curiously symbolic that at just about the time that the 2nd Battalion of the 44th, who had already suffered 160 casualties, rose for the final general advance of the day, their first colonel was himself rising from his dinner table at Copt Hall. At the end of the meal Nicholl's footman, Robert Gale, had placed all the plate in a wicker basket and given it to a groom to take to the scullery, before later putting it in the pantry himself for cleaning and going off for his own dinner.

During their time in America the 33rd had earned themselves a reputation for the efficiency with which they carried out their sentry duties, but standards had clearly slipped at Hendon, and that was the last time that Robert Gale, Thomas Nicholl, or anyone else at Copt Hall would see the colonel's plate. The house was set in its own park providing a good covering of trees, and sometime just after seven, Samuel Halliday, a former servant at the hall who had either been dismissed or let go the previous November, slipped through the gardens, found the back door unlocked, made his way into the pantry and stole the basket and the silver while Robert Gale was still sitting over his dinner.

It seems highly unlikely that this was Halliday's first offence – it was certainly not his last – and yet if he was an old hand in the business he was clearly not a natural. It was no more difficult to slip out of Copt Hall unseen than it was to get in, but having dumped the basket in a nearby ditch, he bundled up the silver in a blue cloth, and set off on the ten-mile walk to the one haunt in Britain that was an even riskier place for Colonel Nicholl's silver than the Copt Hall pantry, and that was Newgate gaol.

There is only one way into this world, as poor, sleepless, half-hinged Sam Whitbread's doctor urbanely told the Whig politician, Henry Brougham, but many ways out of it, and Samuel Halliday had unwittingly already chosen his own sad route. At any time over the last twenty years Halliday would have provided the perfect fodder for Wellington's army, but the irony of his lot was to begin his bungling, tragi-comic spiral into crime at that precise moment when the one viable alternative to the gallows, hulks and transport ships was about to dry up.

The only surprise is that anyone so utterly inept ever got as far as Newgate – the previous week Byron's publisher, John Murray, had been attacked and robbed in these same fields to the north of London – but at some hour that night Halliday found himself and his haul of twenty-seven silver forks, seventeen silver tablespoons, three silver dessert spoons, one silver soup ladle, one silver gravy spoon, two silver butter ladles, two silver teaspoons, one silver fish-slice and one silver salad fork, safely locked up within the walls of London's most notorious crime and distribution centre. 'I was in Newgate as a prisoner, in June last,' one patriotically named inmate-turned-snitch called England Blower was ready to testify, 'and I remember [Halliday] coming to Newgate ... he brought a blue bundle under his left arm; he gave it to the wardsman, named Galler. I did not then see what it contained; but they put it under a bed; and soon afterwards a prisoner of the name of James Hankey, was sent for.'

It is impossible to know the exact arrangement, but what followed would seem to have been a perfect stitch-up, a harmonious collaboration of authority and inmate, with the hapless Halliday caught in the middle. He had been assured by the wardsman-fence that he could dispose of any plate he would bring in, and with James Hankey, a convicted thief with a speciality in coppers awaiting transportation to Australia, always ready to offer his expert services, the hapless Halliday never had a chance. Along 'with two or three others' Hankey retired 'to the necessary' to inspect the bundle, while Galler and Halliday sat down together over a beer to discuss terms. He had never 'seen such things before', England Blower remarked of the 'great quantity of spoons, and forks, and a slice' that had been unwrapped in the 'necessary', and Samuel Halliday would never see them again. When he and Galler had finished their beer, they went back to the bed to recover the silver.

'My God, it is gone,' Galler said.

* * *

It would probably have surprised the twenty-two-year-old John Binstead if anyone had told him this Sunday that Samuel Halliday would come to be his closest friend, but as he mingled among the crowds in Arundel, fate in the person of Fogg the marshalman was already bringing them together.

It was the 600th anniversary of the signing of Magna Carta, and up in the castle, the Duke of Norfolk was entertaining the extended Howard clan. For the last fortnight the papers had been carrying reports of the medieval tournament that he was planning, and for a popular and enterprising young artist like Binstead from just along the coast at Chichester, the great crowds that Arundel was expecting must have seemed the perfect opportunity to show his work.

The tourney proper – the medieval jousting – had not yet started but the first guests had been there since the great opening banquet on Thursday. 'Yesterday' – 15 June – 'being appointed the day for the commencement of the grand Baronial Festivities, the *Morning Post* regaled its readers, 'every arrangement that could give celerity to its completion was facilitated, and finally accomplished with great splendour. It is the intention of his Grace to continue the festivities for twenty-one days. On every Thursday during that period there is to be a Ball, and every week is to be succeeded by fresh visitors. The castle will be opened three days during that period for every person who shall equip himself in a respectable manner, and Monday is talked of as the first day.'

The dinner that Thursday had been served up at five thirty by 'Mr. Waud of Bond-street, in a style of great magnificence', and at six o'clock – just as they were thinking in Brussels about dressing for the Duchess of Richmond's ball – the immense figure of His Grace the Duke of Norfolk, decked out in the uniform of the Sussex Militia, with the Marchioness of Stafford on his arm, entered the hall to the strains of 'O, the Roast Beef of Old England'. Throughout the dinner the Sussex band had continued to play national airs, and after the cloth was removed, and the duke had proposed the toast to the 'Fair of this Company' and to 'The Duke of Wellington', and the band had given 'See! The conquering Hero', he reminded his guests – Howards and Wyndhams and Percys and Grenvilles, seventy-five in all – why they were there. 'While the glorious achievements of this great General beamed upon the mind in glorious resplendence of action', he told them, 'we must not forget from whence the laws under which he had fought and conquered proceeded. He had invited the distinguished party … before him for the purpose of commemorating an event which ought to be reverenced as the foundation of the rights and privileges of the people – he alluded to those illustrious characters, the ancient Barons of England, who compelled King John to sign an instrument which secured to all ranks an equal administration of justice. He hoped the commemoration of such an event would be carried down the stream of posterity, and ever be impress'd on all minds of all ages with respect and adoration.'

In the England of Liverpool, Sidmouth and Ellenborough – an England that was about to fight to restore a Bourbon on the throne – statues of 'Alfred dictating the right of Jury' or 'Liberty supported on the Howard Arms' were pointed stuff, but whatever else was in the air at Arundel this week it was not radicalism. As a younger man the Duke of Norfolk had famously given the toast at a Crown and Anchor Tavern dinner of 'Our sovereign's health – the majesty of the people', but good Whig and Protestant that he still was, this was above all a display of conspicuous consumption in the grand style, a spectacular, family commemoration in stone, glass, music, paint, joust and costume of the Howards and their long role in English history. 'A noble Gothic hall has been built expressly for the occasion', the *Exeter Flying Post* told its readers, '80 feet long by 35, and the height is 30 feet. Mr. Backler has finished a most exquisite work for its Gothic window, emblazoned with heraldic ornaments. The immense range of rooms, all after the purest specimens of the florid Gothic, will be lighted up in the most brilliant style. All the knights will appear in full costume of the Order for those days, there will be tournaments given in the ancient style, succeeded by balls for the ladies.'

'To give full effect to the spectacle, every record has been searched, to discover the costume of ancient times in all its bearing,' *Jackson's Oxford Journal* took up the theme, and although the Barons' room was not yet finished, the *Caledonian Mercury* reassured its readers, it had been hung in scarlet and 'the floor matted so as to form a magnificent, as well as comfortable dining room; On the window at the extremity of the room, facing the Court yard, is a superb painting, representing King John, sitting, attended by the Pope's *Nuncio*, and the Barons, while the King's page, Sir Hugh Montgomery, presents the Duke of Norfolk of that day to the King. The likeness represented is a strong one of the present Duke.'

This Sunday evening it was mainly the great Howard phalanx – Norfolks, Effinghams, Suffolks, Carlisles – that was there to enjoy the turtles killed that morning, but it was the world at the foot of the castle that had brought John Binstead down to Arundel. Sometime during the previous week Binstead had gone up to London, and entering a hosier's in Cheapside with a man called Reader, bought various articles which he paid for with a £10 note – he had nearly £100-worth of them in tens, fives and ones on him – beautifully executed with the finest camel-hair brushes and 'purporting to be of the bank of Messrs Ridge & Co.'

There had been a lot of counterfeit notes in circulation this summer – one of the odder by-products of war had been a steep rise in cases of forgery and a corresponding dip in highway robberies – and war had made smugglers, counterfeiters and customs dodgers of some very respectable people. Since 1797 the Bank Restriction Act had banned the issuing of anything except paper notes by the Bank of England, and with the export of gold illegal and every bit of specie, gold and silver, desperately needed for the army and navy and the huge subsidies with which Britain kept her coalition partners fighting, an enterprising sailor with a piece of Spanish lace or an amiable young artist with some fine camel-hair brushes could do very nicely for himself.

From London to Exeter newspapers had been warning shop owners to be on the look-out for forged notes, but it was not easy. 'Mr. Romanis expressed his unwillingness to change a country note,' *The Times* would report a month later, 'but it appearing that one of the shopmen had some knowledge of Reader, this was considered a sort of guarantee, and the prisoner was accommodated, at the same time affixing a signature (not his own) to the note. On the following day, Mr Romanis presented the note at the house of a respectable banker, in the City, where it was made payable, when it was discovered to be a forgery: search was instantly set on foot for the prisoner, and it was discovered through the medium of Reader, that he had left town for Sussex. A warrant was accordingly procured, and Fogg, the marshal-man, sent to execute it. On his arrrival in Chichester, the residence of the prisoner, he learned that he was at Arundel, then the scene of the late fete.'

The lives of Samuel Halliday and John Binstead were converging towards the same cold December morning, and up at the castle, medieval fantasy and noblesse oblige were coming together for one last chivalric hurrah. The newspapers had been keen to reassure readers that it was a particularly exclusive party that the Duke of Norfolk was entertaining this Sunday, but the one Howard who was not there to talk jousts and costumes with the Effinghams and the rest of them was Major the Honourable Frederick Howard of the 10th Hussars – the younger son of Lord and Lady Carlisle, and the best of the Howards, as Byron saluted him.

As they lingered over their dinner in Arundel Castle, and a dazed Edmund Wheatley turned his back on the battlefield and trudged towards Genappe, Frederick Howard and the light cavalry of Sir Hussey Vivian's 6th Brigade were moving from left to right to form up in support of the Brunswickers on the plateau above and to the west of La Haye Sainte.

It seems wonderfully fitting that at the last great climax of the battle, the advance of Bonaparte's legendary Imperial Guard, they could see almost nothing for the smoke that had turned a June summer's evening into a 'London November fog'. On the left of their squadrons they could make out the pitiful remnants of Ponsonby's and Somerset's brigades, but save for the deafening noise of battle there was nothing to tell them that fifty yards to their front the whole allied line, from Hougoumont on the right to La Haye Sainte and the Brussels road, was under attack.

The exhausted allied infantry had been waiting for this moment – knew it was only a matter of time – but there was still no mistaking the frisson of excitement at the sight of the dark, advancing mass as the Imperial Guard emerged in two dense formations out of the smoke that filled the valley. Throughout the day and ever after, men would think and talk of the battle in the language of the 'ring', and here, at the climax of the fighting, at the end of eight hours 'hard pounding' and 'milling' – the end of a day in which the two 'greatest captains of the age' and the 'two Greatest Nations in the world' slugged it out to a standstill – it seemed almost as if history owed it to Waterloo to cede the last decisive action to the elites of both armies. 'The sanguinary drama was now, with the long and trying day, fast drawing to a close,' wrote Edward Cotton of the 7th Hussars. 'The Imperial Guards, their country's pride, they who had never turned their backs on foe or fled the battlefield, were now, for the first time, about to attack men who, like themselves, acknowledged no victor; the unconquered were to measure their prowess with men who had never been vanquished, the world waiting with anxious expectation the result of this memorable day.'

At the far end of the battlefield, in and around the village of Plancenoit to the rear and right of the French lines, some of the most vicious fighting of the day was going on against Bülow's advancing Prussians, but it was still on the ridge at Mont-Saint-Jean that the battle was to be lost and won. Bonaparte had from the start gambled on the fact that he could hold off a Prussian attack for long enough to rout Wellington, and now with his own reserves running out and envelopment of his right flank only a matter of time, here was his last chance.

With Ney at their head and the drummers beating out their incessant rhythms, the Imperial Guard came up the slope in two diverging masses, one smashing into the faltering Nassauers and Brunswickers near La Haye Sainte, and the other angling farther towards the allied right. The Guard had been kept under wraps by Bonaparte throughout the battle and were still fresh troops, while hidden behind the bank of the covered lane in front of them, lying down in ranks four deep and a thousand yards along, was an army – all British in the front line for this final assault – that had been under incessant attack from artillery, cavalry, infantry and mental and physical exhaustion for eight bruising hours.

'Hard pounding, this, gentlemen, try who can pound the longest,' Wellington had roused his officers, and as the British guns along the ridge opened up with canister on the first, packed ranks of the columns, a thousand Guards under Maitland rose to their feet and poured in a lethal volley at no more than fifty-yard range. As the French faltered under a hail of fire and the cry – 'Now, Maitland, now's your time!' – entered into British mythology, an infantry that had been on the defence all day went in with the bayonet. To their right, in the ground between Hougoumont and Maitland's Guards, the light infantry of Colborne's 52nd unleashed a tremendous fire on the exposed flanks of the advancing French. To the left the situation around La Haye Sainte was stabilised and then reversed, and suddenly – with that unexpected, startling suddenness of a snapping bow string – a check had turned into a retreat, retreat into flight and a French army that had fought with such unremitting bravery all day was disintegrating into a panicking rabble.

Along the whole length of the line, from Hougoumont to La Haye Sainte, a long rolling cheer, taken up in turn by each unit as Wellington rode past urging them on to a general advance, spread the word that men who had had nothing to do but endure thought they would never hear. On the left side of the Brussels road near where the Inniskillings of the 27th lay Captain Kinkaid had begun to think that this would be the first battle in which every man on both sides was killed, and now – out of nowhere it seemed – as the physical and metaphorical fog of war cleared enough to reveal the valley below them, a whole enemy army could be seen in flight and the Prussians advancing from the east.

Blücher had been as good as his word. At the far left of the allied line, where Prince Bernhard of Saxe-Weimar's Nassauers had fought so bravely all day, Papelotte was in Prussian hands. To the right rear of the French position, the flames and smoke belching out of Plancenoit's church and houses marked where the savage hand-to-hand fighting for the village was coming to its murderous end. And on the crest of the Mont-Saint-Jean ridge, Sir Hussey Vivian's and his cavalry's moment had come. At a smart canter and then a gallop Major the Hon. Frederick Howard and the 10th Hussars poured down the slope and fell upon a force of milling Chasseurs. In every account of these last moments of Waterloo a different witness places the engagement at a different spot on the battlefield, but whether it was on the right of the Brussels road or on the left, far in advance of the Guards or behind, whether the impossible Sir John Vandeleur refused his support or a Hanoverian infantry battalion refused theirs – every detail would be angrily thrashed out for decades to come – one incontestable fact is left. Having scattered the French Chasseurs, Vivian galloped up to Howard and ordered him to charge a column of the Guard retreating towards La Belle Alliance. In the dying moments of the battle, with victory already won, the eternal pattern of the day – French cavalry against British square – was about to be reversed. Not, though, the inevitable outcome. A fellow officer of the 10th, Lieutenant Arnold, made one last appeal to a Hanoverian officer to deploy their muskets against what was now a solid square 'but he still refused, saying that he did not care for General Vivian, that he was not his general'. With that, Howard charged. Close beside him, in front of the squadron, rode Arnold and Lieutenant Anthony Bacon. The French – self-preservation or the old disciplines asserting themselves at the last – reserved their fire until they were almost on them and then 'the havoc was frightful'. All three officers were hit in almost the same instant. 'Their praise is hymn'd by loftier harps than mine,' wrote Byron,

> Yet one I would select from that proud throng,
> Partly because they blend me with his line,
> And partly that I did his sire some wrong,
> And partly that bright names will hallow song;
> And his was of the bravest, and when shower'd
> The death-bolts deadliest the thin files along,
> Even where the thickest of war's tempest lower'd,
> They reach'd no nobler breast than thine, young gallant
>   Howard!

Noblesse oblige had claimed its last victim of the day. The Percys, the Wyndhams, the Howards – all guests at Arundel this weekend – had paid their dues. As the last light of a summer's evening, filtered through the duke's stained-glass homage to the Howard dynasty, fell on old Lord Carlisle, the 'best of the Howards' lay dead. The tourney was over.

8 p.m.

A Mild Contusion

In the city of Brussels, it had been a long, frightening thirty-six hours since Charlotte Waldie and her brother and sister had managed to make their escape the previous morning. Over the last three days the town had learned to live with the sound of cannon, and the distant rumble of guns that had once brought them to the walls in panic now seemed almost a comfort compared with the constant, moment-to-moment fluctuations of fear and hope.

It is unlikely that many had the time or leisure to give it a thought, but if any of the town's émigré Britons had paused to think as they watched the city's locals sitting at their café tables on the Charleroi road, 'drinking beer and smoking and making merry, as if races or other sports were going on, instead of the great pitched battle which was then fighting', they might have sent up a Sunday prayer of thanks for the Channel and a navy that through two decades of war had given them the luxury of looking down on foreigners. For the last two days the Antwerp road had been clogged with refugees fleeing the advancing French army, and as rumour had followed rumour through the day (the duke's flank had been turned ... the allies were in flight ... the French were in town ... the scum of Blücher's beaten army were pillaging the countryside …) the dwindling rump of that expatriate world that only on Thursday night had danced at the Duchess of Richmond's ball were desperately searching for a barge or carriage or cart that could get them out of the city.

The first wounded had begun to arrive late in the afternoon, increasing again the anxiety of the city, and even when the only French who appeared in Brussels were prisoners of war, the news that trickled back with the injured was almost universally dire. There was talk again that the Prussians had never come to Wellington's aid, and as Fanny D'Arblay (Fanny Burney) lay in her clothes and boots ready to flee, and the Whig MP, Thomas Creevey's 'young ladies' lay dressed on their beds, and the injured continued to pour in to the town, the Reverend G. G. Stonestreet, Chaplain of the Guards – who had begun the day cashing a bond for £30 and honourably ended it, to his rather pleased surprise, with 'a mild contusion' – settled in to what would be a long night's work.

There were letters to write for wounded officers, and if the men would have to fend for themselves they would probably not have been much troubled by that. Forty years later Sir George Seymour would piously postpone the slaughter of a Chinese navy armed with stink bombs and fireworks from the Sabbath to the Monday, but from Towton to Toulouse – with a brief pause for the God-driven men of Cromwell's armies – the English soldier had been an essentially Godless creature, as happy to do his killing or be killed on a Palm or Easter Sunday as any other day of the week.

It had shocked Stonestreet to find out how casually men could face death, with what levity they could meet their Maker, and yet it had shocked him in the same way as the waltz or a low-cut dress might do. A few weeks before he had joined the rest of Brussels' English community in the Grande Place for the guillotining of three murderers, and one in particular had stuck in his mind, a man who had been kept two years in solitary confinement to prepare him for this moment and had come into the square in the tumbrel laughing and dancing and mocking the priest at his side, before mounting the scaffold with a sang-froid that shocked to the core an Englishman brought up on social proprieties and the exemplary value of capital punishment.

It was probably just as well that he could not have seen what was already happening across the battlefield, the callous brutalities of soldiers and peasants, stripping the dead and dying of all they had, but George Stonestreet had already come a long way in the year since he had fallen in with an old college friend from their Cambridge days. In the way that clergymen did, the two men had soon got on to the subject of money and clerical preferment, and as his friend had just come into a legacy and had no further need of his army chaplain's salary, he had suggested to Stonestreet that he might like to fill his place.

The position might not have been what he wanted, but if England was the best place in the world to live for those who had money, as Stonestreet ruefully told his stockbroker brother-in-law George Trower, it was different for an impoverished clergyman, and with the war clearly coming to an end there might be worse things than a posting abroad and a chance to save for the future. He did not hold out much hope of 'advancing the cause of religion' among the Newgate fodder who would make up his new flock, but George Griffin Stonestreet was not a man to let idle scruples get in the way of sound finance and, with his 'motives sincere', as he assured himself, and 'the co-operation of that Great Power in whose cause I was going forth' confidently expected, the finger of Providence as well as of Prudence was clearly pointing him in the direction of the Low Countries.

Money was in the blood of George Stonestreet if not in his pocket – his father, George Griffin (he had only assumed the name of Stonestreet in 1794) had been a founder of the Phoenix fire insurance company – and neither Jesus College, Cambridge, nor ten years as an indigent curate had made the son shake off the dust of the City. There were doubts in the family as to whether he had done the right thing in joining the chaplains' department, but he had played his cards cannily, extracting from the Bishop of Exeter a blank form that he could fill in at his own leisure, guaranteeing him the return of a 'small piece of preferment' he had held at Honeychurch in west Devon if things did not work out with the army.

Nothing could have seemed more propitious than the day little more than a year ago when he left London for Harwich and the packet for Ostend, a day when the whole city was celebrating the fall of Paris and the imminent end of hostilities. 'The streets were noisy with horns,' he remembered – it must already have seemed a lifetime away as he sat beside makeshift Brussels beds – '& the joyful news resounded that the guilty Paris had fallen before the arms of the Allies … It was almost painful to me to be obliged to quit London in a moment of public exultation. From a boy, I had been taught to take no ordinary share of feeling in public events, & when I stepped into the Harwich Mail, the streets were illuminated & thronged with people, the sound of fireworks & of cannon were heard all around & it seemed to me almost an act of ingratitude to quit the Metropolis on this festival night.'

It was one of those glorious 'Night of Nights' that the young De Quincey rejoiced in, with the night ride on a Victory Mail to make it all the sweeter, and as the coach lumbered eastwards, carrying the news that '*Paris est Pris* through Whitechapel, Mile End, Bow and across the River Lea into Essex' there was only a small cloud to darken Stonestreet's horizon. He had been advised by his City connections to take gold with him to Brussels as English banknotes were at such a wretched rate of exchange on the continent. 'But how,' as he asked himself, 'was this to be done? Not a guinea had been seen in England for years, except now & then as a counter at a whist table; and even if I had them, how were they to escape the vigilance of the Custom House Officers, who had particular instructions to search for & seize all bullion attempted to be exported?'

Twenty years of war had not just made counterfeiters of young Chichester artists like poor John Binstead, but lawbreakers of the great and the good, and in the days before he sailed, Stonestreet had managed to cobble together seventy gold sovereigns from friends in London. On the way down to Harwich he had carefully hidden these about his eminently respectable clerical person, and the next day he had just stopped congratulating himself on successfully evading the customs officers' attentions, when a sweeping bow aboard the Ostend packet to his new commanding officer sent the sovereigns in his hat lining flying across the general's cabin floor.

It was an inauspicious military debut, but with more sovereigns squirrelled away in his shoes, a despatch to carry to Sir James Graham, an enviable knack of survival, and the hide of Jane Austen's Mr Collins, Stonestreet was launched on a career and a style of living that he could never have maintained at home. He had begun his service at the moment when peace seemed assured, and for the best part of a year he had had nothing worse to complain of than the irredeemable shallow-ness of the Belgian population, the embonpoint of their women, their 'swarthy complexions', the 'Jewish cast' of their features, the sad paucity of guillotinings in the Grande Place and the utter absence – one can hear the voice of Mr Collins expounding the virtues of Lady Catherine De Burgh's patronage – of 'a quiet evening with a good family'. 'The Theatre and the Balls seem to constitute the great happiness of the People,' he complained, 'they begin a ball with a *perfect* froideur, they go on with their *dangerous* Waltz (in which all the English women join) and finish with the Galloparde, a completely indecent & violent romp.'

The great influx of British civilian émigrés – Thomas Creevey and his family, the Capels and the other indigent aristocrats who had come abroad in search of cheap living – had irritatingly pushed up local prices, but the news of Bonaparte's escape came 'like a flash of light-ning' out of clear sky. The first reports had reached Brussels on 8 March, and within weeks the city had been transformed, with the arrival of the Duke of Wellington and his personal chaplain – that 'pearl of parsons' and 'great coxcomb', the Reverend Samuel Briscall, as Stonestreet dubbed him – putting an end to the cosy spiritual monopoly he had so far enjoyed.

Stonestreet despised Briscall, and particularly his habit of aping Wellington's haughty manner with subordinates, but he was far too shrewd a courtier to 'think of fighting the Duke' for the post at head-quarters, and had instead set about securing for himself the next best thing on offer. 'I am appointed Chaplain to the Guards,' he reported back to George Trower on 16 May, 'A beautiful body of more than 4,000 men … My brethren are not a little sulky that I have obtained what is considered very justly the best appointment in our department after Head Quarters. At present I combine them both. On Sunday last I performed service at nine to Sir Geo. Byng's brigade, 3 miles from Enghien, at 11 to General Maitland's Brigade (both Guards) at Enghien, afterwards jumped again on my saddle, and rode to Brussels in time to do duty to the English families at Three who gave me some credit for my zeal.'

There were more solid perks that went with the job – £500 a year, fuel and rations for two servants, an occasional '*dejeune* set after marriages of great people', a pair of silver candlesticks at Lord John Somerset's wedding – and if it was all a long way from his placid Emsworth curacy on Chichester harbour, he had, on the whole, good reason to be pleased with the way things had turned out since the escape of Bonaparte. One of the great blessings of his new position with the Guards was the access it gave to some of the 'leading families of the land', and long before the campaign had opened he had indulged himself with dreams of the future: of a triumphant march into France perhaps, the possibilities of a little 'pillaging in Paris' and a return to Brussels, clerical preferment, a 'bigger house' and – who knows? – the one thing he had always wanted, 'a good wife' to share in his fortunes.

It was an agreeable fantasy for a man who combined a prickly sense of his clerical rights with a healthy respect for the good things of this world, and had not 'Old Blücher' sworn at the great cavalry review that 'every man of them should have a Parisian Beauty'? 'The only hope of saving France to society,' a pleasurably alarmed Stonestreet had reported old Marschall Vorwärts' solution to Europe's problems, 'was engendering a new race, and bringing England and France together by a second rape of the Sabine Women!! Such is the bribe and there are those that reckon on it. Indeed there was so much expected when the last allies entered, that I have been informed by a young lady, she was two days *bricked up* in a cellar with meat and wine and bedding. All our lads call for at least three days pillage, but the general idea here is, that *Paris must burn.*'

These were curious ambitions for a chaplain, even an army chaplain, but war had opened up possibilities that went far beyond a pair of silver candlesticks, and over the last three days it had been hard not to rue the missed chance of making a killing out of a little shrewd insider dealing. He knew that his brother-in-law George would feel 'at least £10,000 out of pocket' by his failure to keep him informed, but Stonestreet had been telling him for weeks that they knew in London what was going on in Belgium before they knew it themselves in Brussels. 'The Gentlemen in England seem like other men, insensible of their good fortune,' he had joshed Trower; 'No sooner does any political event of importance take place, than couriers are hurried, their mouths and bags sealed, to London. They traverse provinces and cities, and ... like the English Ladies, never suffer themselves to be brought to bed, but in London ... Besides, you are such a gambling fellow, with so much sly leaning towards Omnium, I do not know how many ⅛ths I may turn the market in the morning.'

George Stonestreet had not been exaggerating when he bandied about figures like '£10,000' because the Trowers were not just marginal figures in the London financial world. In her journals John Trower's wife Sophia might talk casually of a 'loan' as if it might be for the purchase of an extra bit of paddock for their new pony, but 'the loan' she is talking about was the £36 million loan to the government that her husband and his consortium had successfully bid for on the morning of the budget that week.

And George Stonestreet was right about the flow of intelligence. It was nine o'clock. At La Belle Alliance, Wellington and Blücher were shaking hands, and as Stonestreet sat at the bedsides of the wounded through the night, and men across the battlefield came to terms with the fact that they were still alive, and wondered what had happened beyond the tiny world in which each had fought, and whether they would have to fight again tomorrow – and some, indeed, if what they had been through that Sunday could count as a real battle – a mysterious rider was making his way to Ghent and the court of Louis XVIII with the news of an allied victory. There, legend has it, was one of the Rothschilds' agents. Three months earlier the family's network of couriers had been first with the news of Buonaparte's escape from Elba and now again their boats would be waiting at the channel ports. The Trowers would not be the only gentlemen in England this Sunday anxiously watching over their 'eighths'.

9 p.m.

Religionis Causa

It had been a quiet day for William Wilberforce at Taplow after the parliamentary business of the last week, but it could only be the shortest of respites. He was going to have to go back to town in the morning for the Rosebery Divorce Bill, and if it was an ugly business, it was not one that the founder of the Society for the Suppression of Vice could dodge.

Wilberforce would not be reading the report of the case in this Sunday's *Examiner* – he disapproved of newspapers on the Sabbath – but he must have been one of the few Londoners that day who was not wallowing in the lurid details. For the last six months the salacious revelations of Lady Rosebery's adultery had been amusing the capital, and if ever a case was designed to satisfy every conceivable shade of public curiosity – the insatiable appetite for aristocratic gossip, the prurient taste for scandal, the radicals' contempt for their social betters, the moral outrage of the emerging middle classes, the deepest fears of those who detected a country sunk in degeneracy – it was the Rosebery Divorce Bill, *religionis causa*.

Seven years earlier, in 1808, the eighteen-year-old Harriet Bouverie, the granddaughter of the Earl of Radnor and a young woman 'in possession of every charm that could captivate, of every ornament and accomplishment that could constitute the happiness of married life', had met and married the twenty-five-year-old heir to the Earl of Rosebery, Archibald Primrose. For the first years of their married life no couple could have been happier, and with four young children – a boy, Archibald, born in 1809, a daughter also named Harriet in 1810 and two more children in quick succession – and 'a most affectionate, indulgent, and tender husband', the young Countess of Rosebery, as she became in the spring of 1814 on the death of the third earl, seemed to have everything she could possibly want.

'O my friend', the Attorney General told the Solicitor General, the new Lord Rosebery 'was such a man that if any person of the highest rank had a daughter of marriageable age, he could not have found a better husband', and the Hon. Bartholomew Bouverie never had any reason to think otherwise of his son-in-law. During the old earl's last illness Harriet had stayed with her mother at their place in Norfolk, and it was only when Rosebery returned from Scotland to find Harriet changed and the twenty-seven-year-old widower MP for Winchester, Sir Henry St John Mildmay, installed with the run of the house, the nursery and his wife's affections, that the Rosebery world began to crumble.

The husband was reluctant to believe what he saw was going on, but things became bad enough for him eventually to ban Mildmay from seeing his wife, and in the autumn of the same year he took her and the dowager countess with him to their estate near Dalmeny on Edinburgh's Firth of Forth. For a while Lord Rosebery might have hoped that the move had broken her seducer's spell, but unbeknown to the Primroses, Mildmay had followed them up to Scotland, travelling under the guise of 'Colonel de Grey of the Foot Guards', taken a room in an Edinburgh inn, grown a beard – or worn a false one – hired a boatman and, dressed as a sailor, had himself rowed up the Forth under the cover of darkness each evening to meet Harriet.

The Roseberys dined in the country at six each evening, with the ladies leaving the table at seven, only to be joined by the men again at about nine. Lady Rosebery had lately found one sort of pretext or another for slipping away from the dowager countess, and one night in December, Rosebery's younger brother, joining the ladies earlier than usual and suspicious at Harriet's absence, had gone up to her room only to find it locked and noises coming from inside.

Before he could hammer the door down, a flustered Lady Rosebery, her dress undone, had opened it from the inside and there in the guise of 'a common sailor, and armed with a brace of pistols' was Sir Henry Mildmay. The centre of the bed showed a deep depression where the two of them had clearly been lying, but Harriet's only concern was to prevent bloodshed and not detection, and with expressions of remorse and promises that she would quit the house and return penitent to her father's, she managed to get her lover out of the window through which he had climbed.

Lady Rosebery kept to her word, leaving first thing the next day without seeing the family, except that it was not her father's she was heading for but Sir Henry's Mayfair house in Brook Street. The two lovers were traced, inn by inn, along the coach route down to London, but any pretence of secrecy had gone out the window with Sir Henry, and before they could be tracked down they were out of the country and safe on the continent, that abiding refuge of early nineteenth-century bankrupts, runaways, divorcees, homosexuals and hard-up aristocrats bent on continuing the more licentious days of the eighteenth century by other means.

In 1815 the only way of getting a divorce that permitted the remarriage of either party was by private act of Parliament, and then only after it had gone through the Church court and a civil court for criminal conversation first, so by the middle of June the public had had every chance to soak up the details. In the civil court enormous damages of £20,000 against Sir Henry were a fair reflection of popular indignation, and in speech after speech lawyers and politicians at every stage of the process had competed in their denunciations of the adulterous pair.

For the press and public at large, the details of the adultery in themselves had a coarsely comic appeal – the beard, the sailor's outfit, the dent in the bed 'as if pressed by an extraordinary weight', etcetera – but Lady Rosebery's lover was also her brother-in-law and the husband of her recently dead sister, and that gave Moral England all the excuse for vindictive outrage it needed. There was nothing that anyone could actually do either to enforce damages or prevent them from marrying abroad if they chose, but that was not going to stop society, in the form of the two Houses of Parliament, ventilating its outrage over a crime 'than which' – in the ubiquitous Lord Ellenborough's words to the Lords – 'nothing short of the higher felonies could be more atrocious'.

There were those who wanted Harriet stripped of all the usual claims to alimony, to see her sent out on to the streets as 'bare and naked as her crime had left her', but above all they were determined to include a clause that made sure that the offending parties should never be allowed to marry. There was already a standing order in the Lords imposing such bans on all adulterers, but in a case as heinous as this, Ellenborough told the House, 'they owed it to the security of civilised society, to the happiness of families, to the purity and honour of domestic life', to the holiness of the nursery, to the laws of 'nature' and the 'law of God' itself to protect 'the interests of sound morality with a specific clause that publicly signalled the abhorrence of society'.

The only thing to be said in Lady Rosebery's mitigation was that the crime of Sir Henry Mildmay was blacker still, and no one was in any doubt as to what that crime had been. 'Stripped of all its adventitious deformity, of all peculiar and more odious characteristics,' the Attorney General, Sir John Garrow, had asked the Commons, what precisely was the offence? 'It was the crime' – he answered the question himself – 'of depriving a worthy and innocent man of what was most consoling to him in life; it was the crime of depriving four young children of the care and attentions of their maternal parent ... Was there, then, no incest in this crime – was there no blood in it? ... To him it appeared that it would have been more natural and excusable in Sir Henry Mildmay, to have poisoned the mind and debauched the body of his own sister, born of the same womb, and trained by the same hand, than to have planned, conducted and consummated the ruin of Lord Rosebery's family, under all the circumstances by which the ruin was accomplished and attended.'

Morality was on the march, and as William Wilberforce gathered his children around him for family prayers, and respectable Edinburgh settled down to another of that most emollient of clergymen Dr Hill's Sabbath lectures, a young man in his late twenties seated at a dinner table in Piccadilly's St James's Place would have done well to take notice. Ten years before Sydney Smith had suggested that Wilberforce's Society should be renamed the 'Society for the Suppression of Vice among those with an income of less than £500 a year'. The day of the rake was passing, though, and whatever the Duke of Wellington got up to in Brussels, the England of Wilberforce, the Clapham Sect, Sabbath Day observance, Thomas Bowdler's Shakespeare and Hannah More's evangelical tracts demanded better of its leaders as well as its poor.

It would seem unlikely that Byron had been looking forward to an evening at the home of the banker-poet and connoisseur Samuel Rogers, and still less one when William Wordsworth was going to be there. He had only ever met Wordsworth once before and that had also been at Rogers's, but try as he might to be fair to him, try as he did to make up for the juvenile attack of his *English Bards* – and he could see Wordsworth's powers – every effort at generosity or recantation only ended in the same old irritation. 'I still think his capacity warrants all you say of it,' he told Leigh Hunt, 'there is undoubtedly much natural talent spilt over the "the Excursion" but it is rain upon rocks where it stands & stagnates – or rain upon sands where it falls without fertilising

– who can understand him? – let those who do make him intelligible – Jacob Behman – Swedenborg – & Joanna Southcote are mere types of the Arch-Apostle of mystery and mysticism – but I have done.'

There might have been a certain malicious pleasure in meeting the poet of nature in the most self-consciously cultured house in Piccadilly, but then in the summer of 1815 any house that was not his own had its attractions for Byron. Three months earlier he had taken a place across Green Park from Rogers, and if he needed any reminder of the mistake he had made – any reminder of the chaos his life was descending into – then there it was, visible through the trees on the north side of Piccadilly, the sober-fronted, ruinously expensive house of the Duchess of Devonshire that, in some fatal moment of deluded grandeur, he had allowed his wife's aunt and Caroline Lamb's mother-in-law, Lady Melbourne, to take for him and his newly married wife.

It might have amused him once that it had belonged to the duchess – the former Elizabeth Foster who had lived for many years in a *ménage à trois* with the duke and his first duchess, Georgiana – but by the middle of June any amused appreciation of the irony would have been lost on Byron. When he had married Annabella Milbanke at the beginning of the year he had imagined life in terms of some semi-detached co-existence among the hereditary ruins of Newstead Abbey, and instead of that here he was, walled up in a house they could not afford, with a coach and coachman they could not afford, servants they could not afford, a rent of a massive £700 a year and debts of £30,000 to ensure that the bailiffs would never be far away.

For a man of Byron's anxious and touchy pride – a crippled Scottish boy brought up by a ghastly mother in obscure Aberdonian poverty – the embarrassments of the last three months had been humiliating, but the truth was that no amount of money was ever going to reconcile him to marriage. The prospect of renewed war had raised his hopes of getting a decent price for Newstead if he could only sell the place, and yet he knew that even if their money worries could disappear – even if the recent death of Annabella's Wentworth uncle eventually produced something more than a constant stream of hopeful creditors at the door, even if he could bear with her dull, prosing father and put up with his wife's quiet, prim, bourgeois self-sufficiency, even if there were moments when he still loved her – nothing would ever make him forgive her for not being someone else.

That someone else was his half-sister, Augusta Byron, whom he had first met when she was a tall slender girl of seventeen and he a lame, overweight Harrow schoolboy four years her junior. From the first brother and sister had been allies in his endless battles with his ludicrous mother, and as Byron moved on from Harrow to Cambridge and his eastern travels with John Cam Hobhouse, and Augusta slid into helplessly fecund motherhood, the memory of her languorous, indulgent, undemanding unaggressive sexuality – the Zuleika of his 'Bride of Abydos', the 'sleepy Venus' of his *Don Juan* – became fixed in his mind as a fantasy that consanguinity and the shared Byron name made simultaneously safe and dangerously compelling. 'For thee. My own sweet sister', he would write to her,

> In thy heart
> I know myself secure, as thou in mine,
> We were and are – I am, even as thou are –
> Beings who ne'er each other can resign;
> It is the same, together or apart.
> From life's commencement to its slow decline
> We are entwined – let death come slow or fast
> The tie which bound the first endures the last!

This might not have mattered if they had met again at some more stable moment in his life – if there was such a thing – but Augusta had reappeared at the height of his sudden fame when one guttering affair with Lady Oxford and the public melodrama of his relationship with Lady

Caroline Lamb made him particularly vulnerable to her attractions. During the season of 1813 the two were constantly seen out together, and at some point over the next weeks or months – perhaps even days if he was telling his discarded lover, Caroline Lamb, the truth – mutual affection and an infinite capacity for self-surrender on her part and self-destruction on his had turned her from sister into lover.

'*Partager tous vos sentiments*,' she wrote to him in November 1813, enclosing a lock of her light brown hair, '*Ne voir que par vos yeux*' … 'to act only on your advice, to live only for you, that is my only desire, my plan, the only destiny that could make me happy', and it was a sacrifice that Byron was ready to claim. 'To soothe thy sickness,' he had his Zuleika say,

> watch thy health,
> Partake, but never waste thy wealth …
> Do all but close thy dying eye,
> For that I could not live to try;
> For thee alone my thoughts aspire:
> More can I do, or thou require?

It was a heart-wringing question, but the fatal danger for both Augusta and Byron was that he did require more. The vestiges of a Scottish Calvinist childhood had left him with a sense of sin and guilt that prevented him from even naming her in his journals, but that did not stop the rebel outsider in him – the Byron who had always identified with that ur-Byronic hero, Milton's Satan – from trailing their relationship in his letters and flaunting their incest in his verse dramas, in showing her off in London or following her home to Newmarket in a suicidal show of moral and social defiance that pitted the Byrons against the world.

It was never simply or even principally a matter of defiance – the winter idyll of January and February 1814, when brother and sister were snowed in alone at Newstead, had a magic that nothing in Byron's life ever matched – but beyond the snowbound landscape and buried lanes of Nottinghamshire was a world that could neither be defied nor ignored. In the first flush of their affair they had boldly talked of exile together, but Augusta was a mother as well as a sister, and with a deeply troubled daughter who needed her and a child expected that might well be Byron's, the small store of courage and even smaller store of egotism that had been hers began to gutter away.

There seemed only one answer to her, one resort that would put them both beyond temptation and ruin – marriage – and in 1814 the birth of a daughter gave the search for a wife for Byron a new urgency. In a last gesture of defiance they had called the child Medora – the heroine of Byron's *Corsair* – but even for Byron it was the gesture of a beaten man. 'Oh! but it is worthwhile,' he wrote to Lady Melbourne, 'I can't tell you why – and it is *not* an "*Ape*" [a medieval incest superstition] and if it is – that must be my fault – however I will positively reform – you must however allow – that it is utterly impossible I can ever be half as well liked elsewhere – and I have been all my life trying to make someone love me – & never got the sort I preferred before. But positively she and I will grow good – and all that.'

There was no one Byron more admired than Lady Melbourne – 'the best, the kindest, and the ablest female I have ever known', he called her – and two years earlier he had made a half-hearted proposal of marriage to her niece Annabella. He had been relieved rather than disappointed at the time when she turned him down, but if he could not have Augusta it really did not seem to matter whom he married, and with her aunt's help – it was not for nothing she was known as 'the Spider' – he set about courting her afresh.

It was always said of Lady Melbourne that she only had to see a happy marriage to want to destroy it and the thought of creating misery out of nothing must have carried with it its own peculiar pleasure. There is no doubt that she was as fond of Byron as she was capable of being of any human being other than her son, but it is a moot point, as she set about smoothing difficulties and interpreting one to the other, what she would have most enjoyed – the notion of bringing together two people so diametrically ill-suited as Byron and Annabella, the voyeuristic prospect of all those years of marital comedy she could look forward to, or, perhaps most satisfying of all, the pain the marriage would cause her hated daughter-in-law Caroline Lamb.

It was scarcely a job that was worthy of her skills, though, because if ever a woman was wanting to be convinced it was Annabella Milbanke. In the first weeks of their acquaintance back in 1812, Annabella had prided herself on her indifference to the 'Byromania' that was sweeping London, but eighteen months of provincial virtue and lonely moral superiority had been quite enough to bring home how much she had lost in rejecting the most brilliant match in England.

There were subtler temptations, too, for a woman of her nature, because even as a child she had liked to imagine herself as the self-sacrificing heroine of her daydreams, and with her aunt to encourage her she now found the perfect 'cause' in Byron. 'Surely the Heaven-born genius without Heavenly grace must make a Christian clasp the blessing with greater reverence & love, mingled with a sorrow as a Christian that it is not shared,' she wrote to her old spiritual confidante Lady Gosford, intoxicated with the thought of saving a fallen angel; 'Should it ever happen that he & I ever offer up a heartfelt worship together – I mean in a sacred spot – *my* worship will then be most worthy of the spirit to whom it ascends. It will glow with all the devout and grateful joy which mortal breast can contain. It is a thought too dear to be indulged – not dear for *his* sake, but for the sake of *man*, my brother man, whomever he be – & for any poor, unknown tenant of this earth I believe I should feel the same. It is not the poet – it is the immortal soul lost or saved.'

'Early in our acquaintance, when I was far from supposing myself preferred by you, I studied your character,' she was soon writing to

Byron at Lady Melbourne's prompting. 'You were, as I conceived in a desolate position, surrounded by admirers who could not value you, and by friends to whom you were not dear … No longer suffer yourself to be the slave of the moment … Do good. Your powers peculiarly qualify you for performing those duties with success, and may you experience the sacred pleasure of having them dwell in your heart!'

It is hard to know which was the more deluded, Byron in imagining he could bear her prosing cant, or Annabella in thinking she could 'save' him; but with Byron at least there would seem to have been something more to it than this. It is unlikely that he would have been able to forgive *anyone* for not being Augusta, but there was something so wantonly blind in his courting a woman who was the incarnation of everything in society he most despised, that it is as if at some level he was determined to make her and their marriage the cause for a final and irreconcilable split with the 'tight little Island' that was Britain.

He might write of her in his letters and journals as his last hope of salvation, and he might even have thought he meant it, but salvation had never been very high on Byron's list of priorities. Through the summer of 1814 she was away at her father's estate, but on 9 September he finally brought himself to a proposal, sealing and despatching the letter 'with the greatest haste' before he could have second thoughts. 'I am almost too agitated to write,' Annabella had answered from her father's home, Seaham Hall, on the north-east coast – as touchingly honest a letter as she ever wrote; 'But you will understand. It would be absurd to suppress anything – I am and have long been pledged to myself to make your happiness my first object in life. If I *can* make you happy. I have no other consideration. I will *trust* to you for all I should look up to – *all* I can love. The fear of not realising your expectations is the only one I now feel.'

She should probably have been more worried that she *would* meet his expectations but even a fraught week together at Seaham in November was not enough to open her eyes. On 24 December, Byron set off again for the north with his best man Hobhouse, and after a last Christmas with Augusta near Newmarket was married in the Milbankes' drawing room at Seaham on 2 January 1815. 'As soon as we got into the carriage his countenance changed to gloom and defiance', Annabella recalled the first day of her married life, as bride and groom set off on their 'treacle moon' at Halnaby together; 'He began singing in a wild manner as he usually does when angry and scarcely spoke to me till we came near Durham ... On hearing the Joy-bells of Durham ringing for us, he appeared to be struck with horror, and said something very bitter about "our happiness" ... He called me to account for having so long withheld my consent to marry him, signifying I should suffer for it, and had better not have married him at all.'

It was the beginning of a nightmare that grew in Annabella's imagination until nothing else remained, a gothic horror of threats and jibes, of loaded pistols and veiled confessions, of sneering contempt and drunken abuse, of hints of sodomy and incest, which turned their red-curtained marriage bed into a hell for them both. It is clear from her letters rather than her later recollections that these weeks were not all misery, and yet when all the gothic trappings and false memories are stripped away, there can have been no humiliation for a woman of her temperament – for the spoiled child of doting parents, for a girl who had been brought up with a complacent sense of her own worth, for a woman who had startled herself with her own sexual appetite – than to discover that the only thing demanded of her was that she should be someone else.

And six months later, as darkness fell across Green Park and the immeasurable distance that separated her from her husband, that someone else who had haunted her honeymoon with her absence and her marriage with her presence, was still there. She had been there waiting to greet them on their journey south; she had followed them down to London. 'You were a fool to let her come', Byron had warned her the day that Augusta joined them in Piccadilly, and after ten weeks

of misery – ten weeks of wildly lurching fantasies of romantic forgiveness and murderous hatred, of abject self-loathing and pathetic gratitude, of drunken abuse, irrational rages and reconciliations, and all
borne with the brave, public face of a happy and pregnant young bride
– Annabella was going to be a fool no more. She had, at last, snapped.
She had told Augusta to leave. This Sunday in mid-June, in the house
that the Spider had found for them – so respectable, so solid from the
outside – would be the last that the three of them would ever spend
together.

And at Samuel Rogers's this night, if 'Words-words' was talking,
Byron was not listening. Wordsworth family lore recorded that they
argued about Bonaparte and the war, but if they did their meeting
never so much as registered on Byron's consciousness. He had other
things to think about. If he had married to provoke a crisis in his life,
he was about to get his wish. There were three great men destroyed in
1815, Byron liked to say: Bonaparte, Brummell and Byron. Society –
that same society that Ellenborough and Garrow had called into vindictive life to punish Lady Rosebery – would have its revenge on the man
it had once loved. It was only a matter of time.

10 p.m.

Clay Men

The only thing worse than a battle won, Wellington said, was a battle lost, and few that night from either side would have argued with that. Only morning would reveal the full horror of the field of Waterloo, but the screams and parched groans of the wounded and dying, French, British, Dutch, Belgian, Hanoverian, heaped promiscuously on top of each other, the neighing of torn and shattered horses, the sickening thud of the farrier's axe and the sporadic sound of a musket – mercy killing or looter – told their own terrible story.

'My Dearest Mama, We are making some clay men and guns and swords for the army,' a nine-year-old boy had written to his mother from Harrow more than twenty years before. 'The way we do it is this: we go to the Butts and then we get some clay, and we bring it home, and then we cut it with a knife into different shapes. When we want to make a man, we cut him as like as we can, and we pinch a bit for the nose, eyes and mouth. I like school very much. It is time for marbles. All the boys have got some … The man that sells the soldiers to us thinks we are going to fight France. We have twenty dozen amongst us and fight many battles. I am making a castle, and I am your dutiful son.'

The boy was the Hon. Frederick Ponsonby, the second son of the Earl and Countess of Bessborough, the favourite brother of Lady Caroline Lamb, and now Lieutenant Colonel Frederick Ponsonby of the 12th Light Dragoons. Over the last fifteen years the boy who had fought so many battles at Harrow had done little else but fight, and now he lay slipping in and out of consciousness in the hollow below La Haye Sainte, the trampled field around him thick with the dead, their limbs and torsos contorted into every grotesque posture imaginable, as if some malevolent or lumpen child had pinched them out of the Waterloo clay to which they were now returning and flung them down in a fit of rage or boredom.

The 12th had formed the left of Sir John Vandeleur's 4th Brigade to the east of the Brussels road, and at some time after two o'clock Ponsonby had led his squadrons across the Ohain road and at a gallop down the slope in support of his cousin Sir William Ponsonby's shattered Union Brigade. On the far left of that brigade the Scots Greys had got as far up the slope as the Grande Batterie before falling back, and as the exhausted and isolated survivors struggled to make their way back to the allied positions, they found themselves helpless against the nine-foot steel-pointed lances of Jacquinot's light cavalry sweeping down on them from the French right in a classic counter-attack.

Jacquinot had sent in something like seven hundred lances – the one weapon at Waterloo that no one in the allied armies would ever forget – and as Ponsonby's Light Dragoons threw themselves at a French column some thousand strong they in turn were engaged in a ferocious battle with the lancers on their flank. The French artillery had now also joined in the action, pouring grape-shot indiscriminately into friend and enemy – three of their own for every dragoon, Ponsonby reckoned – and within moments he had been disabled in both arms, and was being carted helpless into the French positions by his horse when a sabre blow to the head sent him stunned to the ground. 'Recovering,' Ponsonby recalled, 'I raised myself a little to look round

Peninsular veterans: Sir Colin Campbell and Frederick Ponsonby (right), one of Wellington's ablest and most popular cavalry officers. It was a moot point in Brussels whether his wounds or the nursing by his sister, Lady Caroline Lamb, constituted the greatest danger to Ponsonby's life.

Lady Caroline Lamb. While her brother Frederick Ponsonby lay badly wounded on the field of Waterloo, Caroline Lamb was putting the last feverish touches to *Glenarvon*, the notorious *roman à clef* that would bring about her final exile from society.

David Wilkie's *The Chelsea Pensioners Reading the Waterloo Dispatch, 1822*.
Commissioned by the Duke of Wellington, Wilkie's painting is a brilliant
celebration of the idea of Britain united by the triumph and grief of Waterloo.

'They have ruined my battlefield!' The Duke of Wellington shows what tourists and the Dutch had left of the field of Waterloo to George IV. When he saw the spot where Uxbridge's leg was buried, the King burst into tears. One of numerous images of his hero, Wellington, painted by Haydon.

It was a matter of profound national satisfaction that Bonaparte had surrendered to a British man of war. Not with a bang but a whimper. The British had been unfairly blamed for Bonaparte's escape from Elba, and they were taking no risks the second time around. Here Napoleon begins the long journey into exile that would end only with St Helena and death.

Ball passed thro'
both eyes — but all
the sense of smelling.

He lost the sense
of smelling on the left
to quite gone. His ?
touched —

'Johnnie, how can we let this pass,' the distinguished surgeon Charles Bell wrote to his brother-in-law when he heard the news of Waterloo: 'Here is such an occasion of seeing gunshot wounds come to our very door! Let us go!' Above and left, two of his remarkable illustrations of the work he carried out on both allied and French wounded soldiers in the days after Waterloo.

Above, two British soldiers suffering from facial wounds and, *left*, a soldier of the King's German Legion, called Voultz, who remarkably survived not just the surgeon's knife but also tetanus to make a full recovery.

(being, I believe, at that time in a condition to get up and run away), when a lancer passing by, exclaimed, "*Tu n'es pas mort, coquin!*" and struck his lance through my back; my head dropped, the blood gushed into my mouth, a difficulty of breathing came on, and I thought all was over.'

It was the beginning of an eighteen-hour ordeal for Ponsonby, and a man on the ground of whatever rank and whichever side was fair game to everyone. 'Not long afterwards, (it was impossible to measure time, but I must have fallen in less than ten minutes after the charge),' he continued, 'a Tirailleur came up to plunder me, threatening to take my life. I told him that he might search me, directing him to a small side-pocket, in which he found three dollars, being all I had; he unloosed my stock and tore open my waistcoat, then leaving me in a very uneasy posture.'

The Tirailleur's was merely the first visitation, and having regretfully assured the next looter that he had already been plundered, Ponsonby suddenly found an advancing French officer stooping over him. The officer told him that he was unable to help him for the moment as they were forbidden to move even their own wounded, but that the Duke of Wellington was apparently dead and allied battalions surrendering, and once the battle was won 'every attention in his power should be shewn me. I complained of thirst, and he held his brandy bottle to my lips, directing one of his men to lay me straight on my side, and place a knapsack under my head: he then passed on into the action, and I never shall know to whose generosity I was indebted, as I conceive, for my life – of what rank he was I cannot say, he wore a blue great coat.'

Throughout virtually the whole battle this no-man's land between the two armies was swarming with French sharpshooters, and his anonymous saviour had no sooner moved on than another Tirailleur was kneeling behind him for cover and chatting gaily away to Ponsonby as he fired. The last thing he told him before he slipped away was that the French were about to retreat, but with cannon ploughing up the ground around him, flinging the wounded and dead into endlessly new caricatures of life, even the swelling roar of the allied guns came as a mixed blessing.

Half-conscious or not, though, Ponsonby was soldier enough to be able to know what that sound meant – 'the finest thing I ever heard,' he called it – but as dusk fell and the oaths and defiant French roars gave way to the groans of the dying and moments of still more un-manning silence, it seemed 'the night would never end'. Two squadrons of Prussian cavalry had trampled over him during the allied advance, and with roaming Prussians taking their turn to search him and a dying soldier of the Royals – the air from the poor man's last, convulsive breaths issuing in a hissing sound from a wound in his side – pinning down his legs, it seemed only a matter of time before Frederick Ponsonby joined all those other clay soldiers that lay around him.

Eight, nine, ten ... sometimes conscious, sometimes unconscious, the hours passed for Ponsonby while across the field of Waterloo, among the gardens, orchards and charred ruins of Hougoumont and the shattered walls of La Haye Sainte and Papelotte, among the flattened crops of the hollow and on the plateau where the British squares had stood, along the hedges of the Ohain road and the sandpit by the chaussée, the dead and dying and wounded lay in their thousands under a clear, moonlit night. Propped up against the wall of La Haye Sainte, where he had crawled bleeding from his wounds, the dead Jack Shaw sat with his cheek cradled in his hand. Near him lay Dakin, last seen killing two men with 'cuts five and six', and close to them – his face carved in two as he gave Private Hodgson one last, entreating look for mercy – the bald head and white hairs of the elderly French officer who, for months to come, would haunt the dreams of Benjamin Haydon's 'Achilles'.

Within the yard at Hougoumont, where the Guards lay in heaps, the charred and legless corpses of men who had tried to crawl from the flames told their story, while out in the orchard, wrapped up in his blanket among the shattered apple trees and the 2,000 corpses of both sides – 'the Guards in their usual red jackets, the German Legion in Green, and the French dressed in blue' – William Wheeler lay fast asleep. Keppel was alive too – spattered with the brains of a bugler and epaulette horribly 'mutilated', but alive and glad it was 'fit'. And so was Wheatley, dazed and unsteady still and a prisoner somewhere behind what had once been the French lines. Against the wall of a garden, he had paused to look at 'a foot-soldier sitting, his head back and both his eyeballs hanging on his cheek, a ball having entered the side of his head and passed out at the other. Nothing could equal the horror of his situation, his mouth was open,' remembered Wheatley, 'stiff and clotted, clear blood oozed out of his ears and the purulent matter from his empty sockets emitted a pale stream from the vital heat opposed to the evening cold. So much for honour! thought I. Will it replace his orbs, No. As Falstaff says, "Who was it? He that died yesterday? No!! 'Tis a word coined by an apprentice over his sparkling glass", and the *Morning Advertiser*.'

Who was it? Among the Scots Greys it was the armless corpse of Colonel Jamie Hamilton, the bright and fearless son of the retired soldier William Anderson, adopted by the childless laird of Murdostoun, Lanarkshire, and given his name and made his heir. On the flank above Hougoumont he was the young Edinburgh lad of the 71st, his legs taken off by a cannonball, who twelve hours ago had prayed for his parents' forgiveness. In the 40th it was William Hooper of the company of Grenadiers, decapitated by a shell as they moved up to their positions. On the dead Picton's staff, Gronow's old friend Chambers, killed while taking the surrender of a French officer. In the 16th Light Dragoons, a neighbour of Sir James Hall's, the young Cornet Hay. In the 69th, Hobhouse's regiment, he was Crinnagan, Maxwell, Snell, Delicate. And in the 27th, the Inniskillings – quite literally, lying dead where they had stood in square at the north-east corner of the crossroads of the Ohain road and main Brussels chaussée – he was simply *Legion*.

And on the staff, too, few had got through the battle unscathed. The bloodied and exhausted Major Percy was untouched but Fitzroy Somerset had lost an arm, Sir Alexander Gordon was dying after the amputation of a leg, Canning was already dead, and Curzon, aide-de-camp to the wounded Prince of Orange, lying with his charger on the battlefield. 'I found poor Curzon dead,' a doctor – 'one of the hardest and roughest diamonds,' even in a notoriously unsentimental profession – told Gronow, 'leaning his head upon the neck of his favourite horse, which seemed to be aware of the death of his master, so quiet did it remain, as if afraid to disturb his last sleep. As I approached, it neighed feebly, and looked at me as if it wanted relief from the pain of its shattered limb, so I told a soldier to shoot it through the head to put it out of its pain.'

Behind the lines, weary from their day's butchery, the doctors were also at their trade. The Edinburgh-trained Charles Bell – of 'Bell's Palsy' and 'Bell's Nerve', who had given Haydon anatomy classes – had not come out yet, but in the rear of the British positions, close by the cottage where Sir William De Lancey lay forgotten, Dr Hume was at work. Gordon's life was still in the balance – he had him moved back to the village of Waterloo after the operation – and Hume had just seen him to bed when Captain Seymour arrived with the news that Lord Uxbridge was being brought in from the field with a badly wounded knee. 'I had hardly got to the end of the town,' Hume wrote the next day, 'when his Lordship made his appearance in a gig or Tilbury supported by some of his aides-de-camp. I followed him to his quarters and found on inspection that a grape that had struck him on the right knee close to the lower edge of the patella & entering on the inside of the ligament and having torn open the capsular ligament had made its exit behind fracturing the head of the tibula and cutting the outer hamstring in two.'

'His Lordship was perfectly cool – his pulse was as calm and regular as if he had just risen from his bed,' Hume wonderingly continued, and he showed 'no expression of uneasiness'. He had been on horseback the whole day and 'personally present' at almost every one of the numerous cavalry actions, but 'he was neither heated nor did he display the least agitation. There could be hardly a doubt of the expediency of amputating the limb but as I was not personally known to his Lordship I conceived it was a duty I owed to his family and to himself to do nothing rashly or without evincing to all the world that amputation was not only necessary but unavoidable.'

Hume's caution was understandable – this was the allies' cavalry commander in front of him – and going outside he recruited as many surgeons as he could find to spread the responsibility around. His own knife was blunt from a day's cutting and, borrowing one that had never been used, he went back inside with his new recruits to find Uxbridge in exactly the same posture in which he had left him. With 'the most placid smile' Hume had ever beheld, Uxbridge wished them all a 'good-evening' and, he told them, resigned himself 'entirely to your decision'. He was, of course, anxious 'as any other man' to save the limb if possible, but with his life being of infinitely more consequence to a numerous family he requested that they 'act in such a way as to the best of your judgement is best calculated to preserve that'. 'I replied, "Certainly my Lord, but" – he stopped me and said, "Why any buts, are you not the Chief? It is you I consult upon this occasion."'

There was no more space for wriggling, and having arranged his assistants where he needed them, Hume applied the tourniquet and took his knife in his hand. 'Lord Uxbridge said, "Tell me when you are going to begin." I replied, "Now, my Lord." He laid his head upon the pillow and putting his hand up to his ears said, "Whenever you please."' Hume began his incision by making one cut from above and another below, 'beginning at the inner point or horn of the upper and keeping as nearly parallel as possible'. He completed this first part of the operation by joining the two points on the outside of the thigh, before retracting the skin as far as possible and, 'with one stroke of the knife', dividing the muscles down to the bone. It was now time for the saw, and Hume had got most of the way through the femur when his assistant holding the leg – 'over apprehensive of splintering the bone' – raised the limb and trapped the saw so 'could not be pushed backwards or forwards. I did not perceive what was the cause and said angrily, "Damn the saw" when Lord Uxbridge lifting up his head said with a smile "What is the matter?" These words were the only words he spoke and during the whole of the operation he neither uttered groan or complaint nor gave any sign of impatience or uneasiness … His pulse which I was curious enough to count gave only 66 beats in the minute and so far was he from exhibiting any symptoms of what he had undergone in his countenance that I am quite certain had anyone entered the room they would have enquired of him where the wounded man was.'

History was again turning into the stuff of myth, but there was no sense of this at Waterloo that night. Seldom can a victory have produced so little sense of elation. The cost for everyone had been too great. Through the night one soldier of the 71st fought over and again in his dreams the day's battle and, as to the south, the Prussians pressed on with their savage moonlight hunt, something like a profound depression had settled on the exhausted allied army. In the village of Waterloo the duke would grab a couple hours of sleep before waking to the news of Sir Alexander Gordon's death and the first, tentative casualty lists brought to him by Dr Hume. As he listened to Hume reading out the names the tears rolled down his grime-covered face. 'Well, thank God,' he said, 'I don't know what it is to lose a battle; but nothing can be more painful than to gain one with the loss of so many of one's friends.'

It would be, as Magdalene De Lancey said, a week for weeping. 'I know not why,' Sir Augustus Frazer had written to his wife before the battle, 'but a great mass of armed men always brings to my mind strange associations and reflections; and in the midst of all that the poet calls "the pride and pomp of war", the reflection which we are told made Xerxes burst into tears when his myriads crossed the Hellespont will intrude, that in a few years all these will have passed away.'

'But what nonsense is all this!' he had added, shrugging off the thought; but it did not feel like nonsense now. In a lull in the fighting he had buried his dear friend Ramsey, taking from the body the portrait of his wife that Ramsey always carried next to his heart. There was not a man there who had not been racked with convulsive sobs. And now, as he wrote to his own wife, enclosing the lock of hair he had cut from Ramsey's head before they had put his 'yet warm body in the grave', the full sadness of it all returned. 'Pray get me two mourning rings,' he asked her, 'I will describe them when I next write. All now with me is confused recollections of scenes yet passing before me in idea: the noise, the groans of the dying, and all the horrid realities of the field are yet before me. In this very house are poor Lloyd (leg shot off but not yet amputated), Dumaresque (General Byng's aide-de-camp shot through the lungs and dying); Macdonald ... I dare not enumerate their names ... What a strange letter is this, what a strange day has occasioned it! To-day is Sunday! How often have I observed that actions are fought on Sundays. Alas! what three days have I passed, what days of glory, falsely so called and what days of misery to thousands.'

The day of Waterloo was drawing to its close. 'What will they say of us at home?' had been Corporal Dickson of the Scots Greys constant thought throughout the day, but the question now was: 'What will we say to *them*?' What could Frazer, as he held the snuff box neatly pierced by the bullet that had hit Ramsey in the heart, say to his widow? What comfort had Wellington to offer to Gordon's brother, Lord Aberdeen, when no glory could compensate for his own sense of loss? Which of the Howards at Arundel was going to break the news to Frederick Howard's pregnant wife? In Brussels, the Reverend Stonestreet would still be writing letters. And somewhere out in the night, Frederick Ponsonby could make out the darker shape of one last marauder picking his way through the piles of the dead towards him.

11 p.m.

Went the Day Well?

Behind the porticoed facade of Melbourne House in London's Whitehall, a woman of twenty-nine, dressed in the costume of a young boy, was putting the final touches to the longest suicide note in history. For the best part of five years Lady Caroline Lamb had been threatening to do something along these lines, but not even those who had seen her slash her wrist at Lady Heathcote's ball, or pursue Byron to his own lodgings disguised as a page, can have dreamed of the self-destructive anger that fuelled the solitary, candlelit vigils in Melbourne House through the June of 1815.

Night after night she had been scribbling – a gothic *roman à clef* of savage and vengeful portraits, of brilliant, incoherent tirades and wild attacks, of defiant self-justifications and harrowing self-knowledge, of nonsensical plotting, disguises, murders and political acumen – and now, as the day of Waterloo moved to its end, she was almost finished. She still had to write in her own tragi-heroic end before she gave John Murray the manuscript, and if no one would understand it – if few would ever get that far and those who did see nothing but the ravings of a delinquent child – *Glenarvon*'s Irish tale of political and moral self-destruction spoke with the shrill, half-cracked voice of prophecy.

Before her novel was even published, Lord Byron, the vampiric object of her hatred and vengeance, would be out of the country, a pariah like the Byronic doppelgänger of her novel among the people who had once idolised him, and if Caroline Lamb had looked out across Horse Guards and the park this evening she might have seen a very different kind of outcast making his way back to his apartments in St James's Palace. He was a tall, thin, dangerous-looking man in his mid-forties, his heavily whiskered face disfigured by one closed eye and a sabre scar that gave to his handsome features an ugly, sinister cast that seemed, to his enemies, a chilling gateway to his brutal and caustic soul.

Ernest Augustus, Duke of Cumberland, had been born in 1771, the fifth of the seven large and largely unlovable sons of George III who defaced the public life of the country for the best part of fifty years. As a young man he had been packed off to university on the continent and then into the Hanoverian army, but after fighting bravely in the Netherlands campaign of 1793 he never had the chance to see active service again, being endlessly frustrated by the king or, his brother the Duke of York, of his wish for a significant command in the British Army or any real role in the war.

He had been at the Battle of Leipzig as an observer – and would have been at Waterloo if he had had his way – but with his military career baulked, his talents and fiercely reactionary instincts were left to fester on the extreme fringes of English Tory politics. There were deep suspicions in Whig circles that his influence over the spinelessly malleable Prinny posed a real danger, and with his violent opposition to Catholic emancipation he had become an object of loathing for liberal and radical England, a hate figure for the opposition press and caricaturists of whom anything and everything from incest and sodomy to multiple murder could be and was believed.

In any normal week of the year, in fact, the title of the Most Hated Man in England would have taken some winning – Lord Chief Justice Ellenborough, Lord Castlereagh, Prinny himself, would all have had their supporters – but when Cumberland was in town there was no competition. There was probably little or no truth in most of the accusations levelled against him, and yet there would always be just enough doubt to make sure that the suspicions and libels never went away.

There had been persistent rumours fifteen years before that he was the father of his sister Princess Sophia's illegitimate child, but as he made his way back to his apartments in St James's, it was another and more dangerous scandal that hung over him. The duke had only been in the country a day, arriving alone from the continent early on Saturday morning, following his marriage at the end of May to his cousin, Princess Frederica of Solms-Braunfels. His travelling carriage had broken down on the other side of Dartford on the way up to London, and to the obvious satisfaction of the press he had been forced to hire a chaise for the rest of the journey, 'alighting' as the *Morning Chronicle*'s 'Mirror of Fashion' put it, in St James's Park, and walking through the gardens to Carlton House to spend the day with his brother the Prince Regent. 'The object of his journey,' the paper continued, 'is said to be to endeavour to reconcile the Royal Family to his marriage, and to prevail on Government to make an addition to his establishment on the occasion. He quotes the marriage of the Duke of York as a precedent for an increased allowance; in answer to which it is said that the cases are by no means similar.'

He had spent the whole of Saturday with the Prince Regent and most of Sunday seeing the prime minister, Lord Liverpool at Carlton House before joining Prinny at Windsor, but he had an uphill task in front of him. The vinegary old Queen Charlotte was dead set against his marriage to a woman who had already jilted one of her sons, and scandal stuck to his new bride as tenaciously as it did to Cumberland himself, with dark suspicions of poison surrounding the sudden and all-too-convenient death of her last husband, Prince Frederick William.

Cumberland and Frederica had, in fact, been deeply in love for a year – and would enjoy a long and happy marriage – but not even the novel prospect of a genuine royal love match was going to soften old hatreds. He had not been in the country since before Leipzig two years previously, but memories in Regency England were long and, as he walked now through St James's Palace, he must have known that it was another old ghost lurking in its corridors that would reappear to haunt him.

The ghost – he would make regular appearances in political cartoons satirising the Cumberland marriage debate – was that of a man called Joseph Sellis, whose body lay buried under the road just outside the door to the egg factory near Scotland Yard. Five years earlier, on 31 May 1810, Cumberland had been woken at two in the morning in his St James's apartment by a succession of violent blows, and staggering from his bed, bleeding from sword wounds to his face, throat, arms and hand, glimpsed in the shadows the figure of his attacker fleeing the chamber in the direction of the closet of his Italian valet, Joseph Sellis.

There were a lamp and taper burning by his bed, and in the pools of light he could see the side table and a letter covered with blood and a naked sabre lying on the floor, but it was only when his cries of murder brought his valet Christopher Neale that it was noticed that the door between the duke's bedchamber and Sellis's was locked. The duke's cries for help had by now woken most of the household, and while Guardsmen searched the palace for intruders, Mrs Neale, with the head porter in tow, went round by a second door to Sellis's room.

From inside came the sound of gurgling. Sellis had, it appeared, cut his throat from ear to ear – he was half-dressed and lying on the bed in a pool of blood when they went in – and the next day a hastily convened jury heard evidence from the duke and his servants and brought in the inevitable verdict of suicide. In the early hours of 2 June, Sellis's body was taken down to a spot near the Thames and buried under the high-way in the best approved style, but if the authorities imagined that they were going to bury the doubts and questions with him – or that daily bulletins of the state of the duke's wounds, or throwing open the bedchamber, complete with the bloodied satin sheets to the public was going to win him any sympathy – then they were soon disabused.

There had been odd inconsistencies in the evidence from the start that disturbed even the royal household – Sellis was left-handed, the wound to his throat inflicted by a right hand; he had clearly not killed himself where he lay – and then there was the question of Sellis's motive. It did not seem from the evidence that he had harboured any particular grievance against Cumberland, and when the prime witness, Christopher Neale, was rapidly pensioned off and sent to Ireland, even the most loyal of Tories must have found the claim that Sellis had done it because he was a Catholic or because he had had his travelling allowance reassessed the year before worryingly thin.

With doubts like this circulating even at Windsor, and the Neales vanished, it did not take the opposition press long to come up with another version of what had happened. In some pamphlets it was claimed that the duke had been having an affair with Sellis's wife, but the story that gained most credence, and would wash in and out of the courts for the next twenty-odd years, was that Cumberland and the page Neale had been involved in a homosexual affair; that Sellis had caught them *in flagrante*, had tried to blackmail the duke who had murdered him or had him murdered, faked his suicide, faked his own wounds, packed the coroner's jury with the help of the ubiquitous Lord Ellenborough, and paid Neale and his family to leave the country.

It says volumes for Cumberland's reputation that this could be widely believed – even the fact that the foreman of the jury was the political activist Francis Place was countered with accusations that Place was a government spy – and five years later the ghost of Sellis still hovered between the duke and his hopes of a new marriage settlement. He knew he could rely on the Prince Regent to overrule or ignore Queen Charlotte's objections to his new wife, and Liverpool's government too could be depended on; but Parliament? – the same Parliament that was baying for the head of Sir Henry Mildmay; the same Commons in which William Wilberforce was as concerned with the morals of a royal duke as he was of a countess; the same Commons in which the radical scourge of Tory corruption, Thomas Cochrane, would soon be out of prison and free to speak and vote? Parliament was another matter.

As the Duke of Cumberland walked through the guard in St James's Palace, where the young Ensign Gronow was supposed to be on duty, the day of Waterloo was drawing to its close. Across the park, a light would still be burning where Caroline Lamb was plotting her own alter ego and society's death in a last, fictional orgy of violence and revenge, but in the darkness of the park and across Britain the world could go on in its old course for another day. In Horse Guards and at the Navy Office in the Strand the candles would also still be burning. In Norfolk it had rained all day, in Twickenham it had cleared. In the Dales the weather had been mixed and in Edinburgh the rain had come through the roof during Dr Hill's lecture. At the vicarage in Sunbury the thermometer had touched seventy-two degrees and in London the price of bread was 11¾ the quartern loaf, and three per cent consols stood at 56½.

'All happy families resemble one another,' said Tolstoy, 'every unhappy family is unhappy after its own fashion' and for the vast majority of the country the day had passed unrecorded. People had married, people had died, children had been born. They had gone to church in the morning, they had gone to church in the afternoon, they had gone to evening service, they had not gone at all. They had pottered in their gardens and had almost finished taking in their hay. They had driven through the park to Knightsbridge and taken tea for the first time with the woman they would marry. They had drowned in the Tay going to hear Chalmers preach and been rescued in the Exe. They had read *Waverley* and they had read *The Velvet Cushion*. They were well, they were not well, they were writing up their diaries, they were leaving the day blank. In his chambers the barrister Crabb Robinson had just this minute finished with his law books for the night, and was filling in his journal. He had not got home from the Lambs' until almost one in the morning, he recorded, and had breakfasted with the Wordsworths at nine. Wordsworth had not been there, but he had waited for him and ended not leaving until two. Stuart of the *Courier* had been there, and talking confidently of the allies' success. Scott, too, of *The Champion* – 'a little swarthy man with rather an unpleasant expression of countenance' – just returned from Paris and full of French politics. And Haydon, the painter, whom he had never met before: Haydon had an animated countenance, but had not said much. Both he and Scott had seemed to entertain a high reverence for Wordsworth. They had talked of Wilkie's *Distraining for Rent* and agreed that he was no colourist and not getting any better. Then dinner with the Colliers, tea with Mrs Barbauld – she and her friends had not liked Wordsworth's 'White Doe' – and back home along the river for an hour with his law books, his journal and bed.

A perfectly ordinary end to an ordinary day, and as the Saturday mail-coaches thundered through the night carrying news of the deaths of three soldiers in the Gurkha War six months before, it was the same across Britain. Farington had been writing up his journal too, reminding himself to secure a ticket to see Mr Angerstein's paintings for a friend of Mrs Worsley. Across the park from Melbourne House, Byron would be walking home with that lame, sliding gait of his, oblivious to the fate of his fictional double in Caroline Lamb's *Glenarvon*. In Marlborough Street, Haydon's Centurion would still be waiting for his sleeve to be painted. In Bedford Square, 'Classic' Hallam had come home from Murray's to a new son. At her townhouse Sophie Trower, whose brother in the 16th had charged to the Scots Greys' rescue, was unhappy with a bad cough. Across the garden from Hazlitt, Jeremy Bentham was in the middle of an interminable letter to the Emperor

Alexander on prison reform. At Calne in Wiltshire, that other great seer of the age, Coleridge, had been dictating his *Biographia Literaria*. In Bath, Mrs Piozzi had 'Cramps and Pains all over the Epigastric region which our Ladies call Spasms and the Spaniards Flatos', and in Newgate another week was beginning that might bring news of the Recorder's report.

Down at Arundel, John Binstead was getting acquainted with the marshalman, Fogg, and somewhere near Haymarket, Samuel Halliday was thinking about another expedition to Copt Hall. Up in Glasgow thieves were breaking into a cloth warehouse, and farther north on the east coast, in his newly dug Achany chapel grave, the body of the tacksman, Captain Gordon, was enjoying its last undisturbed night of rest. On the other side of the country, off the west coast on the Isle of Scalpaigh, it would still be light enough to make out the bloody bundle beside the cairn, but in England it was already dark and the Planet Herschel visible in the night sky to the naked eye. 'It souths now a little before midnight,' the *Carlisle Journal* informed its readers, 'is pale & less vivid than the fixed stars near it in Scorpio. It will remain in company with Antares for 2 or 3 years, passing north of it about the middle of 1816, and veering to the east at the rate of 40.18 annually, being nearly seven years in passing one sign and nearly 84 in making an entire revolution. The diameter of herself is 35,220 miles, whereas that of the earth is only 7,970. Its distance from the sun is 1,816,455,000 which is so prodigious that a cannonball from the planet to the sun, moving at the rate of 8 miles a minute would not reach the latter in less than about 430 years.'

Here was a thought to make Xerxes and Augustus Frazer more than weep. Ten miles off the French coast, where the weather was moderate and the breeze south-south-west, the *Bellerophon* and *Myrmidon* were going about their silent, unseen business. Somewhere out in the southern Atlantic, a tiny speck in an immense ocean, the *Baring* transport was carrying a young midshipman, Thomas Whyte, to begin a fourteen-year sentence for killing a man in a drunken brawl at Leith docks. In Botany Bay, Agnes Findlater from Glasgow – guilty of stealing 'two women's slips, two soft muslin Neckcloths … three others of soft Muslin … two pairs of women's stockings, a woman's Bed gown, striped and a white petticoat' – and another 110 females of the *Northampton* were stepping ashore to start their new lives.

The day of Waterloo had ended. On the Scottish east coast, where the Halls would be waiting for word of their new son-in-law, the waves would be breaking against the rocks of Siccar Point. And as an English soldier stood guard over Frederick Ponsonby, and his sister, Caroline Lamb, scribbled herself into oblivion, in a field near the castle at Windsor, where the poor, mad old king lay oblivious to his country's triumphs, William Herschel's giant telescope pointed up to a universe utterly indifferent to it all.

PART II

The Opening of the Vials

'What wonderful changes! The battle of Waterloo is gained! And
Wellington has beat Napoleon in person, and with an inferior
force. The battle has raised the English character even higher
than it ever before stood, and makes one proud indeed of having
been born in the country which produced a Wellington.'

Frances, Lady Shelley

'Jesù, what gotho-barbaric rejoicing – like alleluias of the Druids
chanting round the great idol of straw, full of victims. What
horrors, what slaughters, what a terrible judgement of God on
the blind and brutal fury of the French. How many arms and
legs off, how many brains scattered on the ground, what a
catalogue of martyrs, dead or cut to pieces whilst still alive.
Never have such important and strong tidings come to my ears;
all the other victories pall before it – it is a Trafalgar on land,
which one cannot deny, raises Wellington in a colossal manner.'

William Beckford

For the last two decades the English mail had been the principal
instrument of national intelligence, and if ever there was a time and
event designed to show it up in all its glory, it was the June of 1815 and
the Battle of Waterloo. On any night of the year the departure of the

mails was one of the great sights of London, with the coaches drawn up in double-file the length of Lombard Street, every part of every coach inspected and polished, every horse – 'Horses! can these be horses?' 'bounding leopards', 'cheetahs' rather, wrote Thomas De Quincey – groomed as if it had just stepped out of a royal mews, and in times of 'Victory' it took on a near mystical significance.

Nobody – not even Dickens – has written of the mails as Thomas De Quincey did, no one felt their living role in the life of the nation, no one traced their arterial paths across the body politic with such a loving and almost forensic intentness. By the end of the Napoleonic Wars there were more than a hundred provincial newspapers reaching from Truro to Inverness, and yet for De Quincey it was almost as if some tacit pact had been agreed, and in return for all the riches and goods that fed into the insatiable maw of London from the ports, countryside and manufacturing towns of Britain – in exchange for all those herds that tramped the drover roads towards the great hecatomb of Smithfield – out flowed along the radiating lines of the mail-coaches the news, opinion, propaganda, reports, foreign intelligences, debates, scandals and tragedies that made up the collective life of the nation.

De Quincey loved everything about the mail-coaches – he loved their beauty and the intricacy of their organisation, he loved their speed as they surged through the blackness of the night, he loved the sense of surrogate power as turnpikes opened and panicking carts hurried out of their path, he loved their companionship, he loved the England he could see as dawn broke and the Bath Mail emerged out of the gloom of Savernake Forest – and above all he loved the organic sense of a country united by the joy and grief of war that for twenty years had been the backdrop of his life.

'On *any* night the spectacle was beautiful,' he wrote, but on one of those magic nights when the news of a great battle had reached England – Trafalgar, the Nile, the Glorious First of June, the Basque Roads, Talavera, Albuera – and horses, men and coaches were all decked out in laurels, flowers, leaves and ribbons, then one 'heart, one pride, one glory' connected 'every man by the transcendent bond of his English blood'. 'Every moment are shouted aloud by the Post-Office servants the great ancestral names of cities known to history through a thousand years, Lincoln, Winchester, Portsmouth, Gloucester, Oxford, Bristol, Manchester, York, Newcastle, Edinburgh, Perth, Glasgow – expressing the grandeur of the empire by the antiquity of its towns … What stir! – What sea-like ferment! – what a thundering of wheels, what a trampling of horses! – what farewell cheers – connecting the name of the particular mail – "Liverpool for ever!" – with the name of the particular victory – "Badajos for ever!" or "Salamanca for ever!" The half-slumbering consciousness that, all night long and all the next day' – and longer again for some – 'many of these mails, like fire racing along a train of gunpowder, will be kindling at every instant new successions of burning joy, has an obscure effect multiplying to the imagination into infinity the stages of its progressive diffusion. A fiery arrow seems to be let loose, which from that moment is destined to travel, almost without intermission, westwards for three hundred miles – northwards for six hundred; and the sympathy of our Lombard Street friends at parting is exalted hundredfold by a sort of visionary sympathy with the approaching sympathies, yet unborn, which we were going to evoke.'

'The mail-coaches it was,' wrote De Quincey, 'that distributed over the face of the land, like the opening of the apocalyptic vials, the heart-shaking news' of battles, and for more than a week now this Britain of towns and villages and isolated farmhouses had been waiting for the news that would not come. Night after night, through these middle days of June – as the Duke of Brunswick's coffin was nailed down in Antwerp and ladies lay fully dressed on their beds in Brussels – the women and children of De Quincey's England stood at their windows, waving their handkerchiefs or listening in the dark for the piercing trumpet sound of the mail's approach, and waited and waited in vain.

They were used to living with this suspense – used to those terrible waits between the first joyous news of a Trafalgar and the grim arrival of the casualty returns – but that had never made it any easier, and the tantalising proximity of the Low Countries made it only worse. On the morning of the battle churchgoers in Kent had clearly heard the sound of cannon from across the Channel, but if one imagines the shockwaves of a blast or a stone dropped into a pool at Waterloo, the first ripple of news would have only reached England some thirty hours later, spreading out then in widening circles, traceable in the letters, diaries, and newspapers of the day – the City first, Downing Street on the night of the 21st, London on the 22nd, Liverpool late on Friday 23rd, Keswick the 24th, Jersey and Edinburgh the 25th, the Scottish Highlands in early July – before spreading westwards to Ireland and America and eastward to the Persian Gulf and India, to break finally on the shores of Bombay some four months later. 'We lose not a moment in publishing the following most important and glorious intelligence,' a *Bombay Courier Extraordinary* announced on 27 October, 'by a Dow which has arrived from the Persian Gulf, a letter has been received from the Broker of the Honourable Company, dated the 1st of September, conveying the gratifying intelligence that Lord Wellington had completely defeated Buonaparte near Brussels, and taken the whole artillery consisting of 300 piece of cannon. The packets containing the glorious intelligence had been received by the broker at Bussorah but have not yet reached the government.'

Long before those slow, inexorable ripples had lapped against the shores of British India, though, days even before they reached a waiting England, a newly married young woman had watched them seep beneath the locked door of an Antwerp room where she thought nothing could find her. For the three days since the night of the Duchess of Richmond's ball, Magdalene De Lancey had been living in a cocoon of her own, sealed away from the outside world, her eyes shut to the sights and turmoil of a nervous, jumpy Antwerp, her ears blocked against the clatter of carts carrying the wounded and the distant rumble of cannon that she told herself was the sea.

She had spent the Sunday in a state of unhappy, febrile restlessness, irritable with her maid Emma and physically and emotionally exhausted by a wait that had already gone on longer than she had ever dreamed possible. Over these last days she had told herself time and again that nothing could happen to her husband, and it was only early on the morning of the 19th – twelve hours after the end of the battle – when an officer on his staff arrived with the first lists of dead and wounded to assure her that De Lancey was safe that she realised just how little she had believed it herself. 'I asked him repeatedly if he was sure,' she recalled, 'and if he had seen any of his writing, or if he had heard from him … I now found how much I had really feared by the wild spirits I got into. I walked up and down, for I could not rest, and was almost in a fever with happiness.'

If nothing, in retrospect, could seem crueller to her than the deluded happiness of those moments, they were, for a long time, the only ones she was to know. Captain Mitchell had brought his list to her at nine o'clock on the Monday, and at eleven Emma had come in to tell her that the consul from Brussels, Mr James, was down below along with another of that expatriate community that De Lancey and his new bride had so assiduously avoided in the days before the battle, Lady Dalrymple Hamilton. 'I did not remark anything in her countenance,' Magdalene later recalled – the scene, so laden with ironies, bitterness, and hard, dry-eyed, selfish, frightening sadness, still comes off the page with a terrible immediacy – 'but I think I never saw feeling and compassion more strongly marked than in his expression. I then said I hoped Lady Emily was well. He answered that she was so, with a tone of such misery that I was afraid that something had happened, I knew not what, to somebody. I looked at Lady Hamilton for an explanation. She seemed a little agitated too, and I said, "One is so selfish: I can attend to nothing, I am so rejoiced Sir William is safe ..."'

It seemed 'cruel' to her to impinge their own obvious sadness on her at a time like this – even when Lady Hamilton told her that James had lost a brother and she a nephew – 'but I tried to be polite, and again apologised for appearing glad, on account of my own good fortune'. It had never occurred to Magdalene that they might have come with news for her, and even when Lady Hamilton began to ask if she had plans to return to England or 'any friends in the country' she was so insistent that she 'would not move until Sir William came or sent for me', and 'so obstinately confident that she began'–

There is a break here in the original manuscript which she wrote for her brother Basil – a break more poignant than any tears could be – but then as before there was no time for tears. In the months to come Magdalene would try to persuade herself that Lady Hamilton's motives had been kind in keeping his name off the list that Captain Mitchell had shown her, but at that moment in her Antwerp room, as she listened to the death sentence of all her Brussels hopes, there was only a cold and unforgiving anger that she might have been robbed by that 'kindness' of a last chance to see her husband alive.

That was only the first of a series of reports and counter-reports that brought her very close to madness – he was dead, she was told, he was wounded but with every hope of recovery – and it was another thirty-six harrowing, sleepless hours before she finally reached Brussels to discover that he was alive and lying in a cottage at Mont-Saint-Jean. She had told herself in Antwerp that if she could just see him one last time she would never ask for anything again, and as she sat in a carriage on the Waterloo road, the stench of death all around her, waiting for an old Lothian neighbour to bring confirmation that she could go on, she reaffirmed her pledge: 'I hope no one will ever be able to say that they can understand what my feelings must have been during the half-hour that passed till he returned', she recalled the interminable minutes of waiting: 'How fervently and sincerely I resolved that if I saw him alive for one hour I never would repine! I had almost lost my recollection, with the excess of anxiety and suspense, when Mr Hay called out, "All's well; I have seen him. He expects you."'

De Lancey had been placed at first in an outer room of the cottage, but the faces of stragglers pressing at the windows – British, French, Belgian, Hanoverian, Dutch, Prussian, wounded, prisoners – had disturbed him, and by the time that Magdalene reached him he had been moved to a small inner room. She found him lying on a low wooden frame fastened to a wall, with a sack of chaff for a pillow and his great coat for a blanket, his knees hunched up towards his chest, too weak to move or lift his head. His voice, though, as she took his hand, was stronger and firmer than she had feared. 'Come Magdalene' – his first words and his last complaint – 'this is a sad business, is it not,' he greeted her.

She could scarcely say whether she 'hoped or feared most at first', she remembered, but after thinking him dead 'was ready to bear whatever might ensue without a murmur'. She had every reason to believe that there would soon be nothing but the memories of these hours to hold on to, and 'by suppressing feelings that would have made him miserable, and myself unfit to serve him', she determined 'to lay up no store for regret'. He asked her if she was a good nurse. She told him that she had 'not been much tried'. He then said he was sure he would be a good patient, for he would do whatever she asked till he was well again and then he would 'grow very cross'. 'I watched in vain for a cross word. All his endeavours seemed to be to leave none but pleasing impressions on my mind; and as he grew worse and suffered more, his smile was more sweet, and his thanks more fervent, for everything that was done for him.'

It was a curious place to pick up the threads of their second honeymoon, but no poorer to either of them for that, and for the next six days the wretched Mont-Saint-Jean cottage took on something of the limitless dimensions of their brief Brussels existence. The cottage was hemmed in on all sides by lanes, but not even the constant din of an army on the move, the incessant rumbling of wagons on the Nivelles road, the flow of carriages bearing the wounded back to Brussels or the endless babble of voices at the open windows could penetrate a world that had simultaneously shrunk and expanded to a cramped sick-bed and a room seven feet across.

Not just a world but a whole life had shrunk to the confines of that room and those six days. As she had waited in her carriage for Captain Hay to return she had vowed that an hour was all she asked, and now that it came to the test she was as good as her word, finding in the duties of nurse and wife a strength and maturity that separates by a lifetime of experience the Magdalene De Lancey of Waterloo from the woman who had left Antwerp only that morning.

With leeches and blisters to be applied, doctors to be consulted, bedding to change, provisions to be found, blanket baths to be given – she insisted on doing it all herself – she needed all the strength she could muster to see out a vigil that she soon knew was hopeless. The wound itself seemed to cause her husband surprisingly little pain in these first days, but the slightest cough was agony and beyond lemonade or tea – when she could purloin some milk from a passing Prussian cow – he could take in nothing. 'On Thursday he was not quite so well,' she recalled – well versed by this time in reading the conflicting signs and rhythms of his decline; 'Before this he had been making a gradual progress, and he could move about with more ease. He spoke much better than he did at first. His countenance was animated; but I fear this was the beginning of the most dangerous symptoms, and I saw that the surgeon now became uneasy at the appearance of the blood … That night … Sir William was restless and uncomfortable: his breathing was oppressed, and I had constantly to raise him on the pillow. The pain in his chest increased, and he was twice bled before morning.'

There were other, subtler, but no less telling signs of his gradual withdrawal from this world. On the day that Magdalene arrived, the duke had been to visit him and talk of the battle but De Lancey no longer wanted to see anyone or hear any news. He had told Magdalene that all he wanted was to 'settle down quietly at home for the rest of our lives', but there was no talk now of any future. 'He generally lay thinking,' she remembered, 'often conversed with me, but seemed oppressed with general conversation, and would not listen when anyone told him of the progress of the army. His thoughts were in a very different train.'

On the Friday evening he was very feverish, and at one o'clock in the morning he was bled for the last time. Three hours later Magdalene was called away from his bedside and prepared for the end. The distressed surgeon attending him told her that if she had 'anything particular to say to Sir William' she 'should not long delay'. Was it days or hours, she wanted to know, and on being told that it was not imminent, 'I left him, and went softly into my husband's room, for he was sleeping. I sat down at the other end of the room, and continued looking at him, quite stupefied; I could scarcely see. My mouth was so parched that when I touched it, it felt as dry as the back of my hand. I thought I was to die first. I then thought, what would he do for want of me during the few remaining hours he had to live. This idea roused me.'

After writing a letter to General Dundas asking for help – she hoped that she would be able to control herself when the end came, but did not know 'what effect it might have on me' – she returned to her usual station at her husband's side and took his hand to tell him what the doctors had said. She knew that he was 'far above being the worse' for anything she had to tell him now, but his voice, nevertheless, faltered as he replied it was 'sudden'. 'This was the first day he felt well enough to begin to hope he should recover! He breathed freely, and was entirely free from pain; and he said that he had been thinking if he could be removed to Brussels, he should get well soon. I then asked if he had anything to desire me to do, or anything to say to anyone. He repeated most of what he had told me were his feelings before – that he had no sorrow but to part with his wife, no regret but leaving her in misery.'

That Saturday's vigil seemed to stretch out interminably, but the comings and goings of doctors, and all the talk of blistering, fomenting and further bleeding had as much to do with keeping Magdalene occupied as the patient comfortable. The application of a flannel bath – she had to tear up her petticoat for the flannel – brought him some brief relief, but that night the pain in his chest was intolerable and for the first time, as she lay pretending to sleep in an attempt to free him from at least one care, she had to listen to the uncontrolled groans of a dying man. 'I went and stood near him,' she wrote, 'and he then ceased to complain, and said "Oh, it was only a little twitch." I felt at the time as if I was an oppression to him, and I was going away, but he desired me to stay. I sat down and rubbed it, which healed the pain, and towards morning I put on the blister.'

By nine o'clock he was breathing only with difficulty, constantly asking the 'clock' and pleading for the end of a night that he could no longer bear. He asked Magdalene to lie beside him to ease away the hours but there was so little room she was afraid to hurt him. His mind, though 'seemed quite bent upon it. Therefore I stood upon a chair and stepped over him, for he could not move an inch, and he lay at the outer edge. He was delighted; and it shortened the night indeed, for we both fell asleep.'

It was their last night together. The next morning he lay placidly quiet while she washed his hands and face and brushed his hair. 'See what control your poor husband is under,' he said to her. 'He smiled, and drew me so close to him that he could touch my face, and he continued stroking it with his hand for some time.'

The respite from pain was only brief. By eleven he had again become uneasy, his breathing hard, with a gurgling, choking sound in his throat. To the very end, though, he remained conscious and able to speak. Having asked to have his wound dressed – it had never been looked at – he took her hand, and said that 'he wished she would not look so unhappy. I wept; and he spoke to me with so much affection.

He repeated every endearing expression. He bade me kiss him. He called me his dear wife.'

It was, at last, more than Magdalene De Lancey could take. When Dr Powell and John Hume came in to inspect the wound, she left the room, 'not able to bear to see him suffering'. She had hardly gone, though, when Powell recognised a change in De Lancey's countenance, and sent Emma to fetch her back. 'I hastened to him,' she confessed, 'reproaching myself for having been absent a moment. I stood near my husband, and he looked up at me and said, "Magdalene, my love, the spirits." I stooped down close to him and held the bottle of lavender to him: I also sprinkled some near him. He looked pleased. He gave a little gulp as if something was in his throat. The doctor said, "Ah, poor Lancey! He is gone." I pressed my lips to his, and left the room.'

While the immemorial rituals of death continued below, Lady De Lancey sat alone, too stupefied to hear or think of what was happening. General Dundas had come as she had asked the previous evening, and eventually Emma appeared to tell her that he was waiting to take her to the old apartment in Brussels from which, just ten days earlier, she and her husband had listened at the window to the fading sound of fifes and bagpipes as Wellington's army marched out into the night for Quatre Bras.

As she entered the now silent room, Magdalene De Lancey's thoughts though were not for the thousands of those men who were now dead, nor even for the husband who lay on the cot she had shared with him only hours before. There seemed to her such a picture of peace and 'placid calm sweetness' on his face that her first reaction was one of envy, and the bitter thought that while he was released she was left behind to suffer. 'Those moments that I passed by his lifeless body were awful, and instructive,' she wrote later; 'their impression will influence my whole life.'

* * *

It was one death among tens of thousands – never before or since have so many men crowded into so confined a battlefield – and that sense of depression that hung over Waterloo through the night of the 18th became the universal medium of Brussels life. The surgeon Charles Bell was struck by the defiant, impenitent anger of the French wounded and dying he treated, but there was no corresponding triumphalism. From the night of Quatre Bras, Brussels had grown accustomed to the sight of wounded but nothing had prepared them for this. 'You may form a guess of the slaughter and of the misery that the wounded must have suffered,' Major Frye, a veteran of Egypt, could write even ten days after the battle, 'and of the many that must have perished from hunger and thirst, when I tell you that all the carriages from Bruxelles, even elegant private *equipages, landaulets, barouches and berlines*, have been put in requisition to remove the wounded men from the field of battle to the hospitals, and that they are yet far from being all brought in.'

. While the funeral pyres smouldered on the battlefield, and the burial parties and resurrection men went about their work, and the stench of rotten carcasses made men retch, and brothers searched the field for brothers, a city had become a hospital. Doctors operated on the disembowelled and limbless; friends sat at bedsides, making and changing bandages, feeding, nursing, writing letters; soldiers wept openly in the streets and the world – British, Belgian – looked on with an appalled, compassionate, classless, nationless sympathy at the broken, wounded and emasculated wrecks of victory. 'Poor Lord Hay is the person I regret the most,' wrote Georgiana Lennox, the future Lady de Ros, angry at him for dying when he was so young and full of life; but 'I long to nurse even the poor privates ... Poor Lord F. Somerset is low at having lost his arm; he says all his prospects in life are blighted; poor thing she [his wife] was nearly distracted with anxiety during the action ...'

'We saw Lord Fitzroy Somerset yesterday,' she wrote again, 'he walked a few yards in the Park, he does not sleep and they hope the air will make him pass more comfortable nights. Poor fellow, he is much out of spirits; he does not look so ill as I expected he would, but I really could have cried when I saw him with only one arm.' Only Uxbridge – cheerfully facing 'the fact that he should no longer cut the young men out as a handsome well made fellow, which he had done for many years' – seemed impervious, but a city that wept and shared its sadness was no place for Magdalene De Lancey. She had wanted nothing to do with it in the self-absorbed happiness of her few days there, and it wanted nothing to do with her now in her solipsistic grief. 'Sir W. Delancy is dead after all,' Lady Georgiana Lennox wrote to Lady G. Bathurst on the 27th, passing on what plainly was common gossip, 'I cannot say that I felt much pity for her, which seems inhuman, but she really must be composed of flint ... She wrote a most extraordinary letter before he died, saying she wished General Dundas would go to her as she wished to settle several things relative to his interment. Can you conceive it, and requesting General Dundas would take her to England when her husband was dead. She is a daughter of Lady Helen Halls. I hope I may never see her.'

There would be no need. Within the week Magdalene De Lancey would follow this letter and a thousand others carrying news of the battle and of casualties and of which regiment had done what and whether or not the cavalry had behaved irresponsibly to a waiting England. 'I have not been able to collect all the particulars,' Major Frye wrote home, 'but you will no doubt hear enough of it, for I am sure it will be *said* or *sung* by all the partisans of the British ministry and all the Tories of the United Kingdom for months and years to come, for further details, therefore, I shall refer you to the *Gazette*.'

Frye was right. And it had already begun.

The Days That Are Gone

On Sunday 25 June, the day that Magdalene De Lancey returned to her old Brussels apartment on the Parc, the same wave that had swept away her future in a single moment broke across the Edinburgh world that just three months earlier had celebrated her marriage. Her naval brother Basil was away in the East at the time, and it is in the diary of a Miss Christian Dalrymple – the heir to Lord Stair – that we hear the first muted echo of Magdalene's loss.[1] 'Church twice forenoon,' Miss Dalrymple's entry for the day reads: 'Accounts of a great victory over Bonaparte. Many officers killed. Sir W de Lancey severely wounded. Hill's lectures.'

Nothing could better illustrate the strange time warp within which Waterloo was fought and the news of it received than Miss Dalrymple's diary. On the day of the battle she had been at church in the morning to hear Mr Moodie preach from Philippians, and for the same week that out in Belgium a whole life had been crushed into a few days, a whole world of love, grief and loss shrunk to a shared wooden cot in a Belgian hovel, Miss Christian Dalrymple had a couple of lectures on theology, a visit to the hot baths at Portobello for her limbs, a dose of Cheltenham salts on the Wednesday, a consultation with Dr Waldrof regarding her eyes on Thursday, and a Tuesday evening of playing Loo.

The hypochondriacal Miss Dalrymple was not unusual in any of this – except perhaps in the course of leeches for her eyes that Dr

Waldrof prescribed – and across the country the world had gone on as it always had. In the days before Waterloo, Britain had the air of some nineteenth-century Pompeii on the eve of the eruption, and to look at the newspapers and letters of the early part of the week after the battle – at the announcements for the performance of *Richard II* at Drury Lane or the news that in the churchyard at Kincardine, up on the north-east coast of Scotland, an angry mob had dug up the body of a newly buried suicide, dragged it down to the seashore, flung it into a hole between the high- and low-tide marks, and reburied it under a pile of rocks – is like watching a Britain still unconscious that Vesuvius had blown and the ash that will bury her old world was already darkening the sky.

The battle had not stopped a rusty Robert Southey struggling with his son's Greek, or brought Shelley back from a walking tour in Wales. It had not prompted the young medical student, John Keats, to join Charles Bell in Belgium or put an end to the great Howard clan celebrations at Arundel. It had not dampened the 'brilliant display of fireworks' at Vauxhall under the patronage of the Prince Regent or stopped the Fashionables coming to the Countess of Buckingham's 'splendid *dejeune*' in Grosvenor Square, as if nothing else mattered under the sun, but that sun was already disappearing. On the morning of Monday 19th the crowds in Piccadilly were still queuing to see Lefebvre's portrait of Bonaparte, but even as the papers wondered where the Emperor was, and Magdalene De Lancey struggled against the flotsam of war on the Brussels road, a semi-mythical messenger of Victory and Death out of some drug-fuelled De Quincey dream – a 'Gentleman of Ghent', a Mr C., an agent called Roworth in the pay of Nathan Rothschild, nobody was quite sure who he was – was already on his way to England to spill the last apocalyptic seal over Mrs Piozzi's Regency world.

There had been a badly scrambled account of *a* battle, brought over on the packet *Maria* from Ostend to Colchester on the night of the 18th/19th, but for Regency England's anti-Semites, subsequent mythology and conspiracy theorists alike, only a Rothschild spy has ever properly fitted the bill. In the pre-dawn hours after the battle Wellington had sat down to begin his official despatch to the War Minister Lord Bathurst, but before he had even started – in one variant of the story at least – a courier had already been on the road for hours, racing to bring the news of the victory from Brussels to Nathan Rothschild at his London New Court offices before either government or City had word of it.

On the floor of the 'Change' information was money, and in the age before the telegraph, the network of couriers, riders, cross-Channel clippers, mail-guards, smugglers and carrier pigeons that the Rothschild brothers had established across Europe had made Nathan the best-informed man in England. There is so much myth surrounding the news of Waterloo that it is impossible to be certain about exact times, but while Wellington's aide-de-camp, Major Henry Percy, was still fretting on the tide at Ostend with the official Waterloo despatch, Rothschild's man was already – allegedly – in 2 New Court and Nathan Rothschild in possession of the news.

'The messenger who was employed … was ordered to call on the King of France at Brussels [in fact Ghent] on his way', the Secretary to the Admiralty, the unlovable John Wilson Croker used to recall: 'He did so, then proceeded to the Rothschilds. After they had extracted from him all the information that he possessed, they sent him on to Lord Liverpool, the Prime Minister, in order that the Government might receive tidings of this great event.' Liverpool could make no sense of what the man was telling him, and Croker himself, after he had been sent for, was faring no better when, 'about to give up in despair … and by a sudden impulse', he questioned the messenger as to his interview with the French king. How was he dressed? he asked him.

"In his dressing-gown."

What did he say and do?

"His Majesty embraced me, and kissed me!"

"How did the King kiss you?"

"On both cheeks," replied the messenger, upon which Mr Croker emphatically exclaimed:

"My Lord, it is true; his news is genuine.'"

If this is true, the courier had reached New Court early in the morning of the 20th – *The Times* reported unusual trading activity on the floor of the Exchange that day – but Lord Liverpool had no means of knowing whether Croker was right and kept the news to himself. There was a persistent rumour that Rothschild had in fact learned of the battle by carrier pigeon on the Monday, but whatever the truth of that it was only the following night – a day-and-a-half later – that a chaise and four, carrying Major Percy and the Waterloo despatch, with two captured French Imperial eagles jutting out through the windows, and a noisy and growing crowd in tow, was heard rattling up Whitehall towards Downing Street and Horse Guards.

Percy had not seen a bed in a week – fragments of a man's brains, those of an officer killed next to him, fell out of his sash when he eventually got out of his bloodied uniform that night – and it had been an exhausting journey. He had not left Brussels until the noon of the 19th, and when the HMS *Peruvian* was becalmed mid-Channel he was forced to take to one of the ship's boats, and with the help of the captain and four sailors row himself and the eagles to the Kent coast, where – in a bizarre echo of the Cochrane Stock Exchange fraud – he had beached the boat at Broadstairs and taken a fast carriage for London.

It was ten at night before Percy arrived in Downing Street, where an alarmed Charles Arbuthnot, brought to the window by the sound of a mob, was the first in government to see the eagles. Nobody at Horse Guards seemed sure where Lord Bathurst had gone for the evening, and while a courier was sent to track him down, the dishevelled and bloodstained Percy set off in search of Lord Liverpool, emptying houses of their ball guests and Whites of its members as his chaise with the eagles drove through Mayfair towards Grosvenor Square.

The prime minister had been dining at the cantankerous Lord Harrowby's that night – Bathurst was with Lord Grey and the Earl of Jersey – and it was there that Percy at last found him. In one account he burst into the room shouting 'Victory, a Victory!', but his own, more bathetic version – saved by a relative – has an air of anti-climax about it that smacks of historical truth:

'"You must immediately come with me to the Regent," Liverpool told him, hustling him out into the square where a crowd had again gathered, and into his own carriage.

"But what is to be done with the eagles?"

"Let the footman carry them," said Lord Liverpool.

This did not seem to Percy any way to treat the eagles, and taking them with him, he drove with Lord Liverpool to Mrs Boehme's house in St James's Square, where the Prince Regent and Duke of York were dining. The prime minister took Percy up to the prince and introducing him as Major Percy, announced that he had come "with the news of great victory for your Royal Highness".

"Not Major Percy, but Lieut-Colonel Percy," said the prince. Major Percy knelt and kissed his hand. "We have not suffered much loss, I hope," he then said.

"The loss has been very great indeed," was of course the reply, upon which the prince burst into tears. Major Percy afterwards went to his brother's house in Gloucester Place, and called him up to hear the good news, and then to Portman Square, where he undressed and went to bed for the first time since the battle.'

It was two in the morning before Percy finally got out of his uniform – he was too exhausted to be on time for his appointment with the Duke of York the next day – but by that time small pockets of London already knew the news. In the years to come men and women would arrogate this historic moment to their own lives, and it would have been odd when every family in England had its own Waterloo legend, if an arch-mythologiser, egotist, patriot and hero-worshipper of Benjamin Haydon's stamp, had not pushed his way to the front of events. 'I had spent the evening with John Scott who lived in the Edgware Road,' Haydon wrote, 'I had stayed rather late, and was coming home to Great Marlborough Street, when in crossing Portman Square a messenger from the Foreign Office came right up to me and said, "Which is Lord Harrowby's? The Duke has beat Napoleon, taking one hundred and fifty pieces of cannon, and is marching on Paris."

"Is it true?" said I, quite bewildered.

"True!" said he … Scott began to ask questions. I said, "None of your questions; it is a fact," and both of us said "huzza!"'

It is impossible to know whether any of this is true or not – though if the Prince Regent, the future George IV, could come to believe that he had been at the battle himself it would be hard to hold it against Haydon – and the euphoria was real enough. In the weeks before Waterloo he had been forced to put up with Leigh Hunt's teasing banter as to what Bonaparte would do to his 'Master Wellington', and now the boot was on the other foot, his faith justified, the duke enshrined in the pantheon of deities, the 'vain and impudent French' put in their place, the boasts of the Old Guard that '*Napoleon n'étais jamais battu*' silenced, and the scoffers – 'Terrible battle this, Haydon. A glorious one, Hunt' – routed. 'Sammons my model and corporal of the 2nd Life Guards came and we tried to do our duty,' Haydon noted on the 23rd, 'but Sammons was in such a fidget about his regiment charging, and I myself was in such a heat, I was obliged to let him go. Away he went, and I never saw him till late the next day, and he then came drunk with talking. I read the *Gazette* the last thing before going to bed. I dreamt of it and was fighting all night; I got up in a steam of feeling and read the *Gazette* again, ordered a *Courier* for a month, called at a confectioner's and read all the papers till I was faint.'

Never, as Haydon never ceased to tell people, had there ever been a time like this. And as the guns boomed across the city from the Tower, and crowds jostled and pressed around copies of the *Gazette*, and London came to terms with the best and worst of the news, the mail-coaches in Lombard Street were being decked out in their garlands and ribbons. It was the turn of the rest of the country to learn the cost of victory.

For all the triumphalism of Benjamin Haydon, there would not have been a town in Britain that had not reason to fear, hardly a family as Byron put it, that had escaped 'havoc's tender mercies', and in a society that industrialisation had not yet changed out of all recognition the anxieties would have been multiplied fifty-fold. In many ways the old loyalties and structures that bound the country together had already loosened beyond repair, but the Britain that fought Waterloo was still recognisably a country of defined and integrated communities in which each anxiety would have been a common one and every death a shared loss.

This would be true of the Highlands of Scotland when the news finally reached them, true of the island communities where the memories of Waterloo would echo down the century, true of the close-knit professional world of Edinburgh, true of the parishes of England and Wales and the villages of Ireland, and of nowhere was it truer than of the aristocratic class that had provided Wellington with his officers. Twenty years of war might have done a great deal to dilute the social exclusivity of the army, but for Lord Harrowby's guests one glance at the killed and wounded lists in Wellington's despatch would have been enough to show the appalling price that Sydney Smith's 'Golden Parallelogram' of aristocratic privilege, wit and beauty had paid for victory.

The families of the men on those lists all knew each other, were interconnected by marriage, sat together in Parliament, raced their horses against each other, were members of the same clubs – Sir William Ponsonby, the son of Lord Ponsonby, whose wife's miniature was found on his body, was connected to the Bessboroughs, the Spencers, the Lambs, the Fitzroys, the Greys, the Devonshires – and each death spilled across party and generations to engulf a whole world in a tide of grief. 'I saw a man who was by Sir Wm Ponsonby when he fell,' Lady Capel, Uxbridge's sister, wrote from Brussels – just one of a cache of family letters that preserves in aspic the great surge of collective misery that a single death caused; 'he says he suffered nothing that his death was instantaneous that he never spoke after his first wound, his aide-de-camp came to Brussels more dead than alive. My son saw him immediately and thought he would have fainted as he walked up stairs ... He went next morning & found the body it was known by the *sweet* smile which was still visible on his fine countenance where goodness and kindness were marked with such Strong Lines that it was impossible to mistake him – I saw him a few hours before the final battle and his countenance, his smile, the place where I saw him still haunt me.'

'My dear Lord I can no longer delay to ask how dear Lady Grey is' ... 'tell me how Ly Ponsonby is' ... 'I trembled for the effect the shock might have upon her' ... 'I have now experienced almost the greatest misfortune I could suffer' ... 'Adieu my dear dear Mary you know how I loved William' ... 'Poor Georgiana' – a whole society was coming to terms with loss, anxiety, fear, grief, anger and all those haunting feelings of unresolved and unresolvable guilt that sudden death leaves behind. 'I hired a horse to ride out to enquire concerning a point which occupied my whole soul,' wrote John Cam Hobhouse, still trapped in France three weeks after the battle and unaware that his brother, Ben, had been killed at Quatre Bras. Like so many others he had read the first lists of the dead and wounded and breathed a sigh of relief, only to discover 'how sadly' he was mistaken, and 'what a wound' was to be made in his heart by the loss of 'the most affectionate, the bravest, and the most honourable of men ... I never did anything in my life for my poor brother ... I was not unkind, that is all I can say for myself, either with respect to him or any of my family. I envy him as I do everyone who has lived honourably and ceased to live.'

A century later, an MP standing up in the House of Commons would celebrate the 'Roman virtues' of Britain's women, but in this summer of 1815, as wives and mothers waited for news, or blocked their ears to the news, or refused to believe it, or hoped against hope that it was not true, there was very little sign of any such restraint. 'If you have the least news for God's sake send it me,' a frantic Lady Caroline Lamb – another cousin of William Ponsonby – wrote to Murray, 'the sort of agitation I have been in all day cannot be conceived ... pray let us know when the messenger comes ... if you will send to me it will relieve my mind – I cannot go out anywhere – I was near calling upon you ... The last accounts I heard of my Brother were written by poor General Pack – he said these words & they were addressed to an utter stranger to all of us – Ponsonby is quite idolised by the whole army he is one of our most gallant officers.'

For those out in Brussels or Ghent one of the most familiar sights of these days after the battle was of men openly weeping in the streets, and at home the shock was more than many could bear. 'There are hopes,' reported the *Caledonian Mercury* on 29 June, 'that the Hon. Major Howard, of the 10th Hussars, who had been reckoned among the killed in the late action, is merely missing. The lady of this officer is far advanced in pregnancy, and the account of his death had had so melancholy an effect on her, that she has never spoken since she heard it.'

'When the wife of Major Nogg heard that her husband had been killed,' Lady Frances Shelley noted in her journal, 'she did not speak and died two days later' but as Magdalene De Lancey had bitterly discovered, uncertainty carried its own miseries. 'Vague reports have been made of the numbers slain on both sides,' the *Morning Chronicle* warned its readers, 'and the names of distinguished persons have been too lightly mentioned as having fallen. We should not quote them if our silence could prevent the spread of disastrous intelligence. But to shew how vaguely the names of officers are stated, we shall particularise those of Lord James Hay, brother of the Marquis of Tweeddale, and James Lord Hay, son of the Earl of Errol. Both of these gallant young men were with the Army, and one of them is said to have fallen, yet both are indiscriminately named.'

It was not just the Tweeddales and Errols and Howards who clung on to fading hopes and faced the same agonising wait. 'I can say no more about plays,' the dramatist and blue-stocking, Joanna Baillie, wrote to Walter Scott – she had been in the middle of a letter about Kean and Byron when the *Gazette* and the casualty lists had been brought in – 'and tho' our two young men we have good reason to believe are safe, I can think of nothing else. Everybody around me is anxiously waiting for news of their friends ... Mrs Baillie whose nephew is in the Guards is by me just now, pacing up and down in a most anxious manner, and our good friend and neighbour Mrs Miligan has her eldest son there also. In short we are all less or more in a state of misery till the returns of the killed and wounded are received.'

'We have claimed a victory and illuminated while mo[u]rning in sackcloth would be more suitable,' complained Samuel Kevan, a slater and member of the Reformed Presbyterian Church, in his Sabbath-day journal for the 25th, but the truth was that wherever you turned in Britain parents and wives of every class *were* wearing their sackcloth. 'To the mind's eye haunted by faces it shall never see again, – to voices missed in the circle, to vacant seats at the table, – to widows waking in the morning' – 'to the fatherless, the childless, the husbandless' – what to them are 'the common feelings of hostility or of triumph'? demanded Hunt's *Examiner*, and across the country families bore testimony to its truth. 'The most painful duty I have ever performed is to acquaint you that Dear John is *no more*,' wrote the father of Captain John Blackman of the Coldstream Guards, that other Westminster boy at Waterloo saying his prayers on the morning of the 18th. 'He died in the field of battle, instantly on receiving a shot through his head … To know that his body was found and interred is some consolation, and to be assured he was not mangled, as very many others were, alleviates us a little … God bless his memory.'

'Your letter fills me with the deepest sorrow,' came back the answer from a little village in Shropshire – Bredwardine and London drawn together in the same grief – 'alas in vain were planted, with so much pleasure and innocence, the trees he planted, which he said himself, were to commemorate the era of his military career, they will serve however, with many a pang of deepest sorrow, to call to my sad remembrance, the happy hours in which he planted them in the days that are gone … The bells are ringing, all around me, no doubt for great and glorious victories, but how they mock my feelings.'

'The days that are gone' – a grove of young saplings planted in Shropshire, two miniatures found in a dead son's desk – these were all his family had to hold on to, and yet even for the Blackmans grief in these days was dignified if not softened by a deep and sober pride and gratitude for what their son had done. 'Alas he is fallen, but how bravely fallen,' Sir George Harnage wrote to his parents, 'your boy has done his duty let that be your consolation; long will he live in the memory of his friends and deeply is he lamented – thanks be to the Immortal Wellington, thanks to the ever lamented Guardsman & his brave companions, the chains, the spell, that forged the Infernal Tyrant's power is by their means, for ever broken.'

It was a belief that only private loss can ever validate, and yet when almost everyone was touched at some remove or other, everyone claimed the right to speak. This did not curtail any of the more exuberant public celebrations of course – the church bells, the illuminations, the guns at the Tower, the great bonfire at Calne that Coleridge attended, the 'gotho-barbaric rejoicings' that penetrated even Beckford's extraordinary Fonthill retreat, the Victory ribbons – but even the most die-hard of Tory converts, Robert Southey, seemed almost awed by the sheer magnitude of events. 'Our bells are ringing as they ought to do,' he wrote from Keswick on the 24th, where the Victory Mail had just brought the first tidings of the battle, 'and I, after a burst of exhilaration at the day's news, am in a state of serious and thoughtful thankfulness for what, perhaps, ought to be considered as the greatest deliverance that civilised society has experienced since the defeat of the Moors by Charles Martel.'

Along with this sense of thankfulness was the undeniable fact of national achievement, too, and that, in tandem with the human cost, placed all those who had opposed the war in a difficult position. On the same day that the news of Waterloo reached London, the future prime minister Charles Grey was telling anyone who listened how much the world needed the genius of a Napoleon, but even a confirmed Bonapartist like Lord Holland, whose Holland House was the political and literary centre of Whig England, knew that if victory for the allies was the death of every liberal hope for Europe, defeat would have meant another twenty years of war.

It would not put a stop to the private hostility of William Godwin, to the graceless carping of old Samuel Parr or the drunken stupefaction of Hazlitt and the theatricals of Byron, but while the authentic voice of radicalism would make itself heard soon enough, the world on both sides of the Channel for the moment belonged to the victors.[2] For a politician like Lord Grey – Sir William Ponsonby's brother-in-law – there were double reasons for holding his peace, but the opposition silence in Parliament was the silence of a defeated party only too conscious of its own irrelevancy. In the privacy of letters they might wonder how the march on Paris squared with the government's protestations that the war had nothing to do with restoring the Bourbons, but on the floor of the House the men who had once hounded Wellington over Cintra and carped at every stage of his Peninsular campaign could now only vote him their thanks and add another 200,000 – *nem. diss.*

– to 'the former liberal grants by which its sense of his extraordinary merits had been demonstrated'.

It was never going to be more than a pause in hostilities, though – no more than an undeclared and resented truce – and by the middle of the summer the world was already finding its post-Waterloo equilibrium. From the first day after the battle the field had become a tourist site for anyone prepared to brave the horrors, and while a broken-hearted Lord Carlisle watched Frederick Howard's body being exhumed and Sir James Craufurd stood over his dead son among the charred ruins of Hougoumont, the first waves of pilgrim-tourists – Croker, Walter Scott, Robert Peel – were already streaming across to Flanders to haggle over their souvenir swords and helmets or visit the shrine raised above the buried leg of Uxbridge.

Waterloo was moving from the present into the past, and it is tempting to put a symbolic date to the transition, because on the day that Magdalene De Lancey quitted Brussels for England, Lady Caroline Lamb arrived in the city to look after her brother Frederick Ponsonby. 'I enclose you my drawing and Miss Webster will send you my MSS,' she had written in a hurried scrawl to John Murray before she and her much-tried husband, the future prime minister Lord Melbourne sailed, her attention characteristically wandering between her brother's health and the fictional world of her novel. 'It is in a dreadful state as I had only time to correct the 3rd vol [of *Glenarvon*] which you read all the rest is merely copied from my Brouillon & terrible – I scarce can think but write constantly there as I will to you – direct it to the post office God bless you and all who have been so good & kind – I hope my journey may not be in vain – William's kindness in going with me surpasses everything I ever heard of.'

There was no more than a hope that the seven-times wounded Ponsonby would survive – it seemed a miracle that he had lasted that first night – and whether the same infinite, good-natured patience that had got him through that ordeal could be proof against his sister's arrival was a moot point. 'Lady Caroline Lamb is arrived to nurse her brother Col. Ponsonby, who is doing very well,' Georgiana Lennox wrote home to Lady Bathurst in London on 3 July, happy to spread her disfavours impartially around, 'but she will hurt him I fear. The Surgeon tells her the best thing she can do would be to hold her tongue, in answer to her wishing to know if she had not better read to him all day.'

Caroline Lamb could not have held her tongue to save her own life, let alone her brother's, and it was probably just as well for him that the old dangerous restlessness that ran through her generous and contradictory nature was still alive and well. She probably loved her brother Fred as disinterestedly as she ever loved anyone, but with the duke and the army gone and the social and political world following them towards Paris, the giant sickroom that Brussels had become had lost its charm without losing any of the grim reminders of what had happened there. 'The great amusement at Bruxelles,' she told her hated mother-in-law, Lady Melbourne, one of the unmistakable targets of the *roman à clef* she had just delivered to Murray: 'Indeed the only one except visiting the sick is to make large parties to go to the field of Battle – & pick up a skull or a grape shot or an old shoe and a letter to bring home … there is a great affectation here of making lint & bandages – but where is there not some? & at least it is an innocent amusement … it is rather heart-breaking to be here – however – one goes blubbering about – seeing such fine people without their legs & arms – some in agony – & some getting better. Lady Congham is here … Lady D-Hamilton … Lady F Webster most affected – and Lady Mountmorris who stuck her parasol into a skull at Waterloo.'

The world was moving on – the smouldering burial pits, the protruding skeletal hands that Charlotte Waldie and her sister had visited in the middle of July were now a picnic ground, the skulls subject for jokes at old Lady Mountmorris's expense – and the same process was happening in Britain. 'June 22,' recorded George Ticknor, 'I dined with Murray, and had a genuine bookseller dinner, such as

Lintot used to give to Pope and Gay and Swift ... Those present were two Mr Duncans ... Disraeli ... Gifford and Campbell. The conversation of such a party could not be long confined to politics, even on the day when they received full news of the Duke of Wellington's successes; and after they had drunk his health and Blücher's, they turned to literary topics as by instinct, and from seven o'clock until twelve the conversation never failed or faltered.'

In London the ambitious Mrs Boehme was still blaming Major Percy and his wretched eagles for ruining her ball. In Edinburgh, where the young Elizabeth Grant was recovering from a broken engagement, Hussar jackets were all the rage. In Crieff, Highlanders' bonnets – the same bonnets that Magdalene De Lancey had watched disappear out of the Namur gate on the night of the Duchess of Richmond's ball – were sold out. War was becoming a fashion. But as the tourists flocked across the sea to scavenge among the bones of the battlefield, and Lady Bessborough brought home her son, Fred Ponsonby – one arm useless, an unhealed wound 'through his body, but otherwise healthy and well' as his mother cavalierly reported – events on both sides of the Channel were already facing a reluctant Britain with two inescapable questions: against whom – and for what – had she fought Waterloo?

New Battle Lines

When the news of Bonaparte's escape from Elba first reached Vienna back in March, the allies had planned a concerted campaign in which its various armies would converge on Paris in overwhelming numbers from the north and east to crush French resistance. The pre-emptive strike launched by Bonaparte into Belgium on 15 June had changed the whole configuration of the war, but as Wellington counted the cost of his own victory there were still allied armies marching towards France and still loyal Bonapartist forces in the south and east ready to resist and stretch out the fighting deep into July.

Even for Wellington the campaign as opposed to the battle did not end with Waterloo and 18 June – the Prussian and allied armies had to march in parallel through France, uncertain of what lay ahead, unsure of the temper of the people, in the dark as to where Bonaparte was – and at Cambrai the British met their first show of resistance. 'We had collected what ladders and ropes we could find in the farm houses,' William Wheeler, as irrepressibly jaunty as ever, wrote home on the 25th, 'then we began splicing to enable us to scale the wall if necessary. A flag of truce was sent to the Town but they were fired at, which caused them to return, and a ball had passed through the Trumpeter's cap. We were now ready for storming and were only waiting the order to advance.'

For soldiers who had fought their way up through Spain, Cambrai was routine stuff, and under cover of their field pieces they pushed their trench works close up to the walls and fixed their scaling ladders in place. A more resolute garrison might still have a bloody day of it, but with the regular troops fleeing to the citadel and 'the shopkeepers to their shops', wall, gate and town were soon in British hands. We 'let in the remainder of the brigade, formed and advanced in the great square. We were as was usual, received by the people with vivas, many of whom had forgot to wash the powder off their lips caused by biting off the cartridges when they were firing at us from the wall.'

There had not been much in the way of fighting – the worst incident came that night, when six of the battalion 'fell in with a barrel of gunpowder', blowing themselves up when a corporal, already so drunk that he thought it was a brandy cask, fired into it to make a bung hole – but Cambrai offered an interesting preview of the peculiar problems that peace would land at Wellington's feet. On the day after the siege the army had halted while Louis XVIII – 'His pottle belly Majesty ... the Sir John Falstaff of France' – had arrived to forgive and forget the errant affections of his 'beloved subjects', and a sardonic soldiery stood by while Bonapartists turned royalist to receive 'their father and their king with tears of joy', and old Louis le Désiré 'blubbered over them like a big girl ... called them his children, told them a long rigmarole of nonsense about France, and his family, and his heart, and about their hearts, how he had always remembered them in his prayers, and I don't know what'. What the papers will not mention, Wheeler told his family, was that the 4th Division and a brigade of Hanoverian Huzzars were 'in readiness within half a mile of this faithful city, and if the loyal citizens had insulted their king we should have bayoneted every Frenchman in the place. The people well knew this, and this will account for the sudden change in their loyalty ... from their *Idol Napoleon* (properly named) *the Great*, to an old bloated poltroon.'

It was crucial at this stage that the duke had Louis under his wing, because whatever the common soldier might think of him, Wheeler's fat, blubbering 'Old Bungy' and a moderate French government represented Wellington's best hope of peace. It was still not clear whether Paris would fight or surrender to the allies, but as the British continued their advance down through northern France, Wellington insisted on paying for everything his army needed, determined to do all he could to avoid bloodshed or inflame resentment against his client king.

On their flank, however, it had been a very different story and when the provisional government in Paris surrendered without a battle, Blücher's Prussians entered the city not just as conquerors but avengers. In a letter from Brussels to his brother-in-law in London, George Stonestreet had cheerfully reported Blücher's hopes of a Parisian Rape of the Sabines, and short of wholesale rapine Blücher was ready to make good his threat, ransacking the city for the art treasures plundered over twenty years of French conquest, threatening to blow the bridge named after Bonaparte's victory over the Prussians at Jena, and treating Paris and Parisians with a brutal, Hunnish contempt that – as he was not slow to point out – was no more than payback for the humiliations and ravages France had inflicted on German lands. 'They' – the French government – the Paris-born Duke of Devonshire wrote to Miss Mary Berry on 2 August, 'think everything going as ill as possible for the king & for France; they are incensed with the Prussians who extort immense sums of money & when the Prefets refuse fill their houses with soldiers – they have seized upon the models of the frontier towns & indeed the whole collection at the Invalides, and they are packed up and some gone to Berlin … At the Louvre they have taken about thirty pictures, some by Rubens … & more are coming down every day – having begun there is no knowing where they are to stop.'

It was a very different Paris and a very different occupation from that of the year before, but with Lady Caroline Lamb following the army down for one last exhibitionist fling, and Sergeant Lawrence of the 40th wooing a young woman who had a market stall near their encampment, and Louis le Désiré turning into Louis l'Inevitable, the city did its best to rekindle the mood of 1814. 'The most ridiculous and most characteristic thing is a ballet at the opera and the excessive applause it has,' Devonshire told Mary Berry[1]; 'the story is the Battle of Waterloo, the scene Paris, the Imperial guards beaten come back and inform the national guards of their disaster, a young lady hears her lover is killed, but an English officer arrives with him having saved his life, upon which *tout danse apropos de tout*, white lilies and plenty of Scotchmen are introduced which puts the audience into raptures.'

If there was anything needed to confirm Britain's and Wellington's prestige in France, to add to the lustre of the Waterloo laurels that had been so successfully filched from under Prussian noses, it came in the middle of July with the news that Bonaparte had surrendered to a British man o' war off Rochefort. He had finally left Paris just days ahead of Louis XVIII and the allied cavalry, and moving only with his immediate entourage had travelled incognito down to the coast, hoping to beat the British blockade and a Prussian rope and escape by frigate to America.

It had taken him just four days to reach Rochefort, but it was not long before word of his presence there was leaked, and with contrary winds and Captain Maitland's blockading squadron waiting off the coast, surrender was only a matter of time. He had hoped at first that he would be able to negotiate terms for his exile but Maitland was having none of it, and on 15 July the Emperor threw himself on the mercy of 'the most powerful, the most constant, and the most generous of his enemies', as he wrote to the Prince Regent, and gave himself up to Captain Maitland and the *Bellerophon*.

It was the end of an age – not with a bang but a whimper, not on the battlefield but in the cabin of the old *Billy Ruffian* – and for all the relief that the Tiger was finally caged, his old capital still remained on a knife edge. Through the summer months, allied troops continued to pour into France to batten on the French exchequer, and with the arrest and execution of Marshal Ney and the launch of the 'White Terror' against the surviving rump of loyal Bonapartists, the pre-Waterloo Paris of 1814 and the exemplary Treaty of Paris that had ended the war might have belonged to a different era.

Even the duke's immense prestige took a knocking – when British engineers dismantled the four bronze horses of St Mark's from their triumphal arch he was booed at the theatre – but the change of mood was inevitable. After the Hundred Days and fresh hecatombs of dead at Ligny, Quatre Bras and Waterloo the largesse of 1814 was never going to be repeated, and between a deep Prussian resentment that Prussia had not got its full dues then and a suspicion that they were going to be shafted again, the situation was ripe for a settlement that would undo all the good of the first generous treaty.

There were serious, and potentially combustible, political differences between the allies which went well beyond the question of art works, but for liberal Britain watching from home the shameful thing was that the differences were not as great as they ought to have been. In all the negotiations over France's future, Castlereagh's and Wellington's would certainly be the voices of moderation against wild Prussian talk of dismemberment and extinction, but for all the arguing over the size of reparations and length of occupation or the number of French fortresses to be destroyed or the scale and detail of border changes, peace would reveal that parliamentary Britain and her autocratic allies had fought the Battle of Waterloo for much the same reasons.

From the moment that the Congress of Vienna declared Bonaparte an outlaw the powers had always insisted that the war was against an individual and not a country and that now left them with a problem. On the day of Waterloo, Louis XVIII had been a brother sovereign in exile and France an ally by secret treaty of both Britain and Austria, and if that was the case – as that wily old negotiator and survivor of ancien régime, Revolution, Terror, Empire and Restoration, Charles-Maurice de Talleyrand-Périgord, Prince de Bénévent and erstwhile bishop demanded – what right had they now to punish an ally and effectively doom a legitimate king who was equally the victim of Napoleonic ambition?

There was an unanswerable logic to the objection, and both Wellington and Castlereagh, a decent, talented and honourable man, clearly recognised the political folly of associating the restored monarchy with national humiliation, but all it did was expose the claim that it was only Bonaparte they had fought for the sham it was. A year earlier the allies had been happy enough to reward Bonaparte's fifteen years of aggression and conquest with the island of Elba, but in 1815, France had welcomed Hazlitt's 'child and champion of the revolution' – Victor Hugo's 'Robespierre on horseback' – with open arms, and the French people, the same incorrigible nation that had carried the ideas of the Revolution across Europe and smashed up the old legitimist world – were going to be made to pay.

The real enemy was, and always had been, those forces unleashed in 1789, the real danger, as Austria's Count Metternich recognised, not conquerors – they come and go – but ideas, and if there was any doubt about that the next few years would brutally dispel them. It is often claimed that the Congress of Vienna represented a major step forward in the development of international relations, and yet for all its talk of slavery or the Jews or the theory of 'consent', or rules of navigation, or even peace, the truth is that the ambition and imagination of the Congress and its various diplomatic offspring never soared higher than the preservation of the existing order and the crushing – wherever they saw it, whether in Spain or Poland or Naples or Greece – of any popular movement or constitutional change tainted by liberalism and the ideas of 1789.

The only true legitimacy that emerged from the Congress was the legitimacy of power – the right of the 'director' states to dispose of peoples as if, as Hazlitt protested, they were merely cattle, to police Europe and their own populations as they saw fit, to interfere in the internal arrangements of a sovereign country, to suppress change whenever it came from below – and if Britain rapidly found itself at odds with its partners, it has its share of responsibility for the direction post-war Europe took. As early as 1820, Castlereagh would be protesting against Russian and Austrian plans for military intervention in Spain, but a government that had insisted on creating a buffer state out of Protestant Holland and Catholic Belgium, that had vacillated feebly over the question of Saxony and Poland and would condemn the outbreak of the Greek war of independence against Ottoman oppression, was in no position to take the high moral ground when the system of international policing it had done so much to forge became the tool of European reaction.

For the plain John Bull Englishman, events in Spain or Poland might scarcely so much as register – 'Damn all foreign countries,' one working man would famously tell Gladstone; 'what has old England to do with foreign countries?' – but he would have been wise to have paid more attention. It is a sobering thought, in fact, that public opinion in 1815 was on the side of the Prussians rather than Castlereagh or Wellington in its lust for revenge, but it would not be long before the country discovered that what was good enough for Europe was good enough for Lord Liverpool's Britain and that the same principles that dictated the government's foreign policy could just as easily be turned against its own people.

Britain might have fought the war against Napoleonic hegemony for the same strategic reasons it had historically fought its European wars, but like its allies it would fight the peace against the ideas that had brought Bonaparte to power. During the war there might have been some excuse for the repressive measures that Pitt and his successors took, but fear and necessity had become so much a matter of habit with those in power that the Britain that would finally emerge out of the political mini-ice age of these post-war years would not do so without leaving a long casualty list behind it.

If the worst still lay ahead in 1815 – the years of massive unemployment and vagrancy, of economic depression from which Altrincham's mills would be no more immune than the kelp beds of Harris, of wretched harvests and emigration, of mass political rallies and political oppression – the government wasted no time in putting down its marker. Over the next five years the Peterloo Massacre and the Cato Street Conspiracy to murder Lord Liverpool and his government would relegate it to nothing more than a footnote in legal and radical history, but for two months during the summer of 1815 the condemned cell in a Newgate gaol of a young servant girl was the battleground for the first trial of strength in the war between the forces of reaction and reform.

It is difficult to put one's finger on the moment Eliza Fenning became a 'cause' or precisely how or why it happened – she had, after all, no connections or influence, the poisoning itself was a one-week wonder – and if it certainly had something to do with the fact that she was young and pretty that was only part of it. In the history of the nineteenth century, gallows writers from Dickens to Hardy would offer their queasy testimony to the erotic appeal of its female victims, but the men who championed Eliza Fenning – men like the curmudgeonly Samuel Parr, the great reformer Samuel Romilly, the Hunt brothers, and radical journalist William Hone, the Benthamite child of murder Basil Montagu, and a score of dissenting ministers, chemists and lawyers – did not do so because they had seen her but out of a deep and worried sense that something was rotten in the state of Denmark.

At the heart of this concern was an instinct for justice and fairness that twenty years of oppressive wartime government had not stifled. In the weeks before and immediately after Waterloo the government could afford to ignore any opposition, but in Eliza Fenning all those forces of reform and change that were impotent to effect Britain's foreign policy – all those elements in national life, that, as the Whig lawyer Cockburn said, had 'swallowed' the abuses of power in the interests of some wider patriotism – had found the cause they needed.

It is just possible that had she not become a cause célèbre of London radicalism, her appeal might yet have turned out differently, but in a world not tolerant of dissent she was too dangerous to ignore. The official papers of her case disappeared sometime in the nineteenth century, but the government-paid newspapers from this summer survive, and in the shameful campaign that turned a Sunday school-trained Methodist into a lewd, crypto-Catholic, serial poisoner who could not, even in her death cell, keep her thoughts off the child-rapist Oldfield, it is easy enough to see how the appeal might have gone.

It is clear from her behaviour that she still clung on to the irrational hope of a repeal, but there was something woefully forlorn about hopes grounded in a system that allowed the same 'Black Jack' Silvester who was now warning the Turners against signing a petition on her behalf to take her case for clemency to the Prince Regent. 'Pray come soon,' a distraught Eliza Fenning wrote on 19 July to her parents, more than three months after sentencing, when the confirmation of sentence was at last sent down. 'The report is come for me to be executed on Wednesday next.'

'Dear Parents,' she wrote again on the 22nd, her language characteristically veering between conventional religiosity and a bitterness that in her is always more convincing than the pieties, 'I do solemnly declare, were I never to enter the heavenly mansion of heavenly rest, I am murdered! … I will be happy in heaven, with my dear sisters and brothers, and will meet you by and by … those who swore my life will never enter with me into rest.'

With the confirmation of her sentence and a date of execution – 26 July – the rhythm and scope of Eliza Fenning's life took on their final ghastly shape. From the moment she had been committed to Newgate her existence had been a series of little 'deaths', with each phase of the judicial process marked by a further isolation, an ever deeper burial within the massive walls and troglodyte passageways of the gaol, and now she had reached the bottom.

It was a strange twilight place, the world of the condemned felon, cut off by that vast gulf that separated Newgate's living from its walking dead, and yet at the same time she was now more than ever public property. In the weeks since the trial there had been 'unprecedented' interest in her case, and as the Newgate bell tolled ten on the morning of her last Sunday 'an immense concourse' was already waiting in the prison chapel to enjoy a spectacle that in Georgian London's theatre of the grotesque ranked only second to the gallows. 'The congregation having arranged themselves in a decorous manner,' the *Morning Advertiser* reported the grim ritual – the condemned sermon, the open coffin – that preceded every execution, 'the prisoners under sentence of death, to the number of twenty-one, were brought in by their respective gaolers and turnkeys, and placed on the left of the pulpit. Every eye now fixed upon the black pew in the centre of the chapel, the place set apart for those doomed to undergo the awful sentence of the law: silence pervaded every quarter – it was soon broken by the sighs of the auditory at seeing the unfortunate young girl, Elizabeth Fenning, enter the chapel, attended by those other unhappy victims in floods of tears.'

During these last days in prison a lay preacher had been ministering to Eliza, but the Reverend Horace Cotton had no intention now of ducking his hour in the limelight. Her crime had been one of revenge, he told the congregation, and Satan, having persuaded her 'that revenge was sweet, that he would protect her', – 'Here the unfortunate girl again fainted, and did not recover for a long time' – abandoned her to her fate and 'the penetrating eye of Providence' that 'discovered every secret act of man'.

It is hard to know which is more baleful – the spiritual smugness, the psychological stupidity or the abject surrender to injustice of all those, Anglican or Dissenters, who fought for the soul of Eliza Fenning during these last days – but perhaps they simply knew that the next world was the only one to which she now belonged. Outside the walls of Newgate desperate efforts were still being made to gain at least a stay of sentence, but while the ever-present Lord Ellenborough felt under enough pressure from the press and private representations to hold two last-minute reviews, the Recorder remained as implacable as ever. Corby Lloyd, the Quaker banker, was told by Silvester that he was only interested in Fenning 'because she was pretty'. New evidence would not make a bit of difference. 'He felt so perfectly satisfied of her guilt, (there never being a clearer case),' he continued, 'that he knew no possible reason for delaying the execution.'

Even after this there was time for one more review of the trial and Newgate itself seemed to hold its breath. On the night before an execution even the 'scum of society' were not immune to the horror of morning, but while it was a 'disturbed' night through the prison within the condemned cell, Eliza Fenning seems to have already given up. She had signed her 'Selection of Psalms and Hymns' and sent it to the congregation of the Percy Chapel, Charlotte Street, and on the Tuesday taken a 'heart-rending' farewell from her mother and thrown a last letter to her old cellmate Mary Ann Clark through the window bars. 'Dearest Friend,' she wrote, 'don't grieve, dear girl, my time is but short in this troublesome world, and I soon shall be in eternal rest ... God bless you! And may God send you liberty soon. Here is a lock of hair for you, and another for Young.'

Her courage, inevitably, ebbed and flowed. The next morning – her last – her new spiritual advisor, a Mr Wansbrough, was with her by six, and found her seated on a bench under the eye of a woman keeper, 'elbow leaning on the table next to her ... her head resting on her hands', and 'so dejected that she could not speak'. 'I read to her some parts of Job, that I considered applicable,' he wrote. 'A little before seven o'clock she said that she was bewildered, and that it all appeared like a dream to her. I prayed that God would be pleased to remove her doubts, and confirm her faith, for the tempter was now very busy with her.'

What the tempter put in her head, he does not say, but if it was rage against an unjust fate it perhaps buttressed her courage in ways that Job could not. In a strange way, too, that is recognisable from the annals of the *Newgate Calendar*, the very theatricality of it all seems to have given her a new strength. From the first day she had been committed for trial she had visualised this moment and she was not now going to fail. 'Pray tell my dear parents not to put a bit of black about me,' she had written the night before, the familiar symbolism of the gallows and a young woman's self-consciousness melding strangely together, 'as it will be a token of innocence. A very few leave this world a pure virgin, and when led to the gallows, I shall be led as a shepherd leadeth a lamb to the slaughter, or as a bride to her Heavenly Bridegroom.'

On this last morning she was just as fastidious with her dress, vanity and seriousness touchingly at one. When she knelt on her cell floor in prayer, she took off her gown first so she would not get it dirty. Something about her, too, had eventually penetrated the defence mechanisms of the Reverend Cotton. He came to her cell in one final attempt to get her to confess but, at the last, clergyman and prison apparatchik lost out to the human being. She could have any visitors she wanted, he told her kindly. He also brought with him a smelling bottle, and sent for wine and water to help bolster her nerve.

Sometime after seven she was moved to her final cell, and there at half-past the hour her spiritual advisor joined her. She raised her hands in a gesture of prayer, but could say nothing. 'I cannot speak, sir,' she told him, 'but I pray from my heart.' As they went down on their knees together for the last time – her face 'tranquil', 'the workings of the spirit complete' – there was a knock on the door, and with a staggering step she was led out into the press yard to be prepared for the scaffold.

She was not to hang alone and Oldfield was already there and – the invisible ghost at the feast, unmentioned and unmentionable in almost every account of Eliza Fenning's end – the fifty-seven-year-old sodomite, Abraham Adams. The halter was tied around her and her arms bound. Then the 'cavalcade' of prisoners, warders, sheriffs, chaplain, officers and the rest, 'began to move in solemn and awful procession through the dark passage, with silent and mournful pace; the walls reverberating the words upon the ear, "I am the resurrection and the life, saith the Lord".

Waiting for her outside the Debtor's Gate was a vast crowd, the biggest since the executions of the murderers John Holloway and Owen Haggerty had drawn 45,000 spectators and resulted in more than forty spectators being crushed to death eight years before. Before them they saw a young woman of twenty-two, dressed in a white worked muslin gown, a white worked muslin cap with a white satin ribbon, a white ribbon around her waist, and pale, lilac boots, laced at the front. She was the first to mount the scaffold. 'Before the just and almighty God, and by the faith of the Holy Sacrament I have taken, I am innocent of the offence on which I am charged,' she declared firmly, before obscurely adding in a low voice, 'I hope that God will forgive me, and make manifest the transaction in the course of the day.'

Oldfield, who had asked to be placed next to her on the scaffold – almost certainly to spare unspotted innocence the contagion of Adams's proximity – was less restrained. "'O what a blessed state of immortality awaits all such who die in Christ Jesus!" he cried out mightily unto God ... "O, Oldfield! You are going to heaven." They were almost the last words Eliza Fenning heard. She pleaded with the hangman to spare her the dirty handkerchief over her eyes and asked Cotton to warn her before the platform fell. As in life, though, so in death. 'My dear, it must be done,' Cotton told her as her face was covered and, a few moments later, without warning, the platform crashed and Eliza Fenning dropped to her death. 'Thus perished, by the hands of the executioner, a female twenty-one [sic] years of age,' wrote her spiritual advisor, 'in the prime of her youth, who seemed qualified by nature to fill a superior station in life. Her mind was the most extraordinary I ever knew, possessing great shrewdness, and a quickness of perception which many persons nominate archness. Her temper was warm, her feelings susceptibly alive to everything around her, I have every reason to believe that she died in the faith of Christ Jesus, and is now a bright angel in heaven.'

It is not easy to be sure where to place Eliza Fenning's trial and death, as the defiant swansong of an old brutal world or the first skirmish of post-Waterloo politics. In the figure of Sir John Silvester – a defence lawyer at the trial of Martha Ray's murderer – you can almost smell the concupiscence and corruption of a vanishing age, but in the array of opposition that ranked themselves against Silvester, Sidmouth and Ellenborough and took on the Tory press were those same names that over the next fifteen years would press and fight for change and reform of everything from asylums and the poor law to Catholic emancipation, religious toleration, slavery and Parliament itself.

They had already fired one warning shot across government bows – in an improbable alliance of radicalism and evangelical morality, Lord Cochrane had left the King's Bench to join forces with Wilberforce and defeat by a single vote the motion to increase the Duke of Cumberland's marriage allowance – but Eliza Fenning was their first real show of force.

The authorities were not ready to rest with her death, though, and if it seemed ludicrous to Leigh Hunt that *The Times* could pause from celebrating the slaughter of 'Hecatombs of Frenchmen' to hound the memory of a mere servant girl, Liverpool's government had never been slow to break a butterfly upon a wheel. In the immediate hours after her execution a Newgate turnkey was suborned into signing an affidavit fixing Eliza Fenning's guilt, and over the next week this was printed in government-backed papers and turned into handbills, 'thrown into houses, dropped upon shop counters, exhibited in windows and circulated widely' in an extraordinary London-wide attempt to blacken her name.

This was one battle, though, they were not going to win, and to the heavenly crown that Wansbrough had prophesied for Eliza, her supporters were determined to add immortality of a very different kind. In the immediate aftermath of her death her wretched parents had managed to borrow the 14/6 to recover her body from Newgate's dead house, and from the moment that the authorities lost control of her body they lost control of her reputation, gifting radical England and London's poor a victim of burgeoning mythological status that no smear campaign could contain. 'My aching heart with pity bled,' began one execution ballad,

> When poor Eliza! Cloth'd in white;
> At Newgate dropp'd her lovely head,
> And clos'd her eyes in endless night.
> ...
> Poor hopeless maid! For poison try'd!
> Which caus'd her sad untimely death,
> She vow'd that innocent she died,
> And seal'd it with her parting breath.

This might be no more than the standard, ephemeral stuff of popular Georgian culture – the Last Words, the Confession, the Execution Ballad – but the authorities would have made a bad mistake if they had underestimated its power over the poor, the sad and dispossessed of London to whom Eliza Fenning now belonged. 'SUICIDE,' the *Morning Chronicle* reported on 15 August, almost three weeks after Fenning's death. 'Friday an Inquest was held at the Clayton Arms, Kennington ... on the body of Mary Bailey', a young servant girl of twenty-two – Eliza's age – who was found kneeling by her bed in an attitude of prayer, 'her throat cut in shocking manner with a large carving knife', only minutes after she was seen listening to a 'ballad singer, singing one of those doleful ditties on the death of Eliza Fenning', and sighing to herself 'ah, poor Eliza ...'.

It was not just the poor, the lonely and the insane who identified with her fate, however, but that cohesive, respectable chapel-going community to which she had belonged. Her parents had taken her body from Newgate back to their house by Red Lion Square, and while constables tried to prevent visitors making the pilgrimage up the one flight of stairs to the back room where she lay 'in state', they could not stop the Fennings' world turning her funeral into a defiant protest against injustice, with an immense crowd 10,000 strong – shadowed the whole way by peace officers – following the body and 'six young females, attired in white' supporting the pall. 'Not the slightest accident, however, occurred,' reported the pro-Tory *Times*, 'and the procession of mourners, &c, returned in the same order it came by the Foundling, Lamb's-conduit-street, &c. The vigilance of the officers, in preserving order, was highly meritorious.'

The authorities might have preferred it, in fact, if it had not all been so orderly – there was nothing a government liked more than an opportunity to play the mob card to frighten the decent, respectable, nervous, patriotic servant-owning class back into line – but even so the Fenning case had sounded a note that they knew to fear. Like every government going back to Pitt's in the 1790s, Lord Liverpool's Cabinet saw every protest as part of a wider conspiracy, and in Eliza Fenning they found the sum of all their fears: not just a woman whose foul crime held a particular horror for the nineteenth century, or a servant whose betrayal undermined the whole class system, but a cause that had brought out of the woodwork all those dissident, radical, reforming elements that over the next seventeen years would remorselessly chip away at the foundations of the most perfect constitution imaginable to man.

The battle lines had been drawn. Lord Liverpool's government had not fought and won the war to lose the peace, but neither had the men who stood by Eliza Fenning sacrificed so much over twenty years to lie quietly down now. Within months the hapless Samuel Halliday and

John Binstead would die on the same Newgate gallows, victims of a system devoted to the preservation of property and the status quo. Within four years habeas corpus would be suspended and the notorious Peterloo Massacre – not simply a bad word-play – remind even John Bull that when whole populations could be bartered across the continent and crofting communities brutally driven from their Scottish homes, Peterloo and Waterloo were two sides of the same coin. As an indignant Benjamin Haydon – outraged that a government could turn on the same loyal, brave, steadfast British people who had paid their taxes, fought their battles, and beaten Bonaparte – wrote in his diary, Lord Castlereagh and his ilk had spent too much time with their autocratic Russian and Austrian allies. He had a point. There was little that Lord Liverpool's government, with its spy networks and *agents provocateurs*, its campaigns of vilification and penchant for legalised violence could have learned from Metternich's police. For all that, though, a watershed had been reached. The Tory press, quoting Lord Ellenborough's old mentor, the 'Protestant Jesuit' William Paley, might confidently tell Eliza Fenning's friends that if she were innocent they should console themselves that she had 'died for her country' in the higher cause of the Law. 'The Law', though – Ellenborough's law, Silvester's law, Sidmouth's law – was not going to have it its own way. And at least one of its victims would not be forgotten. By the mid-1840s Eliza Fenning would have been with her siblings in the St George the Martyr burial ground for thirty years, but chemists would still be carrying out laboratory experiments to prove her innocence, and men who had never seen her die would still be writing rhapsodically of the 'beauteous innocent creature', as spotless in her dress 'as her own purity', whose soul had been 'caught up by attending angels and carried to the heaven of eternal bliss'.

Myth Triumphant

'I'll weave a gay garland with Laurels entwining,
Round Roses and Thistles and Shamrocks combining,
I'll weave a gay garland with Olives entwining
To crown our famed Heroes who fought Waterloo …'

To the tune of 'Garland of Love'

'Waterloo, in its ultimate significance, is the considered triumph
of counter-revolution. It is Europe versus France, St Petersburg,
Berlin, and Vienna versus Paris, the status quo versus the new
order … the move to action-stations of monarchy against the
indomitable upheaval of the French people. To subdue that great
people which had been in a state of eruption for twenty-six
years, such was the aim, an affirmation of solidarity between the
Houses of Brunswick, Nassau, Romanoff, Hohenzollern, and
Hapsburg, and the House of Bourbon. Waterloo was the
assertion of the Divine Right of Kings.'

Victor Hugo, *Les Misérables*

'Have not the efforts of the British Nation been gigantic?'
Benjamin Haydon had asked himself five days after Waterloo.
'Think of her Naval Victories – St Jean, St Vincent, Nile, Copenhagen,
Trafalgar, then of Vimeiro, Talavera, Fuentes d'Honoro, Salamanca,

Vittoria, Orthes, Pyrenees. Think of her treasure in coalescing Europe, & now again this battle … Think of her Glories in India, and her subduing all the Colonies of the World. To such Glories she wants but the glories of my noble Art to make her the grandest Nation in the World, and this she shall have if God spare my life. Grant it, Amen.'

By the time that those words were first published in 1853, Haydon and all his hopes had been dead seven years, having cut his throat and shot himself during the murderously hot summer of 1846. There was probably nobody who had felt or captured the excitement of the Hundred Days like Haydon had done, and it is just one more sad irony to pile on those other ironies of his life that the one artist in England whose self-esteem and dedication to History Painting were a match for the new spirit of national pride in the air, was the man without the technique or the painterly imagination to realise his vision.

'Poor Haydon!' Elizabeth Barrett wrote of him after his death, 'think what an agony life was to him, so constituted! – his own genius a clinging curse! the fire and the clay in him seething and quenching one another! – the man seeing maniacally in all men the assassins of his fame! And, with the whole world against him, struggling with the thing that was his life, through night and day, in thoughts and in dreams – struggling, stifling, breaking the hearts of the creatures dearest to him, in the conflict for which there was no victory … Tell me if Laocoon's anguish was not an infant's sleep compared to this?'

None of this had stopped him painting interminable, dreadful portraits of Napoleon in exile – twenty-five at his last count – or endless, equally terrible Wellingtons 'Brooding on the Field of Waterloo', but they had not been what he had wanted for his heroes. From his earliest days as an artist he had despised the 'namby-pamby' business of portrait-painting as unworthy of his genius, and if he was going to paint the great men of the age, he would have shown them as he had done his mighty Curtius, leaping his horse into the void, and not daubed on another jobbing St Helena canvas that he could knock off in two hours for £50.

It would not have made it any easier for Haydon, a man who saw assassins lurking in every room, that it was the great friend, rival and companion of his Paris adventures, David Wilkie, whose celebration of Waterloo had caught the public's imagination. In the summer of 1815, Wilkie had inadvertently upset his wealthy Tory patrons with his *Distraining for Rent*, but the 'Scots Teniers' was nothing if not canny, and when the next summer the Duke of Wellington approached him with a commission no one could have been more biddable. 'I should not perhaps have been disposed to break through the etiquette of writing you before you have written me from the country,' Wilkie wrote to Haydon in August 1816, a letter that is a genre picture in itself: 'had it not been that I have a piece of intelligence to give you of an event that is to me more gratifying than any honour or compliment I have yet had conferred on me. It is that of being waited on by His Grace the Duke of Wellington …' The previous day, he continued, Lord Lynedoch – Wellington's old Peninsula general, Sir Thomas Graham – had arrived to tell him that if Wilkie 'should be at home at four o'clock the Duke of Wellington and a party' would call on him. He had spent the rest of the day tidying his rooms and laying out his canvases for viewing, and – 'last, though not least' – having arranged it so that his mother and sister 'might see the great man through the parlour windows', set himself 'in a sort of breathless expectation' to wait for the hour to come.

The duke had arrived with the Duke and Duchess of Bedford, Lady Argyle and Lord Lynedoch, and at first Wilkie had been discomposed at his silence. It was left to Lady Argyle to explain that he wanted to commission a picture, and she had just begun to say what he had in mind, when the duke, who was 'looking at one of the pictures that happened to be on the ground', swung round on his chair, 'turned up his lively eye to me and said the subject should be a parcel of soldiers, assembled together on the seats at the door of a public house' in

Chelsea's King's road, 'chewing tobacco and talking over their old stories'.

Wilkie assured him that this would make a beautiful picture, 'and that it only wanted some story or principal incident to connect the figures together' and 'proposed that one might be reading a newspaper aloud to the rest'. The duke was immediately taken with the idea and as he and his party prepared to leave, made Wilkie a bow and asked when he should hear from him: 'To which I replied that my immediate engagements ... would prevent me being able to get it done for two years. "Very well," said he, "that will be soon enough for me." They then went downstairs ... and seeing some of my family at the parlour windows, he bowed to them also. As he got upon his horse he observed all the families and the servants were at the windows ... The sensation this event occasioned quite unhinged us for the rest of the day ... The chair he happened to sit upon has been carefully selected out, and has been decorated with ribbons, and there is talk of having an inscription upon it, descriptive of the honour it has received.'

It was just as well the duke was in no hurry for his painting, because it would be another six years before it finally appeared at the Royal Academy's annual exhibition in the summer of 1822. By that time the death of Joseph Farington in the previous year – killed falling down stairs in a church – had broken one of the last links with the original Academy, but nothing that Farington or anyone else had seen in its fifty-eight-year history could have rivalled the excitement or the crowds that turned up when David Wilkie's painting was hung in the place of honour above the fireplace in the Academy's main room.

The duke had every reason to be pleased with the reception – he had paid the highest figure ever paid for a painting, counting the £12,000 out for Wilkie in notes (he did not want his bank to know what a fool he had been, he admitted) – and whether or not he quite knew what he had done, he and Wilkie had touched a public nerve. With the original commission Wellington's idea had gone no farther than paying a tribute to the ordinary soldier, but between commission and exhibition a change had been made, and the notion of the 'newspaper' that Wilkie had tossed into the original conversation had germinated into a central icon that enshrined the whole raison d'être of his painting: '*Chelsea Pensioners*,' it was titled, '*Receiving the London Gazette Extraordinary of Thursday, June 22nd, 1815, Announcing the Battle of Waterloo*!!!'

The painting owes an unmistakable debt to Hogarth, and an even deeper one to the Dutch School of the seventeenth century, but in *Chelsea Pensioners*, Wilkie had done something new. The scene and the characters might belong to any genre painting but here genre and history meet, and the great events and the great heroes of the time – the proper subjects of Haydon's High Art – are located not on the field of battle but in an England of Pensioners and soldiers, of Hussar and Lifeguard, of kilted Highlander and black drummer boy, of the old and young, women, children and babies and – crucially, the great democratising instrument of change – in the pages of a newspaper.

Here in paint is the realisation of De Quincey's hymn to the mailcoach, his 'train of gunpowder ... kindling at every instant new successions of burning joy ... multiplying the victory itself ... multiplying into infinity the stages of its progressive diffusion', uniting the country in a single act of patriotic identification. In his earlier designs for the painting Wilkie had placed his reader to the left of the group seated at the table, but in the final version he is where he should be: at the heart of the scene, the pages of the *Gazette* in his hands picked out by a shaft of sunlight that divides it into dark and light in a kind of visual pun on the news of glory and death it carries.

No two men could be less like each other than the feverish De Quincey and the 'strange, tottering, feeble, pale' cartoon-Scot of Haydon's recollections, haggling over his prints and every last centime of change on their visit to France, and yet for both men war was the great unifying fact of national life. In his mind's eye, De Quincey saw his Victory coach passing through the great and ancient cities of the country that were identified with Britain's history, and in *Chelsea Pensioners*, Wilkie takes the trope a step further, with the deaf old man at the table and the baby held up in his father's arms linking Britain's past and future in a common heritage and a common national destiny.

It was a brilliant painterly conceit and one that for a few brief weeks in the summer of 1815, at least, reflected a profound truth about the way that Britain had reacted to the news of Waterloo. 'How can we be insensible to the distress of those, who to the very circumstances which have occasioned the public felicity, can trace their individual misfortunes?' pleaded the vicar of Kirdford, invoking a sense of common responsibility that went hand in hand with the 'nation' of Wilkie's vision: 'You, my Brethren, can rejoice; you can triumph; but do you not mark the poor mourner, who in the midst of these ebullitions of joy, sees all joy taken away from her for Ever! ... Do you not see her, straining her children to her bosom, and herself all in tears bidding them weep no more – for though their Father is dead, he died to save his country ... It is in our power to diffuse one ray of light into the Mansions of Sorrow ... By our generosity to the Children, we can at least show the ardour of affectionate gratitude with which we cherish the memory of their fathers.'

It was not just the churches either – even the 'Fancy' came up with their own charity fights at the Fives Court to raise money for the widows of Waterloo – but if Wilkie's painting was not a fiction, one reason that people were so desperate to embrace it in 1822 was that seven years of unrest had rendered its ideal of a unified Britain little more than a memory. In the aftermath of the battle a medal – the Waterloo Medal – had for the first time been awarded to every soldier who had taken part in the campaign battles, and yet if you had come across those same veterans seven years later, you would have been just as likely to spot the distinctive crimson and blue ribbon of the medal on the breast of an old Waterloo man-turned-rioter like William Constive as on the soldiers of the 33rd of Foot formed up in square round the scaffold of a harmless Scottish weaver hanged and beheaded for treason.[1]

In the years between Waterloo and Peterloo, in fact, the discipline and drilling of the professional soldier was evident in popular demonstrations from Glasgow to London, but the aura surrounding Waterloo and the 'Waterloo Man' was still real. It would not stop Highland soldiers returning to find their houses gone and landlords' promises forgotten, but what it meant was that when Britain did finally emerge from the political and economic miseries of these years – when the generation that had learned its irremovable horror of change from the excesses of Robespierre and the French Terror had faded from public life – when the politicians whose names had inextricably yoked Waterloo and Peterloo together in the popular imagination had gone to their graves – Ellenborough in 1818; Castlereagh, cutting his own throat, in 1822; Liverpool in 1828 – when Britain had uncoupled itself from its autocratic partners to deliver Greece and South America their freedom – Waterloo, in all its potency, was still there as a powerful, unifying symbol of national achievement and the great foundation myth of nineteenth-century British imperial identity.

It fed off and fed into other national myths, of course, myths that went back to the Henrician Reformation and beyond – myths about the apostolic foundation of her ancient, Erastian Church, about the uniqueness of her laws, the uniqueness of her national character and historic freedoms – but these were specifically English rather than British beliefs. For more than three hundred years these fantasies had provided generations of historians with their unexamined premises and generations of William Wheelers with their invincible sense of national superiority, and Waterloo was an extension of these to a wider Britain, a reconfiguration of ancient myths to meet the demands of a new imperial age and a new British destiny.

No one is likely to read contemporary and nineteenth-century British accounts of the battle and learn that it was Dutch initiative that secured the crossroads at Quatre Bras; no one is going to hear much of the courage with which the allies fought, or the overwhelming impact of the Prussians' arrival, or that British troops scarcely numbered more than one tenth of all the soldiers on the field; no one is going to hear, either, of the allied dead in Hougoumont and La Haye Sainte – or probably hear of Papelotte at all – but what one is going to hear, broadening and extending English myths of superiority to embrace a more inclusive sense of identity, is a hymn to Britain. That great mythologiser of Scottish identity, Walter Scott, had already celebrated the fundamental 'Britishness' of Wellington's Peninsular army, and his 'Field of Waterloo' was an evocation of the same ideal, a vision of ancient 'Albion', 'Erin' and 'Alba' – 'brethren in arms, rivals in renown' – united under one banner and under the common title of 'BRITON' – one indivisible 'Island Empress', 'one race of Adam's offspring' – one country – '*my* Country!' as Scott proudly claims it,

> Period of honour as of woes,
> What bright careers 'twas thine to close!
> Mark'd on the roll of blood what names
> To Briton's memory, and to Fame's
> Laid there their last immortal claims!
> Thou saw'st in seas of gore expire
> Redoubted PICTON'S soul of fire,
> Saw'st in the mingled carnage lie
> All that of PONSONBY could die,
> DE LANCEY change Love's bridal wreath –
> For laurels from the hand of Death
> Saw'st gallant MILLER'S failing eye
> Still bent where Albion's banners lie,
> And CAMERON in the shock of steel,
> Die like the offspring of Lochiel;
> And generous GORDON 'mid the strife

Fall while he watch'd his leader's life –
Ah! Though her guardian angel's shield
Fenced Britain's hero through the field,
Fate not less her power made known,
Through his friends' hearts to pierce his own!'

It was a difficult balancing act that Scottish patriots had to perform, because for all the pride and the deep, Romantic consciousness of 'Scottishness' in the way writers such as Scott, Charlotte Waldie or Joanna Baillie responded to the battle, it was a consciousness that came with one eye firmly fixed on the other side of the border. There was a proprietorial thrill in Antwerp and Brussels that the Highlander was the cleanest, best-behaved and most popular of the troops billeted on the Belgians, but, somehow, in the mere fact of the claim lurked an uneasy and half-submerged awareness that Scotland in some way still needed to prove itself to England. 'Let honour be paid where it is so justly due,' wrote Charlotte Waldie after Quatre Bras, where so many of those 'hardy sons of Caledon' she had claimed as her countrymen only a day before, lay dead; 'Let England be sensible of the vast debt of grati-tude she owes them; and let the names of those who perished there be enrolled in the long list of her heroes.'

Charlotte Waldie would not be disappointed – when Wellington was asked to name the bravest man in his army, he nominated a Macdonell from Glengarry and a Graham from Ulster – and out of the war with France and Waterloo a new British identity was taking shape. Only fifty years before, two uniformed Scottish officers had been booed out of a London theatre simply for being Scottish, and now after the heroics of Quatre Bras and Waterloo it would be a moot point whether Walter Scott or the Highland regiments had done more to alter the way in which England saw Scotland or Scotland saw itself. 'Towards the end of the year the Forty-Second [The Black Watch] returned to England,' recalled James Nasmyth – the same young lad who had watched the defiant march of the freed French prisoners only the year before – 'and in the beginning of 1816 they set out on their march towards Edinburgh.'[2] The crowds had been so immense that it took them two hours to make their way up the High Street towards the castle, and as Nasmyth and his parents and sisters waited, it was only the rolling cheers, the glint of bayonets and 'the tattered colours riddled with bullets' that marked the 'red-coats' path through the seething, crying, hand-shaking masses who had come out to welcome them. 'At last they passed,' Colonel Dick at their head, 'the pipers and drums playing a Highland march; and the Forty-Second slowly entered the Castle. It was perhaps the most extraordinary scene ever witnessed in Edinburgh.'

Here was Scott's vision made flesh – Highland warrior and British redcoat one and the same thing – and if it was part myth, and Tory myth at that (everyone from Lady Frances Shelley to Bonaparte still happily used the word 'English' as if 'English' and 'British' were interchangeable) the fact is that even before Waterloo, Union was a reality within Britain's army. In the last decades of the eighteenth century the influence of the Scottish Lord Bute had been met with a good John Bull-Wilkes-ite backlash in England, but even with Culloden fresh in the memory and the lingering association of Jacobitism and Catholicism still there, the army had remained the one institution that was 'British' in any real sense of the word: the one place in the collective life of the country where a Welsh Picton, a Scottish Cameron, an Irish Ponsonby and an Anglo-American De Lancey could fight under the same banner.

If this was true of Protestant Scotland, it was more importantly so of a Roman Catholic Ireland that for twenty years had been an object of suspicion to an England in fear of rebellion and French invasion. It was remarkable that even after the hatred and bloodshed of the uprising of 1798 only one Irish regiment had to be disbanded, and if the British government and people needed any assurance of the loyalty of the Catholic Irish soldier it was lying there at the crossroads of the Ohain and Brussels roads and on almost every yard of the battlefield.

In the most simple sense the impact of Waterloo here is obvious – England no longer had to worry about Ireland as the historic target of a French or Spanish invasion – but its more intangible effects can be only guessed at. For a generation the English establishment as a whole had been thawing in its historical opposition to Catholicism, and yet it is impossible to imagine that the heroism of the Irish soldier – the legendary reputation of the 88th in the Peninsula, the 27th at Waterloo, the mere title, again, of Ponsonby's Union Brigade – and the rough-and-ready coexistence of seemingly conflicting religious and national loyalties under one flag did not in some way ease the passage towards eventual Catholic emancipation.[3]

This had less to with any overt patriotism – Wellington would have laughed at the notion – than the fact that the army, certainly the army of the ordinary soldier, was a world of its own, with its own rituals, its own codes of honour and its own loyalties. For the tough veteran of the Peninsula such as William Wheeler, the first loyalties were to each other rather than to any abstract notions of country, and yet here again something seems to have happened at Waterloo, some shift in the relationship of the country and her soldiers, some reciprocal awareness of shared identity, that signalled the beginning of the end of Britain's long, historic distrust of her standing army.

It would be a mistake to simplify or sentimentalise this – sixty years later the mother of the future Chief of the Imperial General Staff, Sir William 'Wully' Robertson, could still wish her son dead rather than a redcoat – but this does not invalidate the sense of a genuine shift in the triangular relationship of army, government and people. Over the succeeding, troubled decades the army would continue in its old civil role, but at the end of a war that at its peak might have seen as many as one in five of the population in uniform of some kind, a conflict in which militiamen chosen by lottery increasingly fed into the regular army – in which militia units notoriously sided with bread rioters rather than the authorities – the disbanded soldier of Waterloo was no longer the 'Piccadilly Butcher', or the traditional butt of popular satire, or the detritus of the assizes, but boys and men who belonged to the communities from which they came.

Wellington might have wished it otherwise – he would have given anything for his incomparable, battle-hardened Peninsular army that had fought its way through Spain – but he had to fight with what he was given and not with what he wanted. At the time of Bonaparte's escape from Elba, the bulk of Wellington's old troops had been still in Canada or lying dead at New Orleans, and in their place he had an army of second battalions and raw recruits, of plough boys like Keppel's 'Peasants' who should never have been allowed anywhere near a battle-field, or Hamilton's Scots Greys who in twenty years of war had never seen a shot fired in anger.

The 'infamous army' that fought at Waterloo was probably more representative of the country than any British army before it, and if a Waterloo Medal and two years seniority might be all the common soldier had to show for it then that only tells half of the story. He would have to wait another century and another war to get his equal due, but in the letters and diaries of 1815, in the testimony of officers and the admiration of those tending the wounded, in the appeals and collections raised in parishes, in the sermons preached across the country and the triumphant pride of the tourists who flocked to Belgium, we glimpse a Britain awakening to the nature of its responsibilities and debt. 'The ferocious, the imbecile, the melancholy, the clean, and the unclean, are all blended together,' one naval surgeon, Dr James Veitch, wrote in 1815, protesting at the appalling conditions at one military asylum; 'All is chaos and confusion, and decidedly exhibits a want of proper system in the treatment of men whose suffering gives them a strong claim to attention from the benevolence, humanity, and generosity of that country, in whose service their diseases have been contracted.'

It went further than a mere sense of obligation or pride, though, because if such a thing as 'Britain' did exist anywhere it was on the field of Waterloo with the heirs to Crécy, Agincourt, Poitiers and Blenheim the glue that held it together.[4] 'My LORD,' a baffled William Cobbett wrote in an open letter to Castlereagh, after a bizarre brush with a villainous-looking crowd of gypsies who had given him his first news of Waterloo: 'at the first view of them, I thought of nothing but the robberies which they constantly commit upon us ... but upon nearer approach to them, I perceived the whole caravan' – the ruffian men, the ferocious, pipe-smoking women, even the 'poor asses' – were all decked out in boughs and sprigs of laurel. 'Somewhat staggered by this symbol of victory,' Cobbett had passed them by in silence until he came across a particularly 'ill-looking' straggler who, 'with two half-starved dogs, performed the office of rearguard. I asked him the meaning of the laurel boughs, and he informed me, that they were hoisted on account of the "*glorious victory obtained by the Duke of Wellington over Bony*", that they were furnished them by a good gentleman, *in a black coat and big white wig*, whose house they had passed the day before ... and who had given them several pots of ale, wherein to drink the Duke's health – "And to be sure," added he, "it is glorious news, and we may now hope to see the gallon loaf a *grate* again, as 'twas in my old father's time".'

'History ... is boredom interrupted by war,' wrote Derek Walcott and – spurious or genuine, and it was simultaneously both things – it was war that had kindled the fragmented, often inward-looking, disparate communities that made up the country into a vivid, collective life that was national and British. 'Will these ladies say that we are nothing to *them*?' De Quincey wrote of the Victory Mails and the healing alchemy of war that could unite strangers glimpsed in a passing carriage in a common bond of kinship. 'Oh, no; they will not say *that*. They cannot deny – they do not deny – that for this night they are our sisters: for twelve hours to come – we on the outside – gentle or simple, scholar or illiterate servant – have the honour to be their brothers. These poor women again, who stop to gaze upon us with delight at the entrance of Barnet ... do you mean to say that they are washer-women and charwomen? Oh, my poor friend, you are quite mistaken; they are nothing of the kind. I assure you, they stand in a higher rank: for this one night they feel themselves by birthright to be daughters of England, and answer to no humbler title.'

'The English name stands so high from Ostend [to] here, that it makes one feel proud,' Caroline Lamb wrote home from Brussels at the beginning of July 1815, and after the bitter years of Peterloo, the repressive Six Acts and the Cato Street Conspiracy the whole country was again ready to share in that pride. In the early 1830s, Whig memories were still long enough to deny Captain William Siborne the money to complete his great model of the battlefield of Waterloo, but as Britain came out of the long political crisis of the post-war decades and the Chartist movement for reform came and went without bloodshed, and a suitably sanitised Lifeguardsman Shaw took his place in the pantheon of national heroes, mid-nineteenth-century Britain found itself able to look back on Waterloo through its Victorian-tinted glasses with pretty well unalloyed complacency.

It had reason to do so of course, because Benjamin Haydon was right – the efforts of the British nation had been 'gigantic' – and the nation had more than reaped its rewards. Winston Churchill would later declare that the 'Age of Waterloo' only finally ended with the new century, but even if you were a Briton living only thirty-odd years into that age – sixteen years or so into Victoria's reign – with the memories of the Great Exhibition still sharp, a navy that ruled the waves sailing unchallenged through the Black Sea towards Sevastopol, and an army – under the command of a man who had lost his arm at Wellington's side at Waterloo – about to give autocratic Russia a bloody nose, then you would have been forgiven for thinking that God's plans for his chosen nation were working out just as He intended.

War has always been the great catalyst for change, the ultimate evolutionary dynamic, and the Napoleonic wars were no different from any other in that respect. The peculiar set of circumstances that made nineteenth-century Britain the world's only superpower were already in place at the end of the eighteenth century, but twenty years of conflict involving the collaboration of government and private initiative, the stimulation of industry, the improvement of the infrastructure, the dockyard development of mass-production techniques, naval dominance, the emergence of men of talent and not birth in public life, had all accelerated the process, leaving Britain not just in a position to finance the coalitions that defeated France but to make the ensuing peace a Pax Britannica.

There had also been something deeply in tune with the national psyche, that when Bonaparte finally surrendered it was to a Royal Navy man o' war, Captain Maitland's *Billy Ruffian*, doing what the navy had done for twenty years, but it was Waterloo that satisfied national feeling in a way that only Trafalgar could begin to match.[5] There had been something slightly unsatisfactory about the capitulation of Bonaparte's Paris in 1814 to the Emperor Alexander and an allied force that had no British presence, and for all the dismay at the escape from Elba, the Hundred Days and Waterloo had almost come as a second chance, an opportunity to rectify that wrong and reclaim the military high ground and prestige in a war that British gold had financed, British resolve had maintained and Britain's navy had done so much to win.

A victory of this scale comes at a price, though, because the only thing more dangerous in the long run than a battle lost is a battle won. In the wake of its disastrous defeats by Napoleon, Prussia had put in place major military reforms, but Britain had won at Waterloo and in 1853, as British troops waded ashore in the Crimea under commanders who could not command and with equipment that had not changed and a commissariat that was useless and a medical service that was non-existent, the country was about to discover the price of forty years of resting on its laurels.

It was the same story with Nelson's navy – it would simply take the country another sixty years and the Battle of Jutland in 1916 to realise it – and this complacency ran deep through national life. It is one of the sad paradoxes of British military and naval history that the influence of her two greatest commanders should have had such baleful effects on their successors, but an even greater paradox is that Churchill's Age of Waterloo – an age of gold that, in popular mythology, had begun with the triumph of British liberties over Napoleonic tyranny – could end in the years before the Great War with the Britain that in 1789 had been the most politically advanced nation in Europe locked in combat with a House of Lords as bitterly resistant to change or reform as it had been in 1832.

'What was most impressive in that battle was England,' Victor Hugo insisted in his great digression on Waterloo in *Les Misérables*, 'English steadfastness and resolution, English blood', and above all Englishmen. It galled Hugo that the credit that properly belonged to the 'people' had gone to Wellington, but what irritated him even more was that 'they' did not seem to mind; that 'in spite of their revolution of 1688, and our own of 1789', they were still so hopelessly wedded to notions of hierarchy, heredity and 'feudal illusions', so resolutely determined to 'think of themselves as a nation, not as a people', so willing to accept subordination – the lash for the soldier, contempt for the workman – that they were incapable of even wanting their just rewards.

There is an uncomfortable truth here, and it is a truth that, for all the Gallic hyperbole, goes to the heart of that central paradox of the Age of Waterloo. War is not just a fundamental instrument of evolutionary change but of social and political development as well, and when the First World War could deliver the vote to Britain's women and the Second World War the Welfare State, how was it that a war that had mobilised the energies of a whole nation for more than twenty years could end up with the great mass of people who had fought it in a worse state, politically, than they had been in 1792?

It does not dispose of the puzzle to say that Catholic emancipation came in 1829 or the Great Reform Act in 1832 – all the reforms, from Robert Peel's rationalisation of the penal code to the extension of the franchise to the middle classes were designed to strengthen the system not weaken it – and it is not as though in 1815 there were not the men available to bring about something more than a slow and grudging change. Not since the end of the Roman Empire had Europe been awash with so many tens of thousands of disbanded soldiers schooled in violence, and yet in a hungry and politically oppressed Britain, crying out for redress and filled with a vast reservoir of disgruntled soldiers and seamen equipped with all the habits of discipline and organisation required for armed protest, how, again, was it that noth-ing, essentially, happened?

There is an almost endless checklist of reasons why Britain escaped revolution in these post-war years – working-class dependence on its middle-class leadership, internal rivalries and jealousies, a revulsion of moderate opinion from extreme radicalism after the Cato Street Conspiracy, Methodism, organisational failures, Bentham, an innate habit of deference, an improving economy, rising employment, increas-ing wealth – and to all that must be added the 'anaesthetic' of victory. The role of the abolitionists in bolstering the self-esteem of a population only better off than the slaves they pitied has been eloquently argued, and yet if there was one intangible above that which could reconcile the dispossessed to their fate, one balm for hurt minds or palliative to soothe the degradation of a population cut off from the fruits of Waterloo it was the reflected glory and consolation of their *Britishness*.

In that at least, if in nothing else, the haves and have-nots of the post-Waterloo decades shared something in common, because after twenty years of war, self-interest, fear, suspicion, political principle – or an uninvestigated combination of all four – had left a great swathe of Britain resolutely content with what they had and were. Perhaps the most shocking aspect of the Peterloo Massacre was that the worst of the violence was the work of the local yeomanry and not the regular army, and for the 'manufacturers, merchants, publicans, and shopkeepers on horseback' who trampled and hacked their way through the crowds of women and children – for the clerical magistrates who promised every 'downright blackguard reformer' the rope – for the justices who committed the victims and not the murderers to trial – for yeoman farmers and Tory historians like Robert Southey, who reverenced Britain's incomparable constitution and her Established Church as the bulwarks of the 'common weal' – for Anglican apologists such as George Stonestreet who saw a traitor under every Catholic bed – for all that conservative, patriotic Britain, in love with its own myths, confirmed in every prejudice and every assumption of superiority by victory over Revolutionary and Napoleonic France – the Britain they had was the Britain they wanted.

They loved what Britain had achieved, they loved beating Boney, they loved the stories of Belgians running away, they loved their Lifeguardsman Shaw just as they would love their Lord Palmerston, and above all they loved what Waterloo told them about themselves.[6] 'The doctrine of God's unlimited, particular Providence, in the support, Government, and direction of all things without exception, makes an Eminent Branch of the Christian system,' began one victory sermon in 1815; 'but let me direct your thoughts, or rather let me follow them, whither in all probability they have preceded me, to *Waterloo* – The Spot of Land no doubt designed by Almighty God, for the total defeat and overthrow of our most Inveterate Enemy … Yes, my brethren, God hath arisen and displayed his Omnipotence. And in his great Mercy hath crowned The Christian Banners with Victory and Renown. The Power of God and his faithful servants hath triumphed gloriously … It is God, who disposes of the Interests of Nations, and in so doing serves his own great designs in the government of the universe.'

There has seldom been a war on which God has not been on one side or the other, and usually on both, but the sense of manifest destiny that took hold of Britain in the wake of Waterloo is of a different order. A profoundly Protestant sense of 'election' had been lodged deep in the English psyche for centuries, and Waterloo came as the ultimate confirmation of that belief, the triumphant demonstration not just of Britain and her Empire's special place in God's unfolding purpose but of the fact that nineteenth-century Britain was worthy of that place.

The triumph of the abolitionists, the establishment of the Bible Society, the universal diffusion of Christian education – 'such are the acts which have conciliated our God,' declared the *Sheffield Iris*, 'such are the arms with which we have conquered our enemies' and it was the 'Arm of the Lord of Hosts' that had sustained them 'through this mighty contest'. Not even 'the meanest peasant was so much below the grandeur and the sorrow of the times', wrote Thomas De Quincey of Britain's war with Bonaparte, 'as to confound these battles, which were gradually moulding the destinies of Christendom, with the vulgar conflicts of ordinary warfare, which are oftentimes but gladiatorial trials of national prowess. The victories of England in this stupendous conflict rose of themselves as natural *Te Deums* to heaven.'

It was a neatly circular argument – Britain had triumphed because she had performed God's work and been granted victory in order that she could carry her mission across the globe – and the seventy-two separate campaigns fought by Queen Victoria's armies underlines how willingly Britain took up the challenge. Forty years after Waterloo God-fearing, evangelical young officers would see war in the Crimea as a portent of Christ's Second Coming, and in poems, letters and sermons, history and destiny link hands in a theme that shades from the crassest philistinism and xenophobic disdain at one end of the spectrum to the most ecstatic visions of Thomas De Quincey at the other.

*   *   *

And it is De Quincey, finally – bizarrely – the opium-addicted child of Romanticism, whose youth was set against the backdrop of war and the mail-coach, and whose last years were lived out in the age of industrialisation, steam and the train – who has left the most extraordinary testament to the place of Waterloo in the psyche of the British people. As an old man he would look back to those war years and think of a young woman who, each morning, as dawn broke and the Bath Mail burst out of the gloom of the Marlborough forest, would be waiting at the roadside to pick up her customers' commissions.

Over the years 'Sweet Fanny of the Bath road', standing in all her steadfast beauty and innocence 'among the roses and dewy thickets and roe-deer', had become for him the symbol of the Britain that fought that June of 1815. In his dreams he would see her assailed by the monsters of Napoleonic tyranny, until somewhere in the depths of his mind she merged with the nightmare memory of another girl who he had seen nearly crushed to death by a mail-coach. 'Immediately, in a trance,' he wrote thirty-seven years after the incident – thirty-seven years in which that young woman's image, frozen for a moment in the moonlight, 'fainting, praying, raving, despairing' had haunted his dreams – years in which he had followed her on Coleridgean ghost-ships across oceans and over quicksands in desperate attempts to save her from her fate, 'I was carried over land and sea to some distant kingdom, and placed upon a triumphal car amongst companions crowned with laurels … Tidings had arrived, within an hour, of a grandeur that measured itself against centuries', a grandeur 'too full of pathos, too full of joy that acknowledged no fountain but God' to express itself in any other language than that of tears and hymns of praise and gratitude.

'The tidings', the 'sacred word', was Waterloo, and for two hours the Victory coach thunders into the night carrying with it the news of Europe's redemption – through 'a mighty minster forty leagues long and reaching into the clouds – past chantry chapels and hymning white-robed choirs – through a soaring, purple marbled necropolis of terraces and towers – between bas-reliefs of battles and sarcophagi that hold the noble dust of Crécy and Trafalgar's heroes – league after tireless league until, suddenly, out of the mist, an infant girl stands helpless in the mad careering path of their horses. "Oh baby!" I exclaimed, "shalt thou be the ransom for Waterloo? Must we, that carry tidings of great joy to every people, be messengers of ruin to thee?"'

As De Quincey rises to his feet in horror, a trumpet sounds from the stony lips of a 'Dying Trumpeter' woken into life and the infant child – the price of Victory – the price England has paid for redeeming Europe – Christian England herself – is whisked away from under their horses' hoofs, to reappear again, grown now into womanhood, high aloft in the vast recesses of the cathedral, her face bathed in the crimson hues of stained-glass windows and the martyred blood of England's warriors, while the dead of Crécy and Trafalgar and a hundred English battles unite with the living in one tumultuous song of praise. And 'I heard a voice from heaven, which said, "'Let there be no more fear, and no more sudden death! Cover them with joy as the tides cover the shore!" … As brothers we moved together; to the skies we rose – to the dawn that advanced – to the stars that fled: rendering thanks to God in the highest – that, having hid his face through one generation behind thick clouds of war, once again was ascending – was ascending from Waterloo – in the visions of peace.'

Never could Revelations, opium, gothic Romanticism, genius, vision, dream, fear, illness, submerged memory and the fractured pieces of a lifetime's learning come together to produce something so completely central to the way that ordinary men and women saw the world. Victor Hugo would certainly not have liked its message, or England made head or tail of what on earth De Quincey was on about, but behind all the extraordinary flights of imagination – the stony trumpeter, the Campo Santo of the nation's dead, the transformation of an English country lane into the fan-vaulting of his mighty cathedral, a chance moment of horror into a whole, swelling fugue – here, at the bottom of it all, stripped of its pageantry and the strange private symbolism of a young girl who is one moment Fanny, another De Quincey's dead sister and another the young woman of his moonlit nightmare, are the prosaic, Protestant patriotic, beliefs of the average nineteenth-century Englishman in the divinely sanctioned destiny of England.

It is a strange thought that only a vial of opium separates De Quincey from the world of Gilbert and Sullivan, but there was nothing in his or Haydon's vision of British greatness that would have discomfited the vast crowd of over a million who gathered on a raw November day in 1852 for the funeral of the Iron Duke. 'What makes the difference between the obsequies of the Duke of Wellington and of any other great men?' *The Times* asked: 'Grief, of course, in the usual sense of the term, is out of the question ... but sentiments sublimer far than sorrow are awakened by such spectacles as that of yesterday. Through the countless thousands then gathered along the streets of London ran the strong currents of feeling and of thought which go to form the spirit of a nation ... When the independence of England and the world was assailed Providence sent us a champion, and as the myriads of his countrymen yesterday watched with deepest interest the transit of his body to the tomb, many a heartfelt prayer must have been uttered that, should ... this land of freedom be once more threatened, God may grant us another Wellesley to lead our armies and win our battles.'

'Ahmedugger, Assaye, Argaum, Gavilghur, Roleia, Vimiera, Douro and Oporto, Talavera, Busaco, TorresVedras, Fuentes d'Onor, Ciudad Rodrigo, Badajos, Salamanca, Vittoria, Pampeluna, Pyrenees, St Sebastian, Nivelle, Nives, Orthes, Toulouse, Quatre Bras, Waterloo' – the battle honours adorning the hideous, eighteen-ton, bronze funeral carriage could leave no doubt of what was being honoured here, or on what the greatness of the greatest imperial city the world had ever seen rested. Thirty-seven years before, the *Sheffield Iris* had invoked the

'Lord of Hosts' in Britain's civilising mission, and as regiment after regiment who had fought under the duke at Waterloo and through India, Spain, France and Belgium, filed between the packed and black-draped stands, who could have doubted that the Lord of Hosts was still with them or that Britain had manifestly honoured its covenant with its God?

A world empire, the abolition of slavery, the spread of the Gospel, a navy that scoured the seas to uphold its writ, an army whose triumphs on the field of Waterloo had given Europe nearly forty years of peace, who could doubt it? 'There' was the sombre green of the Rifles, *The Times* noted; there the 33rd; there the 17th Lancers and the 13th Light Dragoons, there the 8th Hussars, the Scots Greys, the Blues and the Life Guards, there the one-armed Raglan and there, 'most wondrous of all, with bald, uncovered head, apparently unconscious of the fact that age stands exposure to cold less successfully than youth', the Marquis of Anglesey, Uxbridge as was. This was a nation celebrating itself and the military cornerstone of its greatness and prosperity. In the cities of Gloucester, Birmingham and Carlisle the Quakers might keep their shops open in protest at 'the wickedness' of commemorating a life of killing, but if anyone else was harbouring their doubts and remembering the human and political cost of that triumph – if any of his Irish troops marching with the great funeral car recalled how late and reluctantly he had come to Catholic emancipation – or any minds went back to the days of 'Captain Swing' or the night the reform mobs smashed the windows of Apsley House and the duke's words to Mrs Arbuthnot – 'The People are rotten, rotten to the core' – then this was not the day to acknowledge them.

It would have been strange if it had been any different, because the men and women at his funeral were not just celebrating an individual, they were celebrating themselves. In the modern theory of political life the rationale of the state lies in the service of its people, but the Britain that had triumphed at Waterloo was not a 'nation state' in that modern sense but its evolutionary antecedent in which the energies and talents of the whole people – from Wellington to Wheeler, from the Whig grandees gathered at Arundel to celebrate the 600th anniversary of Magna Carta to the crowd clustering around the Waterloo despatch in David Wilkie's painting – were there to serve the state.

It had been a brilliant system for fighting a war – for two decades it had harnessed the will, resources and taxes of a whole nation – and in peace it had been a soothing panacea. Thirty-odd years after the Peterloo Massacre, the children and grandchildren of the men and women killed that day seemed no nearer winning their political rights than they had been in 1819, but the Britain to which they belonged had never been greater and in the celebration of the man whose victory at Waterloo had laid the foundation of that greatness – the chapter and verse of all that they understood by the term 'British' – they saw their apotheosis and not their servitude.

It was a dangerous illusion. The duke had dedicated himself so completely to the state, on the battlefield and in Cabinet as minister and prime minister, had been such a towering figure in the life of the nation, that by some strange inversion he had become that state. As surely as Bonaparte had been the imaginative embodiment of Revolutionary France, the Iron Duke had become the incarnation of the Britain whose inflexible determination had defeated Bonaparte. He was not, though; he was just its greatest and most blinkered servant. 'What would the duke have done?' his old subordinates used to ask themselves, and only too soon Britain would have its chance to find out what it would do without him.

That, though, lay in the future. Hazlitt could have told them, but Hazlitt was long gone, and as the November evening closed in, and the crowds drifted away, it was perhaps fitting that it was one of the classic trimmers of his age who was left among his ghosts beside the library fire of the Athenaeum. As a young man, Henry Crabb Robinson had run through the streets of Colchester shouting out the news of the collapse of Pitt's treason trials, and as he sat there now, full of years and respectability, reading Thackeray in the club he had helped found, did his mind go back to a night thirty-seven years earlier, when he had climbed the stairs of the Lambs' house in Inner Temple Lane and 'cut' Hazlitt?

It was half a lifetime ago and a lost world. 'Where are they gone, the old familiar faces?' Lamb had asked over half a century before, alone with his own childhood ghosts. 'All, all are gone, the old familiar faces', and now Lamb himself was with them. He had died in 1834 and poor, insane Mary thirteen years later, and one by one they had dropped away – the young Charles Lloyd in his straitjacket, Basil Montagu just last year – until only a handful of them were left, so respectable that if they had passed their younger selves in Hare Court they would scarcely have known each other.

The young, defiantly Byronic Benjamin Disraeli, whose father Isaac had been at Murray's with George Ticknor on the day of Waterloo, might regret the days when disinherited sons would race their father's horses at Newmarket and steal their fathers' mistresses, but Crabb Robinson's journey was the journey of the age. Oswald Leicester, who had founded the first Methodist Sunday school at Altrincham, had died a Church of England priest. Francis Place, the 1790s radical who was the foreman at the Duke of Cumberland inquest, lived to be a constable at the Chartists' marches. John Cam Hobhouse, the Westminster firebrand sent to Newgate in 1819, was now the first Baron Broughton. The Countess of Rosebery – execrated as a harlot in both Houses of Parliament – would become the grandmother of a British prime minister. Thomas Cochrane, one-time scourge of the Establishment, honours and rank restored, would end in Westminster Abbey; and Byron – even the dead were not exempt the Victorian airbrush – would metamorphose from the pariah of English society, forced into exile in 1816 on the scandalous collapse of his marriage, into the idealised champion of Greek freedom.

Respectability – the evangelicals' gift to the nation – was in the air, settling like a November fog on the streets of London. The London that in 1815 had echoed to the shouts of Corn Law rioters and the smash of glass at the Chancery Lane house of Eliza Fenning's employers had become the one city in Europe where Metternich could take refuge from the upheavals of 1848. The forces of conservatism in Britain had won and won so completely that more than a million people had lined the streets of the capital to pay homage to the man whose genius on the battlefield and stubborn resistance at home had done so much to thwart their political aspirations.

And in the Athenaeum, Crabb Robinson, the disciple of William Godwin, finished his Thackeray. From the other side of the city, just as they had done to announce the victory at Waterloo, the guns of the Tower boomed out through the gloom to signal the end of Wellington's obsequies. As the duke's horse – boots reversed across the saddle – was brought back alone along the funeral route, old soldiers would be hovering around Siborne's great model of Waterloo, on display in the Banqueting House opposite where Caroline Lamb had sat scribbling that night in Melbourne House. It was almost twenty-five years now since she had died there, half out of her mind. Her much-loved brother Frederick was dead too, though not before he had found himself at a dinner in Malta sitting next to the French officer who had saved his life with brandy while he was lying wounded on the field of Waterloo. Wheatley had married his Eliza Brooks – perhaps the cachet of Waterloo had made him seem more acceptable to her family – but he had also died. That engaging military Mr Collins, the Reverend Stonestreet, was still alive and full of clerical honours, but he was an exception. Thomas Chalmers had gone, taking down the Church of Scotland with him; and Frederick Maitland on board his ship the *Wellesley*; and William Wheeler; and Basil Hall, insane in the Haslar Hospital at Portsmouth, and his sister Magdalene, the plaything of an indifferent universe to the last. She had eventually married another friend of her brother's, only to die in 1822.

Salic Law and the accession of Queen Victoria had turned the Duke of Cumberland into the King of Hanover but he had been gone a year now, rumours and suspicions of murder and treason dogging him to the end. The world of Caolas Scalpaigh to which Eury MacLeod belonged had also disappeared as completely as she had herself – within ten years of Waterloo, economic ruin and emigration had seen to that – leaving for the island's crofters only memories of broken promises and men who never returned. And Waterloo itself? 'They have ruined my battlefield,' Wellington had complained when he saw the giant memorial pyramid that had been raised out of what had once been the ridge that his army had defended for eight hours. But he need not have worried. It had always been more than a place. Each year on 18 June, deep into the 1890s, field marshals, generals and statesmen would come in their droves to the house of Lady de Ros, the Georgiana Lennox of Brussels fame, to pay their respects and bring their bouquets of flowers. And each year Lady de Ros, the young girl Wellington had taken in to the ball on the eve of Quatre Bras, would go in her carriage to Portland Square to take the old Earl of Albemarle – the junior ensign in Wellington's army, George Keppel as he had once been – a sprig of laurel. Where Captain John Blackman had been buried, snowdrops would be coming out in the new year. In Belgian homes, cups would bear the grateful inscriptions of English parents indissolubly tied to this corner of a foreign field. In English houses branches of elm, carefully labelled, would carry the memory of 'Wellington's tree' down the generations. In the Wyndham household they would sit in draughts because no Wyndham had closed a door since Hougoumont. In an ancient ruined church on the east coast of Scotland, open to the elements, a plaque would record the death of a Colonel William De Lancey. At Waterloo itself, Sergeant Cotton of the 8th Hussars, surrounded by his relics, would smile tolerantly at the idea that the French had ever threatened Mont-Saint-Jean. And at night, wrote Victor Hugo, when Cotton's tourists and pilgrims had all left, 'at night a sort of visionary mist rises from it, and the traveller who chooses to look and listen, dreaming like Virgil on the field of Philippi, may catch the echoes of catastrophe. That monumental hillock with its nondescript lion vanishes, and the fearful event comes back to life.' The battlefield 'recovers its reality, the lines of infantry wavering across the plain, the furious charges, the gleam of sabres and bayonets, the flame and thunder of cannon-fire. Like a groan emerging from the depths of a tomb the listener may hear the clamour of a ghostly conflict and see the shadowy forms of grenadiers and cuirassiers and the image of men departed – here Napoleon, there Wellington. All gone but still locked in combat, while the ditches run with blood, the trees shudder, the sound of fury rises over the sky and over those windblown heights – Mont-Saint-Jean, Hougoumont, Frischermont, Papelotte, Plancenoit – the spectral armies whirl in mutual extermination.'

And, perhaps, amidst the chaos and violence of battle, and the 'Ha! Ha!' of William Verner's Constantia, spooked to the end of her long life by the sound of gunfire or smell of powder, the voice of a British soldier – the accent cockney, or Irish brogue, the Highlands, the north of England, the West Country, Knightsbridge?

Were you at Waterloo?
I have been at Waterloo,
'Tis no matter what you do.
If you have been at Waterloo.

Notes on the Text

The Tiger is Out

1. *'All the town was out to see them'*: It was not just French prisoners who were returning home. 'One of my father's amphibious crofters disappeared,' the son of Sir Hector Mackenzie of Gairloch, on the west coast of Scotland, remembered, 'leaving his wife and family to the care of Providence, without a clue to his being dead or alive, for some five years. One day my father, superintending some job near the bay, noticed a man coming towards him with a true sailor-like roll. Intimate with the cut of every man on the estate, says he, "Surely that is dead Donald McLean's walk;" and, on coming near, it certainly was Donald himself, in naval attire. "Halloa, Donald!" says he, "where on earth are you from?" speaking, as he always did to his people, in Gaelic. Donald pulled up, and saluting, replied in two words, also in Gaelic, "*Bho Iutharn,*" the English of which is simply "From hell." … Donald had been grabbed by a press-gang, had survived five years of it, and found his widow and children glad to see him again' (J. H. Dixon, *Gairloch and Guide to Loch Maree, 1886*, Fort William, pp. 984, 9112–3). Since the Peace of Amiens there had also been soldiers, sailors and civilians held in France, some for ten years or more. 'Charles Scott, a seaman in His Majesty's Ship under my command,' Captain Frederick Maitland of the *Bellerophon* informed the Admiralty, 'having applied to be paid for HM Ship *Lidd*, and for the period he was Prisoner in France, from the year

1804 to 1814, is informed he is suspected to have served in Arms against his country, and therefore cannot be paid till he brings Proof to the contrary. There are now on board the ship two men … who knew him in Valenciennes Prison from the year 1805 to the year 1809, when he attempted to make his escape, and are ready to make oath, that they afterwards saw his name in a hand bill as being condemned to slavery for having made the said attempt; Scott further states that he was condemned to 5 years slavery, four of which he served in L'Orient Dockyard in chains, as a convict, and was released at the Peace' (Adm 1./2179/239).

3 a.m.: A Dying World

1. *And beside the track*: If there is something about the history of 'Aurora MacLeod' and her child, something about its hopelessness, that seems to encapsulate the fate of the doomed island communities, it was not the whole story. In many ways the pattern of abandonment, displacement, ignorance and economic despair might seem to say it all, but the truth of the Gaelic tragedy lies as much in its brutality and violence as in its sadness, and in the peat-brown depths of a deserted lochan at the northern end of the island, the mouldering remains of another child could have told another story. The child – it was never known, or at least never recorded, whether it was a boy or a girl – had been born to a twenty-three-year-old servant girl called Elizabeth MacIver in the house of the customs officer for Stornoway. She had come to work for Mr Syme Tod and his wife the previous Martinmas, and although there had been gossip about her from the start, had given perfect satisfaction until on the morning of the 16 March – just as news of Bonaparte's escape from Elba was reaching Scotland – her empty bed and bedding were found stained with blood and Elizabeth MacIver gone. The other servants in the house had suspected she was pregnant from the day she arrived, but she had always denied it, and when she was found at her sister's and brought up before the Sheriff Substitute, Elizabeth MacIver

held to her story. She had gone to her sister's with nothing but a bad back, she insisted, but when the next day she was dismissed from her service and questioned again, she finally admitted to a 'carnal connexion' the previous June and July with the Stornoway schoolmaster John Fraser. 'Now moved by a just sense of deep contrition for the heinous crime recently committed,' she confessed, 'that on the evening of Wednesday last … she was privately delivered of a still-born child in the House of Mr Syme Tod and concealed it there in a box' in the kitchen. She had gone to her sister's that night, and a few days later had returned to the Tods' house after dark to retrieve the body, and thrown it into the sea 'near the Castle of Stornoway', before returning to her sister's. She would have known perfectly well that concealment of a pregnancy was a crime in itself, but over the next weeks – battered down by repeated questioning, haunted by the image of her dead child, driven to a final self-destructive anger against a world that had pinned her down, it is impossible to know which – she made one last statement. 'In the presence of John Mackenzie Esq. Sheriff Substitute of Lewis,' the English transcript reads, 'on being further examined and Interrogated [she] Declares that on the Evening of Wednesday the Fifteenth day of March last, she was privately Delivered of a full time child … that finding the child was in life she strangled it by putting a string or cord around its Neck … [and] proceeded to a Pond between two Dykes near Brayhead, and threw it therein.' The harsh, Calvinist world of the Kirk had borne its predictable fruit. Despair and violence – the two poles of the nineteenth-century Highland experience – were there together in the dock and it was not just liberal lawyers who saw in the fate of Eury MacLeod and Elizabeth MacIver more than just personal tragedies. Was it any wonder, Scottish judges on the Northern circuit speculated, that the incidence of concealment and infanticide seemed at their highest where the law of the Kirk was at its sternest? It seemed to the Lord Justice Clerk – no enemy to Tory values – that a little more charity from ministers might mean a little less crime, but over these next decades charity – from Kirk or landlord – would not be a quality in rich supply in the Scottish Highlands.

3 p.m.: The Walking Dead

1. *The blaspheming rapist William Oldfield*: A different system operated in the provinces, where the royal prerogative had effectively been delegated away, but for Old Bailey cases the royal 'fount of mercy' still flowed from the king or Regent. At the end of every assize the Recorder for London would draw up a list of prisoners sentenced to death, which he would then take in person to the prince and his Cabinet advisors for confirmation or commutation. For all the rich constitutional and symbolic trappings that hung around the prerogative, though, the result was a lottery – one man might hang because the government needed five for a decent show, or be reprieved because eight on the same gallows could seem too bloody – and no one could know what would happen when the sentimental, indolent 'Prinny' woke from his doze to exercise his right to mercy. 'I was standing close to [the king] at the Council,' the diarist and courtier Charles Greville recalled one such meeting of George and his senior ministers, convened to decide which names were to be 'ticked off' for execution, 'and he put down his head and whispered, "Which are you for Cadland [the previous year's Derby winner] or the mare?" [meaning between Cadland and Bess of Bedlam] so I put my head down too and said "The horse!" and then as we retired he said to the Duke, "A little bit of Newmarket"' (Gatrell, p. 552).

The Days That Are Gone

1. *Her naval brother Basil*: Basil Hall's story is a particularly cruel example of the way in which people learned of Waterloo. He was returning on his ship from India when they fell in at the entrance to the Channel with another man o' war, and a 'precious copy' of the *Gazette* containing Wellington's despatch gave them their first news of the battle.

'Within five minutes after landing at Portsmouth,' Hall remembered, 'I met a near relation of my own. This seemed a fortunate rencontre, for I had not received a letter from home for nearly a year – and eagerly asked him, "What news of old friends?" "I suppose," he said, "you know of your sister's marriage?" "No, indeed! I do not! – which sister?" He told me. "But to whom is she married?" I cried out with intense impatience, wondering greatly that he had not told me this at once. "Sir William De Lancey was the person," he answered. But he spoke not in the joyous tone that befits such communications. "God bless me!" I exclaimed. "I am delighted to hear that … I see by the despatch, giving an account of the late victory, that he was badly wounded – how is he now? I observe by the postscript to the Duke's letter that strong hopes are entertained of his recovery." "Yes," said my friend, "that was reported, but could hardly have been believed. Sir William was mortally wounded, and lived not quite a week after the action"' (De L, p. 30).

2. *the theatricals of Byron*: On the morning after the arrival of the Waterloo despatch, George Ticknor had paid his first call on the Byrons in Piccadilly, and while he was there, talking of America, 'English Bards', Walter Scott and Byron's old family quarrel with Lord Carlisle – Major Frederick Howard's father – Sir James Bland Burgess had burst into the room 'and said abruptly, "My lord, my lord, a great battle has been fought in the Low Countries, and Bonaparte is entirely defeated." "But is it true?" said Byron, – "is it true?" "Yes, my lord, it is certainly true; an aide-de-camp arrived in town last night; he has been in Downing Street this morning, and I have just seen him as he was going to Lady Wellington's. He says he thinks Bonaparte is in full retreat towards Paris." After an instant's pause, Lord Byron replied, "I am d—d sorry for it," and then, after another slight pause, he added, "I didn't know but I might live to see Lord Castlereagh's head on a pole. But I suppose I sha'n't now." And this was the first impression produced on his impetuous nature by the news of the Battle of Waterloo' (Ticknor, p. 60).

New Battle Lines

1. *'The most ridiculous and most characteristic thing'*: In such a climate it was unlikely that the inimitable George Stonestreet would not be feathering his clerical nest, but even that was fraught with difficulties. 'I was dining yesterday with Gen Howard and was sitting as his Vice over a turkey,' he reported to George Trower, and was in the middle of carving the bird, and particularly looking forward to his share, when an aide-de-camp rushed in, saluted nobody, and told him that he had to come immediately – would brook no argument – would allow no delay for the turkey and give no explanation other than that 'My General and Lady Sarah Lennox', the Duke of Richmond's daughter, were waiting outside for him. Even Stonestreet could see that there was nothing to be done, and with one last reluctant glance at the turkey, followed the aide and, climbing into a fiacre, found himself with Sir Peregrine Maitland of Waterloo fame and a sobbing Lady Sarah Lennox. '"Here we are," said the General, "We have just run away from the Dukes – we shall be pursued – will you marry us instantly" … "What I said (to myself), steal a young lady out of a Duke's family – the ex-Viceroy of Ireland – the friend of Wellington – the offender too a good staid widower of near 40 – this is a terrible piece of larceny – I too am to be an accomplice" … all this you know was "aside", for it was not pretty to tell him what term belongs to gentlemen and what term too, to ladies – who do these sort of things.' It was an exquisite problem – he could not afford to offend his general, he could still less afford to offend a brace of dukes, and then there was always the possibility of a little piece of 'portable property' in the shape of candlesticks or a bit of plate to think of – but perhaps most important of all there was still that turkey waiting. Maitland had told him that the only way of avoiding bloodshed was to marry them straight away – 'he could refuse the duke's challenge as a son-in-law but not otherwise' – but even with that to factor in, caution got the better part of clerical valour, and giving them the name and address of another chaplain who might be more

biddable or braver, saw the runaways off and returned to the dinner table. 'But the turkey was gone! Cheese, dear, tasteful repast to a ploughman or cricketer, but too vulgar and mortifying, and I reserved my disappointment for ample revenge on the dessert.' The Reverend Stonestreet was not out of the woods yet, however, and the next day Maitland was back to say that the chaplain had disappeared, that no French priest or notary could be found, and that Stonestreet would have to apply to Wellington for a special licence for them. For under-standable reasons he was not eager to do this, but an order was an order, and braving the duke's 'overbearing stare' and abrupt questioning – 'I stand bullying very well,' he proudly told Trower – at last succeeded in getting Maitland the licence he wanted. 'It turned out the luckiest thing in the world – that he [Stonestreet] had made so many difficul-ties,' he later reported, because it gave everyone time to cool down. 'Four days after the wedding the Bride return'd to the world; made her debut at a grand family dinner, all branches delighted … I think I drew my head very well out of the scrape. For however powerfully interest work'd to get *their* pardon, I think I should never have had mine' (BL Add Mss 61805 ff).

Myth Triumphant

1. *In the aftermath of the battle a medal*: Even if Napoleon was right, and 'it is with baubles that men are led', the Waterloo Medal had been an unusually imaginative act of inclusive unity. The soldiers who had fought their way up through the Peninsula would have to wait another thirty-odd years for similar recognition, and the Waterloo Medal – not just the first British medal awarded to every soldier regardless of rank, but the first medal that carried the name of the recipient around the rim, the first that was given to the widows and families of the dead – reflects a genuine sense of responsibility, debt and communal identity that seems something new in the life of the nation. 'I was under the necessity of talking to my wife in French, as she could not understand

English,' Sergeant Lawrence recalled his arrival back in Britain, when he and his new French wife were trying to sail, walk and hitch their way from Leith to the childhood village in Devon he had not seen in sixteen years campaigning. They had just got into a cab with another gentleman and Lawrence was explaining this to him when the man noticed the Waterloo medal on his breast. '"I see you have been in the battle of Waterloo, sergeant?" ... He wished to know where I was bound for, and when I told him, he politely asked me to spend a week at his house on the way, saying that I should not want for anything, but I told him the reason of my hurry, thanking him for his kindness, and his stage having expired at this period he got out. But he would insist on giving my wife five shillings and paying our fare: we then shook hands heartily and parted, he wishing us good-speed on our journey' (Lawrence, p. 162).

2. *recalled James Nasmyth*: Such homecomings were not always the case, though, and the young William Keppel and the 'Peasants' of the 14th of Foot had come home in December 1815 to find 'Waterloo men at a discount' and a Britain 'saturated with glory ... brooding over the bill that it had to pay. An anti-military spirit had set in,' Keppel recalled, 'and if we had been convicts disembarking from a hulk we could hardly have met with less consideration. "It's us as pays they chaps," was the remark of a country bumpkin as our men came ashore. A brigade of artillery, their muzzles crammed with French contraband, had just slipped through the fingers of the customs officers undetected, and they did not get much kinder notice from them either' (Keppel, II, p. 68).

3. *eventual Catholic emancipation*: There is a need for caution here – Wellington, himself, had consistently voted against Catholic Emancipation before necessity brought him round – and popular anti-Catholicism was probably as rampant in the post-war period as it had ever been. In the 1820s the Catholic priest and historian John Lingard was exploding all the most cherished foundation myths of English

Protestantism, but that was not going to stop a man like the chaplain to the rabidly anti-Catholic Duke of York, (as he had subsequently become) George Stonestreet – that excellent barometer of enlightened self-interest – from producing a 130-odd-page diatribe against popery and the corrupting threat of foreign influence.

4. *heirs to Crécy, Agincourt, Poitiers and Blenheim*: As Wilkie's painting had suggested, they were also the progenitors of the Alma, Inkerman and Mons. It is impossible to look at a map of the Waterloo campaign and not be as conscious of the First World War as Wellington's men were of Marlborough's, and nineteenth-century Britain and its regiments wallowed in a tradition that linked its armies across time in an unbroken line of bravery and stoic endurance. 'On one occasion,' a nineteenth-century historian of the Reverend Grindrod's Altrincham proudly recorded, 'two men were whipped, one after another. One of them, after having received his portion, begged with a self-abnegation and gallantry worthy of all praise, that he might receive his companion's lashes, as he was sure he was unable to bear the punishment. No wonder that with men made of such sterling stuff Wellington won Waterloo. No wonder that their descendants conquered at Inkerman, and charged through the Russian hosts at Balaclava!'

5. *when Bonaparte finally surrendered*: It would not have been Britain, though, if having fought the 'usurper', 'monster' and anti-Christ for the best part of twenty years, they had not streamed down to Torbay in their crowds to catch a glimpse of the man. 'As I went over Westminster Bridge last week,' complained an astonished Hester Piozzi, 'I saw we were building a new mad-house twice as big as the old Bethlehem Hospital; and sure no building could be so wanted for Englishmen … this Man, this Buonaparte, whom to dethrone such torrents blood were willingly spilt; whom, to depose such treasures of money had been willingly spent, no sooner surrenders himself than we make an idol of him,

crowd round for a glance of his eye, and huzza him as if he were our defender. Had not Government prudently prevented his touching shore, hundred, nay thousands, would have drawn him up and down in triumph' (Piozzi, IV, p. 392). 'I come as Themistocles, to sit at the heart of the British people,' Bonaparte famously wrote to the Prince Regent, and with Charles Lamb not the only one wondering how long it would take for the British people to decide that he would make a far better job of ruling them than their own wretched Hanoverian, it was small wonder the government were taking no risks. Castlereagh had never been happy with the allies' choice of Elba for Bonaparte's first exile, and at the beginning of August he was transferred at Plymouth from the *Bellerophon* to the *Northumberland* and taken south to St Helena to begin an exile under the ghastly Sir Hudson Lowe – the first man Wellington had sacked when he got to Brussels – that most people thought punishment enough for a lifetime of crime.

6. *they loved what Waterloo told them about themselves*: It is impossible to put a strict date to these kind of attitudes, of course, but there is an intriguing sidelight cast on them in the journal of an English, Roman Catholic antiquarian called John Gage, who found himself in Brussels in the days after the battle. There was nothing unusual in the habit of seeing Britain as a second Rome – West's portrait of the death of Wolfe had made the connection explicit – but here, in the grounds of Hougoumont, is a moment when the stock comparisons of the classically educated Englishman of the time, the almost reflex habit of dignifying British achievements by reference to a classical past, suddenly seem no longer needed, because nothing could possibly add a lustre to what Britons have done and borne. 'In the Hougoumont garden Sir James Craufurd's son had been buried the morning after the battle in part of his clothes, and in a blanket with every decency the moment would allow. We had one of the Guards with us for our guide and he directed us to the spot, and we had no difficulty in finding the body.

Raphael, to paint the horror of civil war, in his battle of Constantius and Maxentius, has represented a father taking up his sons, who had fought on opposite sides. None but a father can feel the sentiments which are there expressed, none but a Raphael paint them! This picture loses its force when I look upon the scene in the Hougoumont garden: a father opening the winding sheet of a beloved son who had fallen in battle eight days before! I retired down the garden and indulged feelings I could not repress' (T. A. Birrell, *Across the Narrow Sea*, BL 1991).

Reference Notes

Prologue

'There exists …': Victor Hugo, *Les Misérables*. Translated by Norman Denny, London, 1982, p. 317.

'Well!' he wanted …: J. Wardroper, *The World of William Hone*, London, 1997, p. 22.

'He didn't …': T. F. Fremantle Diary, 13 June 1815, D-FR/82/1-14, Centre for Buckinghamshire Studies.

'And what should …': Rudyard Kipling, 'The English Flag', *St James's Gazette*, 3 April 1891.

The Tiger is Out

'The pilot who …': G. Ticknor, *Life, Letters and Journals Vol 1*, Cambridge, Mass., 1876, p. 49.

'May security, confidence …': Adam Zamoyski, *Rites of Peace: The Fall of Napoleon and the Congress of Vienna*, London, 2007, p. 418.

'What times …': H. Piozzi, *The Piozzi Letters*. Eds E. & L. Bloom, London, 1989, Vol V, pp. 339–44.

'God knows how …': *Glasgow Herald*, 17 March 1815.

'What a dreadful …': Sir Samuel Romilly, *Memoir of Sir Samuel Romilly*, London, 1818, Vol 3, p. 160.

'In 1814 a war …': Henry Cockburn, *Memorials of his Time*, London & Edinburgh, 1856, pp. 168–70.

'All the town …': *James Nasmyth: An Autobiography*. Ed. Samuel Smiles, London, 1891, p. 59.

'We are at …': *Liverpool Mercury*, 24 March 1815.

'I am for …': W. Derry, *Dr. Parr: A Portrait of the Whig Dr. Johnson*, Oxford, 1966, p. 299.

'vain, insolent …': Benjamin Haydon, *Autobiography of Benjamin Robert Haydon*. Ed. Edmund Blunden, Oxford, 1927, p. 284.

'I don't much …': Charles Lamb, *The Complete Correspondence and Works of Charles Lamb*, London, 1868, Vol I, p. 234.

'It seems …': *Morning Chronicle*, 26 September 1796.

'When pressed …': H. C. Robinson, *Diary, Reminiscences and Correspondence of Henry Crabb Robinson*. Ed. T. Sadler, London, 1869, Vol I, p. 250.

'Dear God! …': William Wordsworth, 'Composed upon Westminster Bridge', September 1802. *Works*, London, 1994, p. 269.

Midnight: Belgium

'he cannot live …': C. A. Eaton, *Waterloo Days: The Narrative of an Englishwoman Resident in Brussels in June, 1815*, p. 56.

There had always been …: Cockburn, p. 258.

'He was the …': Elizabeth Grant, *Memoirs of a Highland Lady*, Edinburgh, 1988, Vol II, p. 50.

'On us who saw …': J. Playfair, *The Life of Dr. Hutton*, Transactions of the Royal Society of Edinburgh, 1805, reprinted 1997, p. 72.

'We divided …': Lady Magdalene De Lancey, *A Week at Waterloo in 1815*. Ed. Major B. R. Ward, London, 1906, p. 27.

'To tell you the truth …': Ibid., p. 12.

'on his way out …': Ibid.

'I never passed …': Ibid., p. 40.

'We little dreamt …': Ibid., p. 43.

'I saw an aide …': Ibid.

'he was safe …': Ibid., p. 46.

1 a.m.: Cut

'Child Roland …': William Hazlitt, 'The Life of Napoleon', *Selected Writings*. Ed. John Cook, Oxford, 1991, p. 240.

'dumb, inarticulate …': Hazlitt, 'My First Acquaintance With Poets', ibid., p. 211.

'like a stream …': Ibid., p. 213.

'I had no notion …': Ibid., p. 211.

'pollute the air …': T. Paulin, *The Day Star of Liberty*, London, 1998, p. 179.

'to be a true …': Hazlitt, 'Illustrations of *The Times* Newspaper', *Selected Writings*, p. 52.

'Hating,' he acknowledged …: Ibid., p. 52.

'shut up in …': 'My First Acquaintance With Poets', ibid., p. 212.

2 a.m.: Dance of Death

'hope, confidence …': Eaton, p. 13.

'Old men …': Ibid., p. 40.

'It was a solemn …': Ibid., p. 59.

'The Brunswickers are …': Augustus Frazer, *Letters of Colonel Sir Augustus Frazer, KCB*. Ed. Major-Gen. E. Sabine, London, 1859, p. 550.

'Duchess, you may …': Elizabeth Longford, *Wellington: The Years of the Sword*, London, 1969, p. 416.

'Nobody can guess …': Ibid., p. 411.

'Our movements …': G. G. Stonestreet, British Library, Add Mss 61805.

'as it was the place …': Longford, p. 417.

'There was the sound …': George Gordon Byron, Lord, *Childe Harold's Pilgrimage*, Canto III, Stanzas XXI–XXIII, *The Poetical Works of Lord Byron*, London, 1855, Vol 1, p. 96.

'Soon afterwards …': Eaton, p. 21.

'Where indeed …': Frazer, p. 550.

'In no battle …': E. Cotton, *A Voice from Waterloo*, London, 1862, p. 30.

3 a.m.: A Dying World

'Within the bay …': Bill Lawson, *Harris in History and Legend*, Edinburgh, 2002, p. 68.

'All the broad …': Ibid., p. 9.

'At the time …': The National Archives of Scotland, JC 26/370.

'That albeit …': Ibid.

4 a.m.: I Wish It Was Fit

'What a sight …': William Wheeler, *The Letters of Private Wheeler*. Ed. B. H. Liddell Hart, London, 1951, p. 169.

'It was as bad …': Cotton, p. 25.

'another truant …': George Keppel, Earl of Albemarle, *Fifty Years of My Life*, London, 1876, Vol I, p. 351.

'plenty of us …': Sir Henry Keppel, *A Sailor's Life under Four Sovereigns*, London, 1899, p. 1.

'Holding the King's …': Albemarle, Vol II, p. 4.

'terrible licking …': Ibid., p. 42.

'afterwards General …': Ibid., p. 16.

'had hardly …': Ibid., p. 13.

'Well, Pearce …': Ibid., p. 18.

5 a.m.: A Trellis of Roses

'The writer who …': *The Examiner*, 18 June 1815.

'mawkish, unmanly …': Fiona MacCarthy, *Byron: Life and Legend*, London, 2002, p. 431.

'Adonis in loveliness …': Nicholas Roe, *Fiery Heart: The First Life of Leigh Hunt*, London, 2005, p. 163.

'I turned it …': Leigh Hunt, *The Autobiography of Leigh Hunt*. Ed. J. E. Morpurgo, London, 1948, p. 243.

'mudshine': *The Examiner*, 1 January 1815.

'Capt. Bontein …': *The Examiner*, 18 June 1815.

'It is well known …': Ibid.

6 a.m.: The *Billy Ruffian*

'The following account …': *The Alfred*, June 1815.

'small rain …': Log of the *Bellerophon*, The National Archives, Adm 51/2024.

7 a.m.: *Le Loup de Mer*

'Lord Gambier's plan …': David Cordingley, *Cochrane the Dauntless*, London, 2007, p. 216.

'His Lordship's …': Donald Thomas, *Cochrane: Britannia's Last Sea King*, London, 1978, p. 187.

'the goodness of Him …': Ibid., p. 188.

'I have the honour …': Ibid., p. 212.

'partiality, misrepresentation …': Cordingley, p. 259.

'You have before had …': Ibid., p. 246.

'His appearance …': Robinson, Vol I, p. 226.

'I will never …': Cordingley, p. 248.

'according to the …': Ibid., p. 250.

'justice he wanted': Thomas, p. 259.

8 a.m.: The 'Article'

'It is very difficult …': *The Examiner*, 18 June 1815.

'When Greek meets …': Frazer, p. 539.

'hundred times …': Wheeler, p. 160.

'I never remember …': Ibid., p. 161.

'By God! …': Thomas Creevey, *The Creevey Papers*. Ed. Sir Herbert Maxwell, London, 1903, p. 228.

'in the expression of …': Wheeler, p. 170.

'As much as …': Ibid., p. 148.

'When I look …': Ibid., p. 158.

'called Legion …': Edmund Blunden, Introduction to Sir Fabian Ware's *The Immortal Heritage: An Account of the Work and Policy of the Imperial War Graves Commission during Twenty Years, 1917–1937*, London, 1937, p. x.

They waited …: A. Lagden and J. Sly, *The 2/73rd at Waterloo: Being a Roll of All Ranks Present*, Brightlingsea, 1998.

9 a.m.: Carrot and Stick

company or fun …: Fremantle, 18 June 1815.

'The teachers are …': E. Grindrod, *Rules for Altrincham Methodist Sunday School*, 1815, Greater Manchester County Record Office, C18/10/2/3/1.

'What is the people?': Hazlitt, 'What are the People?', p. 3.

'disgusting' and 'unsubdued passions': E. H. Thompson, *The Making of the English Working Class*, London, 1981, p. 441.

'The Scholars must …': MCRO c/18/10/2/3/1.

'for the purpose': Ibid.

'more lowly path …': Thompson, p. 442.

'Break their wills …': Ibid., p. 412.

'I have left …': Ibid., p. 90.

'Believe me …': T. W. Wansbrough, *An Authentic Narrative of the Conduct of Elizabeth Fenning, by the Gentleman who attended her*, London, 1815, p. 26.

10 a.m.: The Sinews of War

'some providential accident …': Gronow, Frederick Llewellyn, *Waterloo Recollections*, Leonaur, 2007, p. 111.

'Early in June …': Ibid., p. 107.

'a continuous wall …': Ibid., p. 112.

'On the opposite …': Wheatley, p. 63.

'longed to see …': Alessandro Barbero, *The Battle: A New History of the Battle of Waterloo*, London, 2006, p. 90.

'swelled-faced …': Wheatley, p. 64.

'Tom, you are …': Ed. Christopher Hibbert, *A Soldier of the Seventy First*, Moreton-in-Marsh, 1996, p. 106.

'I have often heard …': Wheeler, p. 153.

'For the second time …': Captain John Blackman, *Captain J. H. Blackman Papers*, National Army Museum, 1988-07-52.

'tranquil and composed …': Frazer, p. 543.

'It is an awful …': Wheatley, p. 64.

'It will be lower …': John Cam Hobhouse, *Recollections of a Long Life*, London, 1910, Vol I, p. 299.

It was 'strange': Nick Foulkes, *Dancing into Battle: A Social History of the Battle of Waterloo*, London, 2006, p. 194.

'A ball': Wheatley, p. 64.

11 a.m.: The Sabbath

'dust and bustle …': R. & S. Wilberforce, *Life of William Wilberforce*, London, 1838, Vol IV, p. 261.

'In my last …': Thomas Chalmers, CHA-6.16.91, New College Edinburgh.

'fragments of burning …': Mary Cosh, *Edinburgh: The Golden Age*, Edinburgh, 2003, p. 487.

'For you will …': Chalmers, CHA-6.16.91.

'On the fast day …': S. J. Brown, *Thomas Chalmers and the Godly Commonwealth in Scotland*, Oxford, 1983, p. 50.

'publicans and harlots …': Chalmers, CHA-6.16.91.

'Call of Providence …': Brown, p. 92.

'with despair …': Wheeler, p. 153.

'Perhaps at this very …': Wilberforce, Vol IV, p. 261.

12 noon: Ah, You Don't Know Macdonell

'Ah, you don't know …': Longford, p. 450.

'The dead and the wounded …': Gronow, Llewellyn, p. 124.

1 p.m.: Never Such a Period as This

'I wish thou …': Charles Lloyd to Mary Lloyd, 18 June 1815, Temp Mss 403/4/7/1/33, Library of the Religious Society of Friends in Britain.

'a time of much …': Elizabeth Fry, Journal, BL Add Ms 47456.

'I am convinced …': Samuel Lloyd, *The Lloyds of Birmingham*, London, 1907, pp. 124–5.

'speculative principles …': Ibid., pp. 124–5.

'I found a most …': Charles Lloyd, Temp Mss 210, No 33.

'Sammons was …': Benjamin Haydon, *Autobiography of Benjamin Robert Haydon*. Ed. Edmund Blunden, London, 1927, p. 290.

'finest of all …': Ibid., p. 292.

'Apollyon …': Ibid., p. 241.

'In the history …': Ibid., p. 279.

'tell me …': Alethea Hayter, *A Sultry Month: Scenes of London Literary Life in 1846*, London, 1965, p. 184.

'would not cloud …': Haydon, p. 218.

'Designing my *Entry* …': Ibid., p. 270.

'I am full of …': Ibid., p. 272.

'He bore it …': Ibid., p. 277.

'singular compound …': Ibid., p. 226.

'O God …': Benjamin Haydon, *The Diary of Benjamin Robert Haydon, Vol 1, 1808–1815*, p. 254.

2 p.m.: Ha, Ha

'Reader have you seen …': Hazlitt, 'The Fight', *Selected Essays*, p. 119.

'Why?' demanded Hazlitt …: Ibid., p. 120.

'His height …': Pierce Egan, *Boxiana: Or Sketches of Ancient and Modern Pugilism*, London, 1813–29, Vol II, pp. 382–4.

'had heard of battles …': Ibid., p. 384.

'No one but …': Wheatley, p. 70.

'Hast thou given …': Job, Chapter 39, verses 19, 23, 24, 25.

'felt a strange thrill …': Llewellyn, p. 194.

'like a bit …': Haydon, p. 292.

'In the melee …': Foulkes, p. 229.

'Ye who despise …': Hazlitt, p. 124.

'On that great day …': Tom Moore, Egan, p. 382.

3 p.m.: The Walking Dead

'Confused by his …': Charles Dickens, *Sketches by Boz*, London, 1836, p. 257.

'steady, honest …': J. Watkins & W. Hone, *The important results of an elaborate investigation into the mysterious case of Elizabeth Fenning*, London, 1815, p. 3.

'I am the wife …': A. Knapp & W. Baldwin, *The New Newgate Calendar*, Vol VI, London, 1824, p. 119.

'an extreme violent pain': Ibid., p. 119.

'Mr Marshall, the surgeon …': Ibid., p. 126.

'message for her mistress …': Ibid., p. 126.

'to form a liquid …': Ibid., p. 120.

'I washed it …': Ibid., p. 125.

'I now lay …': Watkins, Appendix, Letter I.

'Gentleman, you have …': Knapp, pp. 125–8.

'carried from the bar …': Ibid., p. 129.

'As to exercise …': Watkins, Appendix, Letter X, passim.

'Be careful of …': Ibid., Letter XXV.

'Some one …': Ibid., Letter XXV.

4 p.m.: The Finger of Providence

'everywhere to be found …': De Lancey, p. 115.

'indeed look very bad …': Barbero, p. 231.

'a ball came …': De Lancey, p. 14.

'The Duke bade …': Ibid., p. 51.

'ever advancing …': See Capt. Siborne, quoted in Cotton, p. 104.

'But as he spoke …': De Lancey, p. 51.

'Nothing else …': Ibid., p. 52.

5 p.m.: Portraits, Portraits, Portraits

'One of the most …': *Morning Post*, 29 April 1815.

'The *Distraining for Rent* …': Ibid., 1 May 1815.

'The colouring of …': *The Entertaining Magazine or Expository of General Knowledge for the Year 1815*, p. 261.

'The seventh day …': Byron, *Childe Harold's Pilgrimage*, Canto I, Stanzas LIX and LXX, *Works*, p. 186.

6 p.m.: *Vorwärts*

'Not an individual …': Wheatley, p. 86.

'Impelled by curiosity …': Ibid., p. 48.

'About two o'clock …': Ibid., p. 66.

'when a passe-parole …': Ibid., p. 68.

'About four P.M. …': Llewellyn, p. 117.

'Charge after charge …': Wheatley, p. 67.

'it struck the front …': Barbero, p. 263.

'About four o'clock …': William Lawrence, *Sergeant Lawrence: With the 40th Regt. of Foot in South America, the Peninsular War & at Waterloo*, Leonaur, 2007, p. 145.

'screaming like a …': Llewellyn, p. 66.

'Would it not …': Llewellyn, p. 70.

'A thought struck me …': Wheatley, p. 71.

'I could see …': Ibid.

7 p.m.: Noblesse Oblige

'I was in Newgate …': Records of the Old Bailey, Ref t18150913-4.

'with two or three …': Ibid.

'being appointed …': *Morning Post*, 19 June 1815.

'While the glorious …': Ibid.

'A noble Gothic …': *Exeter Flying Post*, 16 June 1815.

'the floor matted …': *Caledonian Mercury*, 17 June 1815.

'purporting to be …': *The Times*, 14 July 1815.

'Mr. Romanis …': Ibid.

'London November fog …': Ed. Gareth Glover, *Letters from the Battle of Waterloo: Unpublished Correspondence by Allied Officers from the Siborne Papers*, London, 2004, p. 98.

'The sanguinary drama …': Cotton, p. 128.

'but he still refused': Glover, p. 106.

'Their praise …' Byron, *Childe Harold's Pilgrimage*, Canto III, Stanza XXIX, *The Works of Lord Byron*, London, 1994, p. 207.

8 p.m.: A Mild Contusion

'drinking beer …': Foulkes, p. 138.

'a mild contusion …': G. G. Stonestreet, BL Add Ms 61805.

'advancing the cause …': Ibid.

'The streets were …': Ibid.

'But how …': Ibid.

'The Theatre and …': Ibid.

'I am appointed …': Ibid.

'leading families …': Ibid.

'every man of them …': Ibid.

'The Gentlemen of England …': Ibid.

9 p.m.: *Religionis Causa*

'a most affectionate …': Sheriff's Court, Bedford Street, 10 December, Report of Proceedings, *Morning Post*, 12 December 1814.

'O my friend …': Ibid.

'than which …': Hansard, 1 June 1815.

'they owed it …': Ibid.

'Stripped of all …': Hansard, 14 June 1815.

'Society for the …': Sydney Smith, *The Works of The Rev. Sydney Smith*, London, 1840, Vol I, p. 84.

'I still think …': Ed. L. Marchand, *Byron's Letters & Journals*, Vol IV, London, 1982, p. 324.

'For thee. My …': Byron, *Epistle to Augusta*, Stanza XVI, *Works*, p. 90.

'To soothe thy …': Byron, *The Bride of Abydos*, Canto I, Stanza XIII, ibid., p. 258.

'Oh! but it is …': L. Marchand, *Byron's Letters & Journals*, Vol IV, p. 104.

'Surely the Heaven …': Charles Mackay, *Medora Leigh: A History and an Autobiography*, London, 1869, p. 54.

'Early in our …': Ethel Mayne, *The Life and Letters of Anne Isabella, Lady Noel Byron*, London, 1929, p. 58.

'I am almost …': Ibid., p. 111.

'As soon as …': Malcolm Elwin, *Lord Byron's Family*, London, 1975, p. 250.

'You were a fool …': Mayne, p. 183.

10 p.m.: Clay Men

'My Dearest Mama …': Earl of Bessborough and A. Aspinall, eds, *Lady Bessborough and Her Family Circle*, London, 1940, p. 73.

Frederick Ponsonby: BM Add Ms, 19390/11-13 and passim.

'the Guards in their …': Llewellyn, p. 124.

'a foot-soldier …': Wheatley, p. 74.

'I found poor Curzon …': Llewellyn, p. 130.

'I had hardly …': John Hume, Surgeon's Hall, Edinburgh GD 1/5.

'Well, thank God …': Barbero, p. 415.

'I know not why …': Frazer, pp. 546–81.

'What will they say …': Llewellyn, p. 200.

11 p.m.: Went the Day Well?

'The object of …': *Morning Chronicle*, 19 June 1815.

'a little swarthy …': Robinson, Vol I, p. 256.

'It souths now …': *Carlisle Journal*, 24 June 1815.

'two women's slips …': The National Archives of Scotland, JC 26/367.

The Opening of the Vials

'What wonderful changes …': Ed. Richard Edgcumb, *The Diary of Frances, Lady Shelley*, London, 1912, p. 83.

'Jesu, what gotho-barbaric …': Eds. William Beckford and Boyd Alerand, *Life at Fonthill 1807–1827*, London, 1957, p. 178.

'Horses! can these …': Eds. Thomas De Quincey and Robert Morrison, *The English Mail-Coach: Confessions of an English Opium Eater and Other Writings*, Oxford, 2013, p. 192.

'On *any* night …': Ibid., p. 192.

'We lose not …': *Bombay Courier Extraordinary*, 27 October 1815.

'I asked him …': De Lancey, p. 53.

'I did not …': Ibid., p. 54.

'I hope no one …': Ibid., p. 67.

'Come Magdalene …': Ibid., p. 68.

'On Thursday he …': Ibid., p. 82.

'He generally lay …': Ibid., p. 80.

'I left him …': Ibid., p. 85.

'This was the first …': Ibid., p. 87.

'I went and stood …': Ibid., p. 95.

'seemed quite bent …': Ibid., p. 97.

'See what control …': Ibid.

'he wished she would not …': Ibid., p. 98.

'I hastened to him ...': Ibid., p. 99.

'You may form ...': Llewellyn, p. 23.

'Poor Lord Hay ...': BL Add Mss 6305722-2.

'Sir W. Delancy ...': The Hon. Mrs J. Swinton, *A Sketch of the Life of Georgiana, Lady de Ros: With Some Reminiscences of her Family and her Friends, including the Duke of Wellington*, London, 1921, p. 190.

'I have not ...': Llewellyn, p. 24.

The Days That Are Gone

'Church twice forenoon ...': National Library of Scotland Ms 25467.

'The messenger who ...': Eds. John Wilson Croker and L. J. Jennings, *The Croker Papers*, Vol I, London, 1884, p. 59.

'You must immediately ...': A. Hayward, *Diaries of a Lady of Quality from 1797 to 1844*, p. 167.

'I had spent ...': Haydon, p. 281.

'Sammons my model ...': Ibid., p. 282.

'I saw a man ...': University of York, Borthwick Institute of Historical Research. Halifax/A1/4/29.1.

'I hired a horse ...': Hobhouse, p. 299.

'If you have ...': BL Add Ms 43466.

'There are hopes ...': *Caledonian Mercury*, 29 June 1815.

'When the wife ...': Shelley, p. 83.

'Vague reports ...': *Morning Chronicle*, 21 June 1815.

'I can say no more ...': Joanna Baillie, *The Collected Letters of Joanna Baillie*, p. 337.

'We have claimed ...': BL Add Ms 42556.

'To the mind's eye ...': PAR 116/7/1, West Sussex Record Office.

'The most painful ...': John Blackman, Capt. J. H. Blackman Papers, National Army Museum 1988-07-52.

'Alas he is fallen ...': Ibid.

'Our bells are ringing ...': Eds. R. Southey and Rev. Charles Southey, *The Life and Correspondence of Robert Southey*, London, 1849, Vol IV, p. 115.

'the former liberal ...': Annual Register 1815, p. 50.

'I enclose you ...' BL Add Ms 43466, June 1815.

'Lady Caroline Lamb ...': BL Add Ms 63057, f225.

'The great amusement ...': BL Add Ms 45,546 f85.

'June 22 ...': Ticknor, p. 62.

'through his body ...': BL Add Ms, 75925.

New Battle Lines

'We had collected ...': Wheeler, p. 176.

'They' – the French government: BM Add Ms 37726 ff109-11.

'The most ridiculous ...': Add Ms 37726 ff109-111.

'Damn all foreign ...': L. C. B. Seaman, *Victorian England: Aspects of English and Imperial History 1837–1901*, London, 1973, p. 101.

'Pray come soon ...': Watkins, Appendix, Letter XXVI.

'Dear Parents ...': Ibid, Letter XXVIII.

'an immense concourse ...': *Morning Advertiser*, 26 July.

'because she was pretty ...': Watkins, p. 80.

'Dearest Friend ...': Ibid., Letter XXX.

'elbow leaning on ...': Wansbrough, p. 19.

'Pray tell my ...': Watkins, Letter XXIX.

'Before the just ...': Gatrell, p. 355.

'O what a blessed ...': Watkins, p. 22.

'Thus perished ...': Wansbrough, p. 25.

'thrown into houses …': Watkins, p. 106.

'My aching heart …': Gatrell, p. 353.

'Friday an Inquest …': *Morning Chronicle*, 15 August 1815.

'Not the slightest …': *The Times*, 1 August 1815.

Myth Triumphant

'Waterloo, in its …': Hugo, p. 317.

'Have not the …': Haydon, *Diaries*, Vol I, p. 456.

'Poor Haydon …': Hayter, p. 184.

'I should not …': Haydon, *Autobiography*, p. 327.

'strange, tottering …': Ibid., p. 258.

'How can we …': PAR 116/7/1, West Sussex Record Office.

'Period of honour …': W. Scott, *The Field of Waterloo*, London, 1815, Stanza XXI.

'Let honour be paid …': Eaton, p. 21.

'Towards the end …': Nasmyth, p. 69.

'The ferocious …': Dr Sharpe, *Report … for the better regulation of the Madhouses in England*, London, 1815, p. 198.

'My LORD …': William Cobbett, *Political Register*, 1 July 1815.

'Will these ladies …': De Quincey, p. 194.

'The English name …': Countess of Airlie, *In Whig Society, 1775–1818*, London, 1921, p. 171.

under commanders who …: G. Corrigan, *Waterloo: A New History of the Battle and its Armies*, London, 2014, p. 320.

'What was most …': Hugo, p. 315.

'manufacturers, merchants …': Thompson, pp. 749–55.

'The doctrine of God's …': PAR 116/7/1.

'such are the acts …': *Carlisle Journal*, 12 August 1815.

'the meanest peasant …': De Quincey, p. 174.

'I was carried …': Ibid., pp. 213–22.

'What makes the …': *The Times*, 13 November 1852.

'There' was the sombre …: Ibid.

'They have ruined my battlefield …': Longford, Vol II, p. 79.

'at night a sort …': Hugo, p. 316.

Select Bibliography

There is a vast and growing literature dedicated to the Battle of Waterloo and Bonaparte's Hundred Days, but I have restricted myself here to those primary sources and commentaries that are either of particular relevance to this story or have shaped the way in which I have approached it. Some of the early printed accounts are only available in research libraries, and where appropriate I have indicated whatever modern reprint or anthology has made the material most easily available. The documentary sources for this book are scattered around libraries and archives across Britain, and are separately indicated in the endnotes.

Annual Register, Or a View of the History, Politics, and Literature, for the Year 1815 (London, 1816)

Barbero, Alessandro, *The Battle: A History of the Battle of Waterloo* (London, 2006)

Beckford, William, *Life at Fonthill 1807–1822* (ed. Boyd Alerand, London, 1957)

Bell, Charles, *Letters of Sir Charles Bell* (London, 1870)

Bobbitt, Philip, *The Shield of Achilles: War, Peace and the Course of History* (London, 2002)

Breton, B., *The Story of St George's Altrincham* (Altrincham, 1999)

Brewer, John, *Sentimental Murder: Love and Madness in the Eighteenth Century* (London, 2004)

Brougham, Henry, *The Life and Times of Henry Lord Brougham, Vol II* (London, 1871)

Burney, Fanny, *The Journals and Letters of Fanny Burney* (ed. P. Hughes, Oxford, 1980)

Byron, George Gordon, *Byron's Letters and Journals, 12 Volumes* (ed. Leslie A. Marchand, London, 1982)

Cobbett, William, *Selected Writings, Vol 111* (ed. Lenora Nattrass, London, 1998)

Cockburn, Henry, *Memorials of his Life* (Edinburgh, 1856)

Colley, Linda, *Britons Forging the Nation* (London, 1992)

Cordingley, David, *Cochrane the Dauntless: The Life and Adventures of Thomas Cochrane* (London, 2007)

Corrigan, Gordon, *Waterloo: A New History of the Battle and its Armies* (London, 2014)

Cosh, Mary, *Edinburgh: The Golden Age* (Edinburgh, 2003)

Cotton, Edward, *A Voice from Waterloo* (London, 1862)

Creevey, Thomas, *The Creevey Papers* (ed. Sir Herbert Maxwell, London, 1903)

Croker, John Wilson, *The Croker Papers* (ed. Louis Jennings, London, 1884)

Crumplin, M. K. H. and Starling, P., *A Surgical Artist At War: The Paintings and Sketches of Sir Charles Bell 1809–1815* (Edinburgh, 2005)

De Lancey, Magdalene, *A Week at Waterloo in 1815* (ed. Major B. R. Ward, London, 1906)

Dixon, J. H., *Gairloch and Guide to Loch Maree* (Fort William, 1886)

Farington, Joseph, *The Diary of Joseph Farington* (ed. K. Cave, New Haven, 1984)

Foulkes, Nick, *Dancing into Battle: A Social History of the Battle of Waterloo* (London, 2006)

Frazer, Augustus, *Letters of Colonel Sir Augustus Frazer, KCB* (ed. Major General E. Sabine, London, 1859)

Hardman, J., *Study of Altrincham and its Families in 1801 and 1851* (Altrincham, 1989)

Haydon, Benjamin, *Autobiography of Benjamin Robert Haydon* (ed. Edmund Blunden, Oxford, 1927)

Haydon, Benjamin, *The Diary of Benjamin Robert Haydon* (ed. Willard Pope, Cambridge Mass., 1963)

Hayter, Alethea, *A Sultry Month: Scenes of London Literary Life in 1846* (London, 1965)

Hazlitt, William, *Selected Writings* (ed. John Cook, Oxford, 1991)

Hibbert, Christopher, *A Soldier of the Seventy-First* (Moreton-in-Marsh, 1996)

Hobhouse, John Cam, *Recollections of a Long Life* (London, 1910)

Holmes, Richard, *Wellington: The Iron Duke* (London, 2003)

Hone, William, *The World of William Hone* (ed. J. Wardroper, London, 1997)

Hugo, Victor, *Les Misérables* (translated by Norman Denny, London, 1982)

Hunt, John Henry Leigh, *The Autobiography of Leigh Hunt* (ed. J. E. Morpurgo, London, 1948)

Ireland, George, *Plutocrats: A Rothschild Inheritance* (London, 2008)

Jones, Edwin, *The English Nation: The Great Myth* (Stroud, 1998)

Keegan, John, *The Face of Battle: A Study of Agincourt, Waterloo and the Somme* (London, 1978)

Keppel, George, *Earl of Albemarle: Fifty Years of my Life* (London, 1876)

Knapp, Andrew and Baldwin, William, *The Newgate Calendar* (London, 1826)

Knight, Roger, *Britain Against Napoleon: The Organization of Victory 1793–1815* (London, 2013)

Lamb, Lady Caroline, *Glenarvon* (ed. Frances Wilson, London, 1995)

Lawrence, Sergeant William, *The Autobiography of Sergeant William Lawrence* (ed. G. N. Bankes, London, 1986)

Llewellyn, Frederick, *Waterloo Recollections* (Leonaur, 2007)

Lloyd, Christopher, *Lord Cochrane Seaman – Radical – Liberator: A Life of Thomas, Lord Cochrane 10th Earl of Dundonald* (London, 1947)

Lloyd, Samuel, *The Lloyds of Birmingham* (London, 1907)

Longford, Elizabeth, *Wellington: The Years of the Sword* (London, 1969)

Longford, Elizabeth, *Wellington: Pillar of State* (London, 1972)

Mayne, Ethel Colburn, *The Life and Letters of Anne Isabella, Lady Noel Byron* (London, 1929)

McGann, Jerome J. (ed.), *Byron: The Complete Poetical Works, 7 Volumes* (Oxford, 1993)

Mercer, Cavalie, *Journal of the Waterloo Campaign* (London, 1870)

Muir, Rory, *Wellington: The Path to Victory, 1796–1814* (Yale, 2013)

Nasmyth, James, *An Autobiography* (ed. Samuel Smiles, London, 1891)

O'Keefe, Paul, *Waterloo: The Aftermath* (London, 2014)

Paulin, Tom, *The Day Star of Liberty: William Hazlitt's Radical Style* (London, 1998)

Piozzi, Hester, *The Piozzi Letters: Correspondence of Hester Lynch Piozzi* (ed. Alan Bloom and Lillian D. Bloom, University of Delaware Press, 1989)

Richards, Eric, *The Highland Clearances: People, Landlords and Rural Turmoil* (Edinburgh, 2008)

Robinson, Henry Crabb, *Diary, Reminiscences, and Correspondence of Henry Crabb Robinson* (ed. T. Sadler, London, 1869)

Rules for The Management of the Altrincham Methodist Sunday School (Manchester, 1815)

Selincourt, Edward de, *The Letters of William and Dorothy Wordsworth* (Oxford, 1970)

Shelley, Frances, *The Diary of Lady Frances Shelley* (ed. Richard Edgcumbe, London, 1912)

Siborne, Major General H. T. (ed.), *Waterloo Letters* (London, 1891)

Southey, Robert, *The Life and Correspondence of Robert Southey* (ed. Rev Ch. Southey, London, 1849–50)

Stirling, A., *Coke of Norfolk* (London, 1871)

Thomas, Donald, *Cochrane: Britannia's Last Sea-King* (London, 1978)

Thompson, E. P., *The Making of the English Working Class* (London, 1981)

Ticknor, George, *Life, Letters & Journals, Vol 1* (Cambridge Mass., 1876)

Wansbrough, T. W., *An Authentic Narrative of the Conduct of Eliza Fenning* (London, 1815)

Wheatley, Edmund, *The Wheatley Diary: A Journal and Sketchbook Kept during the Peninsular War and the Waterloo Campaign* (ed. Christopher Hibbert, London, 1964)

Wheeler, William, *The Letters of Private Wheeler* (ed. B. H. Liddell Hart, London, 1951)

Wilberforce, William, *Life of William Wilberforce* (ed. R. and S. Wilberforce, London, 1838)

Wynn, Frances Williams, *Diaries of a Lady of Quality* (ed. A. Hayward, London, 1864)

Zamoyski, Adam, *Rites of Peace: The Fall of Napoleon and the Congress of Vienna* (London, 2007)

List of Illustrations

Plate section 1

Page 1: The Duke of Wellington by Sir Thomas Lawrence (*Private Collection/Photo © Mark Fiennes/Bridgeman Images*)

Page 2: Napoleon Bonaparte by Robert Lefebvre, oil on canvas, 1809 (*Musée de la Ville de Paris, Musée Carnavalet, Paris, France/ Bridgeman Images*); Blücher by Sir Thomas Lawrence, oil on canvas, 1814 (*Supplied by Royal Collection Trust/© Her Majesty Queen Elizabeth II 2014*)

Page 3: Magdalene De Lancey and William De Lancey, from *A Week At Waterloo 1815*, John Murray, London 1906 (*© The British Library Board*); Charles and Mary Lamb by Francis Stephen Cary, oil on canvas, 1834 (*© National Portrait Gallery, London*)

Page 4: William Hazlitt, replica by William Bewick, 1825 (*© National Portrait Gallery, London*); James Henry Leigh Hunt by Samuel Laurence, oil on canvas, c.1837 (*© National Portrait Gallery, London*)

Page 5: Benjamin Haydon, engraving by W. Read (*© Mary Evans Picture Library*); Thomas Chalmers by David Octavius Hill, and Robert Adamson, calotype, 1843–8 (*© National Portrait Gallery, London*); Lord Cochrane, from a picture by P. E. Stroehling (*© National Maritime Museum, Greenwich, London*)

347

Pages 6–7: *Closing the Gates at Hougoumont, 1815* by Robert Gibb, oil
on canvas, 1903 (© *National Museums Scotland*)

Page 8: *Shaw the Life Guards-man's heroic attack on the French
Cuirassiers*, from *History of the French Revolution, and of the wars
produced by that event* by Christopher Kelly, London 1820–22
(© *The British Library Board*); Colonel James MacDonell by
Henry Raeburn, oil on canvas (*courtesy Museum of the Isles*);
Edmund Wheatley, *A Self-Portrait*, from *The Wheatley Diary: A
Journal and Sketch-book kept during the Peninsular War and the
Waterloo Campaign* (ed. Christopher Hibbert)

Plate section 2

Page 1: *Distraining for Rent* by Sir David Wilkie, oil on panel, 1815
(*courtesy Google Art Project*); *Fare Thee Well* by George
Cruikshank (*Private Collection/Bridgeman Images*)

Page 2: Elizabeth Fenning (*photo by Hulton Archive/Getty Images*)

Page 3: Frederick Ponsonby and Colin Campbell by Jan Willem
Pieneman, 1821 (*courtesy English Heritage/Mary Evans*); Lady
Caroline Lamb by Sir Thomas Lawrence, oil on canvas (© *Bristol
Museum and Art Gallery, UK/Bridgeman Images*)

Pages 4–5: *The Chelsea Pensioners Reading the Waterloo Dispatch, 1822*
by Sir David Wilkie, oil on wood, 1822 (*Apsley House, The
Wellington Museum, London, UK/Bridgeman Images*)

Page 6: *The Duke of Wellington describing the field of Waterloo to King
George IV* by Benjamin Haydon, oil on canvas, 1844 (© *Royal
Hospital Chelsea, London, UK*)

Page 7: *Napoleon on board HMS Bellerophon* by Sir William Quiller
Orchardson, colour litho (*Private Collection/© Look and Learn/
Bridgeman Images*)

Page 8: Injured soldiers by Charles Bell, watercolour, 1815 (*courtesy
Wellcome Library, London*)

Acknowledgements

The best part of writing any book is the research, and I am especially grateful to everyone who has helped in tracking down material for me and patiently answering questions. The source material for a book of this kind is inevitably widely scattered, and there is nowhere – from the Seallam Visitor Centre on the Isle of Harris and the Highland Archive Centre in Inverness down to the West Sussex County Record Office on the South Coast at Chichester – where I have not met with more tolerance and kindness than anyone who was as unfamiliar with English Parish Bastardy Records as he was with Gaelic genealogy had any right to expect. The endnotes will, I hope, underline the extent of this debt. The passages from the sermon of Thomas Chalmers are quoted here with the kind permission of New College, The University of Edinburgh. My thanks, also, to the West Sussex County Record Office, to the Borthwick Institute of Historical Research, York University and to the Library of the Religious Society of Friends for allowing me to quote from material held in their collections. I am particularly grateful to Lisa McQuillan for her help at the LSF.

It is impossible to exaggerate how much this book owes to all the previous writers on the subject, but, again, I hope the endnotes and bibliography will spell that out. From the moment, almost, that the battle was over both soldiers and civilians recorded their impressions and memories of Waterloo and its aftermath, and two hundred years of argument and counter-argument over every aspect of the battle, campaign and background – military, political, diplomatic, biographical, and social – have left a legacy that would be impossible to escape even if one wanted to do so.

On a more personal note, I would like, as always, to thank all the friends and family who were prepared to talk about this book, read it in draft, point me in the direction of sources and tramp over the battlefield with me. I would particularly like to thank Colin Young for his help with some tricky genealogies and, especially, John O'Reilly, who scoured the county archives of southern England, turning up letters and diaries enough to fill another volume.

I am very grateful to everyone at William Collins involved with this book, to Arabella Pike, Kate Tolley, and to Kate Johnson for her patience with a manuscript that cannot have been easy to edit. I would also like to thank Derek Johns, who oversaw its beginning, and Natasha Fairweather its end. Above all, my thanks, as ever, go to Honor for all her help and support. Finally, I would like to dedicate this book to my mother. She died while I was finishing it so was never required to honour an unlikely promise to read it, but she was very keen on the title.

Index